SKETCH OF
THE SEMINOLE WAR

AND SKETCHES DURING A CAMPAIGN

WILLIAM W. SMITH
LIEUTENANT OF THE LEFT WING

ENHANCED EDITION
EDITED BY
DEBRA KAY HARPER
WITH INTRODUCTION, CONTENTS,
ENDNOTES, AND INDEX

INTRODUCTION BY FRANK LAUMER

SEMINOLE WARS FOUNDATION, INC.
DADE CITY, FL

The Seminole Wars Foundation, Inc.
Dade City, FL

www.seminolewars.us

ISBN: 978-0-9821105-5-3

Our appreciation to Jackson Walker for his kind use of the
cover paintings:
"Charge with Every Man" (Main Image)
"The Flower Hunter" (Inset, William Bartram)
www.jacksonwalkerstudio.com

THIS BOOK IS DEDICATED TO

FRANK LAUMER
1927-2019

Thank you for your friendship, mentoring,
kindness, affection, and appreciation.
You meant the world to me, and you are missed
every day. You will continue to be the wind
beneath the Foundation's wings.

Debbie Harper has been Treasurer and Board Member of the Seminole Wars Foundation, Inc., for over a decade. She previously published the *English/Seminole Vocabulary; as Documented During the Second Seminole War 1835–1842.* She has a background as a research librarian and is retired as a Business Analyst from the Southwest Florida Water Management District. She is certified in Electronic Records Management, has edited publications for the Foundation, and has assisted Frank Laumer with his research and writing on the Seminole Wars. In 2017, she was project manager and co producer of the video for the *Frank Laumer Legacy Award.*

Frank Laumer is the author of *Massacre!* and *Dade's Last Command,* histories of the destruction in 1835 of the command of Brevet Major Francis Langhorne Dade by Seminole Indians. He is the editor of *Oceola Nikkanochee* by Andrew Welch and *Amidst a Storm of Bullets, The Diary of Henry Prince in Florida 1836-1842.* His novel *Nobody's Hero* is the story of Pvt. Ransom Clark, a survivor of Dade's battle, and was published in 2008. He is past president of the Dade Battlefield Society and the Seminole Wars Foundation.

The Seminole Wars Foundation

The Seminole Wars Foundation, Inc. was founded in 1992 with the goal of preserving sites significant to the Seminole Wars, establishing educational programs to disseminate information about the wars, and to publish books and other matter pertaining to these important but little understood conflicts.

The Foundation has been instrumental in the preservation of the Camp Izard battle site, has purchased portions of the Fort Dade site and funded excavations upon it, and has assisted in the purchase and preservation of the Fort King site in Ocala. Foundation members have given numerous talks to civic organizations, student groups, and the general public.

For further information contact the Seminole Wars Foundation at www.seminolewars.us or on Facebook.

A list of our publications can be found on page 312.

Acknowledgements

John and Mary Lou Missall

Without you, this book may not have been completed. You stepped up and gave me the needed guidance when my world was falling apart. I thank you for your patience, assistance and the resuscitation I needed to complete this.

Dr. Ray E. Giron
1943-2011

Doctor of Veterinary Medicine.
Former Board Member, Seminole Wars Foundation.
Property manager and military authenticator on many motion pictures such as, *Glory, Gettysburg, Rough Riders,* and *Gods* and *Generals.*

Ray commenced this project after receiving scanned images of Smith's book from the U.S. Army Archives. Those images, along with Ray's highlighted notes brought to life the authenticity of the story. Knowing that this was his book, left in my care, I am honored to help bring his vision to light.

Map of General Scott's Campaign

CONTENTS

Cause of the War—Council at Camp King—Hoithle-mattee, or Jumper, violently opposed to the Treaty for Removal—Oseola—Sketch of his person and Character—His equivocation and artifice—Murder of Charley Omathlie and massacre of Gen. Wiley Thompson, the Indian Agent—Previous Reports of Hostilities and Alarm at St. Augustine—Assaults and Depredations—Attack upon, and burning of Col. Warren's Wagon Train—Battle of Black Point—Skirmish—Indians surrounded by Gen. Call, and sustain a loss.

Destruction of plantations on the coast of Mosquito, south of St. Augustine, by Philip and his bands; remark on the slave population; their fidelity and attachment to their masters; massacre of Mr. Woodruff at Volusia; alarm at St. Augustine; measures for defence; distress and scarcity of provision; coincidence of the Seminole war with the Yemassee war in Carolina; Volunteers from Savannah arrive at Picolata; the progress of the Indians unchecked; delay of assistance from the Government; defect of the army; negligence, of the department of war; Gen. Clinch waits for a reinforcement, and for Gen. Call to join him, in order to march against the Indians.

A reinforcement is despatched from Tampa Bay to Gen. Clinch; Massacre of Major Dade's detachment; Battle of Withlacoochee

NOTES ON THE ENHANCED EDITION

In publishing this new edition of *Sketch of the Seminole War* by William Wragg Smith, the Seminole Wars Foundation hopes to improve upon what was already a valuable book. Although the work had been out of print for quite some time, in recent years a facsimile edition has been published and is readily available. The problem with the original and facsimile editions is that they lack many of the things modern-day scholars have come to rely upon. Most important, because Smith didn't make an index, the facsimile editions are also lacking one. It was also felt the book needed endnotes in addition to Smith's footnotes. People, events, and places generally known to readers of the time but now obscure needed to be identified or information about them clarified. Finally, an Introduction was required to provide background both on the Second Seminole War and on Smith, who originally published the work anonymously. Thankfully, he was astute enough to extensively subtitle each chapter, making the Table of Contents useful to researchers.

Facsimile editions are little more than photographic reproductions of the original edition. To add endnotes and the occasional editorial comment, it was necessary to re-type the entire document. This introduces a problem: Because of differences in typeface, font size, page size, and margins, the page numbers would not come out the same. This, in turn, poses a problem for anyone who is looking up something another author referred to in Smith's original book. If a citation is said to be on page 137 of Smith's original edition, then it needs to be on page 137 of all editions of the book, including this one.

To resolve this issue, each page was broken in the same place as the original. Unfortunately, this does not produce a perfect result, and the reader will notice that very often the bottom line on a page does not extend all the way to the right margin. Also, the last line usually falls far short of the bottom of the page. Unfortunately, font size could not be increased over what would cause the longest page to wrap into the following page.

Another issue that resulted from creating a new document was the matter of typographical errors in the text. In a facsimile, there is no question as to who made the mistake; you're seeing it as it was originally published. In something that is re-typed, the reader can't be sure where the error originated. The most obvious such errors are in spelling. Webster's dictionary was still a new thing at the time, and education in America was far from standardized. For the most part, Smith's spelling is good, but he used what we would today consider "British" spelling, such as colour, neighbour, centre, lustre, practise, authorised, and defence. Words that the reader will easily recognize as such are not marked with a [sic]. The original edition also contained an "Errata" page, listing errors that were discovered after publication. The editor has located those errors in the text and put the corrections in brackets, leaving the original error in place.

To avoid any confusion, footnotes in the text are Smith's originals; endnotes are the editor's additions. Likewise, anything in brackets are insertions by the editor.

The Seminole Wars Foundation hopes you enjoy this new edition and that our enhancements help in your understanding of this tragic and largely forgotten conflict.

WILLIAM WRAGG SMITH

INTRODUCTION

The child who would become "A Lieutenant of the Left Wing" was born to Charlotte and William Loughton in 1808 on his parent's estate, the Smith-Wragg Plantation near Charleston, South Carolina. His father, William Loughton Smith, had studied law in England, and been admitted to the bar in 1784. Elected to the First U.S. Congress in 1789, he was reelected four times, serving until 1797 when he was appointed United States Minister to Portugal and Spain. He returned to Charleston in 1801 and four years later married Charlotte Wragg. When he died in 1812 their son, William Wragg Smith, was four years old.

The boy grew up on the family's estate with his mother, an older step-brother and sister. In later years he would be described as a gentleman planter, lawyer, naturalist, translater and poet, but in 1836 news of the "massacre" of two companies of American soldiers by Seminole Indians in Florida shocked the nation and the call went out for volunteers. William Wragg, now aged twenty-seven, enlisted and left Charleston for Florida as a lieutenant of the South Carolina Volunteers.

In his first encounters with Black Seminoles, slaves who had escaped to freedom in Florida, he was surprised and "puzzled." Referring to conditions at home he wrote, "A large majority of our slaves preferred to remain in the happy and secure state of servitude…". There would be other surprises to come.

Frank Laumer

SHORT BIOGRAPHY OF W.W. SMITH

William Wragg Smith was born on October 2, 1808, the son of William Loughton Smith (Oct. 2, 1758 - Dec. 19, 1812) and Charlotte (Wragg) Smith (May 14, 1774 – Feb. 6, 1852).[1]

His father was born in Charleston, S.C., attended preparatory schools in England, studied law in London, and pursued higher studies in Geneva, Switzerland, during the American Revolution. He returned to Charleston in 1783, was admitted to the bar the following year, and commenced practice in Charleston while engaged in agricultural pursuits on his estate near Charleston.[2]

In 1836, twenty-seven-year-old William left South Carolina for Florida as a lieutenant in the South Carolina Volunteers, commanded by Col. Abbott Hall Brisbane. They were to serve under regular army Gen. Abraham Eustis's left wing in Gen. Winfield Scott's 1836 campaign. This book is an account of his experiences and observations during this campaign.

Smith was known as "a gentleman of education and culture, who contributed by his investigations and publications to the knowledge of botany of the low country of South Carolina." He was founding member of the Elliott Natural History Society and served as vice president, and was a member of the Charleston Library Society, of which Joel R. Poinsett (Secretary of War during most of the Second Seminole War) was President.[3]

He was the author of several works, including:

- "Sketch of the Seminole War and Sketches During a Campaign, by a Lieutenant of the Left Wing." (1836)
- Translated "The Last Canto of Childe Harold's Pilgrimage, translated and amplified from the French of Alphonse de Lamartine" [and other minor poems]. (1842)

- "Flora of the Lower Country of South Carolina Reviewed." (1859)
- "Autumn Coloring, Fall of the Leaf, Winter Habit of Trees and Shrubs in the Lower Country of South Carolina." (February 1, 1860)
- "Melody," a poem. (opposite page)

William Wragg Smith died on May 28, 1875 and is buried at Mount Olivet Cemetery, Maspeth, New York. His third wife, Mary Theresa (Hedley) Smith (1825(?) - 1892) and seven others are listed on the headstone. If they are the children, they were born in 1843, 1850, 1852, 1854, 1856, 1858, and 1862.[4]

MELODY

Ah! When, in fancy dreaming,
I gaze thee, dear maid,
All nature's holy seeming
Appears in thee portray'd!

The stars of heaven shine not
More brightly than those eyes;
While Love and Hope divine
Their tender mysteries.

The music of the forest
Is glad when thou art glad;
But, sweetest, when thou sorrow'st,
The trees, they too, are sad!

These flowers around us springing,
Will die-will die I'm sure;
These birds all gaily singing
Will sing – will sing no more,

Whenever, dearest maiden,
Those accents case to speak,
And Beauty's blossoms fade in
That fresh and rosy cheeks.

William Wragg Smith [5]

PREFACE

I first came across *Sketch of the Seminole War and Sketches During a Campaign* when I was compiling a pamphlet for publication by the Seminole Wars Foundation on the *English/Seminole Vocabulary, as documented during the Second Seminole War 1835-1842*. Mr. Smith's book contains quite an extensive compilation of Seminole words and was a big part of the pamphlet.

My assistance with research and editing publications for both the Foundation and Frank Laumer (noted historian, author, and co-founding member of the Seminole Wars Foundation) led me to take on the task of creating the *Vocabulary* for publication. Not only did I believe it would prove a useful work, I wanted to assist in the Foundation's goal of publishing pertinent material relating to the wars. As I soon learned, one project usually leads to another.

Further prompted by my background as a research librarian, I discovered that Smith had not been reprinted since the original edition, *and* that it had been published anonomously. This intrigued me. Why does everyone, including the World Catalog have Smith as the writer? Why had he written this important historical document without taking credit? Besides the compilation of Seminole words, the explanation of the events prior to Smith's tenure in Florida (articulated in "Part the First") chronicals the events that led to his participation in the war. "Part the Second," *Sketches During a Campaign* gives a first-hand account of his involvement in the campaign, in the trenches, leading his fellow South Carolina Regiment. Frank and I worked closely on the project for several years, but sadly, my dear friend passed away mere weeks from its completion.[6]

The book has since been reprinted, but only as a facsimile of the original document. I hope the reader will find the enhancements in this edition aids his or her understanding of the work and further brings to life a period of time and events in history that have been long overlooked. The Second Seminole War was the longest, costliest, and one of the deadliest wars the United States fought against Native Americans and works relating to it need to be widely disseminated and understood.

For those who wish to study first-hand accounts of the Second Seminole War, there are a handful of books that are required reading. The first is John Sprague's *The Florida War*, followed by Jacob Motte's *Journey into Wilderness*, John Bemrose's *Reminiscences*, Henry Prince's diary *Amidst a Storm of Bullets*, and a few others. One of the less well known of these accounts is William W. Smith's *Sketch of the Seminole War*, first published in 1836. Although Smith was only in Florida for a few months of what would turn out to be a seven-year conflict, he was present at a critical time, and was privy to information that others lacked. He was also a keen observer of details, dedicated to understanding the causes of the conflict, and very much interested in his Seminole adversaries.

The Second Seminole War was part of the much larger problem of how to reconcile the wants of the rapidly growing American nation with the rights of those aboriginal nations who had lived here for centuries. The solution decided upon by President Andrew Jackson and Congress was to remove all Native American nations from the eastern portion of the country and resettle them out west. Caught up in this effort were the Seminole Indians, who resided in what was then the largely unsettled Florida Territory. As government pressure on them increased, Seminole resolve to remain in their homeland only became stronger.

Tensions increased until December 1835, when war seemed to explode upon the Territory. On the 28th, a column of 108 soldiers under the command of Maj. Francis L. Dade was virtually wiped out as it passed through the Seminole heartland. A few days later, a force of about 750 men under Brig. Gen. Duncan Clinch was repulsed at the Withlacoochee River. All across the peninsula, isolated homesteads and prosperous plantations were attacked, torched, and their occupants murdered or forced to flee for their lives. Florida, it seemed, was in flames.

News of the outbreak travelled as swiftly as it could in those days, yet it still took about two weeks to reach New Orleans, where Maj. Gen. Edmund P. Gaines was on an inspection tour. Gaines was head of the Western Department of the United States Army, and most of the fighting in Florida had taken place within his jurisdiction. Gathering about 1,100 men (mostly Louisiana Volunteers), Gaines travelled to Florida in hopes of quelling the Indian uprising. In that he failed, being held under siege for over a week on the north side of the Withlacoochee. The Seminole, a small tribe with only about 1,500 warriors, seemed unstoppable.

When news of the war was received in Washington, President Jackson, initially unaware of Gaines's actions, ordered Maj. Gen Winfield Scott to take command of the war in Florida. Scott planned an elaborate campaign consisting of three columns, or "wings," that would converge on the Seminole strongholds near the Withlacoochee River on the west side of the peninsula. In total, Scott's army would be made up of approximately 5,000 men, predominantly volunteers from the neighboring states. One column would march north from Tampa, another south from the Ocala area, and a third, the "Left Wing," would cross the peninsula from the St. Johns River in the east. Lieutenant Smith and his fellow South Carolina Volunteers would be part of this wing, commanded by Brig. Gen. Abraham Eustis of the regular army.

The military establishment of the time was very different from what we have today. The regular army was pitifully small for such a large nation, only around 7,000 men. When emergencies such as the one in Florida arose, the government depended upon state volunteer forces made up of patriotic citizens enlisted for short periods of time. These were not professional soldiers, and throughout the Seminole War period, there was considerable tension between regulars and volunteers, with each type of soldier having little respect for the other.

In the end, General Scott's massive campaign proved yet another failure for the army. The precise timing required by the three columns quickly fell apart, and the Seminole easily escaped the trap by fleeing into the unmapped wilderness. Smith and his fellow South Carolinians went home disappointed but satisfied they had done their duty. The war against the Seminole continued without them, lasting six more years, wasting thousands of lives and millions of dollars.

Debra Kay Harper

SKETCH

OF THE

SEMINOLE WAR,

And

SKETCHES

DURING A CAMPAIGN.

BY A LIEUTENANT.

OF THE LEFT WING.

CHARLESTON
DAN J. DOWLING,
SOLD BY J. P BEILE AND W. H BERRITT; AND
BOOKSELLERS IN THE PRINCIPAL CITIES.
1836.

TO BENJAMIN ELLIOTT, ESQ.,

Dear Sir:

When one appears as a writer before the public for the first time, the least that he can say, by way of preface to his work, the better perhaps for him. In the first place, few will deign to grant him a hearing; and in the second, those few who do, will not believe a word that he says. It is a contempt of court to open his mouth to say any thing, before the stern Judge has condescended to put his spectacles on his nose, and take a glance at the evidence of his case. Then he may permit him to say something about himself.---

To you, however, Dear Sir, to whom I would simply inscribe these unpretending pages, the result of two or three month's employment, I yet may be permitted to address a few words as an apology for the present offering.

You may recollect that when I last had the pleasure of meeting you, previous to my departure for Florida, you remarked, flatteringly, that you hoped, should I return, I might turn my recollections of the Florida excursion to a literary account. With the view of fulfilling, in some slight degree, and to the best of my abilities, this expectation, (however unworthy of it I might have thought myself,) I began to make Notes of whatever occurred; and having once begun, I was induced to continue, though, I confess, I was disappointed in much of my materials, and was besides a lazy journalist; and when I found myself prevented by sickness from going the whole way upon the Campaign, I had concluded that as others would see so much more than I would, and some one better qualified than myself would no doubt give a detailed narrative of the campaign, I might as well drop the subject. On the return, however, of the Army, to the astonishment of every one, they had met with so little adventure, and as we had had some of equal importance, and as novel, perhaps, where we remained, I was encouraged still to keep it in mind: and flattered myself, that, with the aid of some casual notices of the new country I had visited, and of such few original collections as I had made, relative to the Seminoles, I might be enabled to render some of my pages interesting. For the rest, I had to rely on such incidents, as, occurring more immediately among ourselves, furnished matter for "SKETCHES."

I thought afterwards, to preface these with a First Part, or Introduction, giving an historical Sketch of the War, up to that time—the materials for the first few pages of which I gathered from conversation with those who had been on the spot, at the period mentioned, on whose authority I relied for the descriptions I have given, but the greater part of this account, or "SKETCH OF THE SEMINOLE WAR," is the result of the tedious labor of compilation, except where I may have interspersed a few remarks and notes of my own. In the second part, I have sought to vary my pages, as much as the nature of the subject admitted, and to approach as near as I could, the standard of "Light Reading," without sacrificing those notices of the natural objects of a country, which one should not pass over. For a too frequent indulgence, perhaps, in some of these, which may not suit the taste of some readers, and the omission of others, I have to plead the natural bias, which inclines us to regard certain objects in nature more than others, and that my pretensions are not scientific, but I have dwelt on these, as affording in their contemplation, a pleasure to myself. If they are meagre and limited, I must be excused on that score, by the general nature of the plan of these Sketches:

Having premised these Remarks, permit me, Dear Sir, to you—the patriotic Citizen—the zealous Carolinian—the Venerator of the intellectual repositories of our Ancestors, and Preserver of the valuable records of the Past—the Friend and Encourager of Youth—and the Promoter of the Literary prospects of the Future,

TO INSCRIBE,
In simple Testimony of my High Respect,
THIS HUMBLE VOLUME,
I remain, with sincere friendship and respect,

THE AUTHOR.

CHARLESTON, August, 1836.

Part the First:

——

SKETCH

OF THE SEMINOLE WAR

CHAPTER I.

Cause of the War—Council at Camp King— Hoithle-mattee, or Jumper, violently opposed to the Treaty for Removal—Oseola—Sketch of his person and Character—His equivocation and artifice—Murder of Charley Omathlie and massacre of Gen. Wiley Thompson, the Indian Agent—Previous Reports of Hostilities and Alarm at St. Augustine—Assaults and Depredations—Attack upon, and burning of Col. Warren's Wagon Train—Battle of Black Point—Skirmish— Indians surrounded by Gen.Call, and sustain a loss.

As the following sheets are intended to connect a summary account of the prominent and earlier events of the Seminole War, which occurred previous to the Author's arrival in Florida, with lighter details or sketches of whatever fell beneath his eye and contemplation, and appeared worthy of being mentioned, in the late Campaign, I shall begin with a succinct relation of the origin of those desperate outrages which, at this late period of our power and prosperity, when the Indian had become so limited and rare on our borders, that every day gave him a more romantic interest, suddenly overwhelmed with ruin a fair sister territory, seated upon the confines of populous States and settled for more than two centuries, and led to the bloody tragedies as were ever recorded in the annals of the olden Indian time – rendering the name of Seminole conspicuous among the tribes of the Aborigines.

In pursuance of the policy which the government of the United States has for some years past adopted in its relation with the Indian tribes within its limits and jurisdiction, their gradual removal out of its territories to a country assigned them west of the Mississippi, where they might enjoy their national Independence, follow their peculiar habits, and live free from the contaminations of the white man, a council was held at Paine's* [Payne's] Landing[7] in June, 1832; and, under the authority of Col. Gadsden,[8] and with the consent of the Seminole nation, a deputation of Chiefs, accompanied by the Indian Agent, were sent to examine the country allotted them in the Arkansas, and instructed to report to them its nature—they returned and signed a treaty for the Seminoles, in which they agreed to relinquish their lands in Florida to the United States, and to remove to the banks of the "White River" in Arkansas—the section of country apportioned out for them, which adjoins that of their neighbours the Creeks, within a specified time. Some were to go that year, and the rest in the two following years—at the expiration of the period when they should have removed it was found that many were opposed to the treaty and declared that they would not go; they denied the right of the commissioners to bind them by the treaty at Paine's Landing, and affirmed that they were sent, only to examine the country and were not empowered to make a treaty. On the 27th of December, 1832, two hundred and fifty of the warriors met in council, half of

_____

*This was not the first Council held for this purpose.

whom were in favor of, and half against removing. One of the chiefs said that he had one hundred and fifty kegs of good powder and that he for one would not go until that was all burnt out —they were generally armed with rifles, and their conduct was such as to create much apprehension among the settlers in the neighborhood, who, for fear they might break out into some violence, lived ten or twelve families together in one place, armed ready to defend themselves.

After they had been allowed a longer time than was expressed in the treaty, and would not remove peaceably, it was found necessary to employ force, and in January, 1835, a company was ordered to Fort King*[9] under command of Captain Drane,[10] and shortly after, four other companies, the whole to be under the command of Gen. Clinch.[11]

The matter was finally urged in a council held on the 20th April following at Camp King in which Gen. Wiley Thompson,[12] the Indian Agent, called upon the chiefs to confirm the treaty for removal, and threatened them, that in case they refused, and would not consent peaceably to go at the appointed time, which was the January following, to force them at the point of the bayonet; but out of 13 chiefs who were all that were present, there were not more than 8 who confirmed the treaty. The opposition on the part of the dissentient chiefs, was vehement, and attended with their usual bold oratory—Among them was one, who was distinguished for his open and undisguised opposition to the treaty from the beginning, for his stern and uncompromising

---

*Fort King, or Camp King, is situated within the reserve 14 miles from the boundary line; 25 miles south of Micanopy, and about 35 miles nearly west, from Volusia.[13]

character, and his sworn hatred to the white man.

This was Hoithle Mattee, or Jumper,[14] as he is better known by his English name; a tall, fine looking, hard featured Indian, who seems to have preserved undiminished and unpolluted, the noble features, and independent character of the early Seminole. He was between fifty and sixty years of age, and his wisdom and eloquence were such as to cause him to be made Micanopy's*[15] chief orator ("Yatikka-Cluckko") and private secretary—the "Sense-bearer" of the nation, as he was called in their language, or as the negroes more simply designated him, the "Lawyer"—his military talents were considerable also, and this war was not the first occasion on which he had become known, having been a chieftain of some note, during Gen. Jackson's expedition,[16] to whom he was so obnoxious, that at one time $500 was offered for his head.— Hoithle-Mattee, or Jumper, stood up in the council, and with the erect bearing, and frowning front of a Grecian or Roman orator, expressed himself openly, and without disguise, and thundered a torrent of eloquence in the ears of the agent—he concluded his vehement harangue in these emphatic words, "I say there is no good blood between Hoithle-Mattee and the white man— every branch that a white man hews from a tree on our soil, is a limb lopped from Hoithle-Mattee's body—every drop of water that a white man drinks from our springs, is so much blood drawn from Hoithle-Mattee's veins."

---

*King or Governor of the Seminoles.

On the same side, and owning secretly the same sentiments, but studiously avoiding the same bold avowal of them, was Hassé Ola,* or as his name is more euphonically pronounced Oseola,[17] known as well by his English name of Powell.

As this personage subsequently attained much notoriety, and has attracted as much attention as the famous Philip,[18] Tecumseh,[19] or Black Hawk[20] did in their time, the following short sketch, and few particulars relating to him, may prove interesting. Oseola is a half breed, (his father an Englishman,) of the red stick tribe of Creeks—in person, he is middle-sized, of rather slight make, but active and well proportioned; with the exception that he is slightly hump backed, which defect is an Indian, renders his appearance more remarkable. He is not much over thirty years of age—his complexion is rather lighter than that of the Seminoles generally, who are not as dark as many other tribes of Indians, his eye is deep and restless, and his features indicate hardihood and concealed cunning; his voice is remarkably clear and shrill; he has black hair like a full blood Indian, though not as coarse; his dress is usually simple and neat, without much pretension to ornament or style; like other chiefs, he usually wears a scarlet or blue handkerchief, or shawl, wound gracefully around his head in the manner of a turban, and surmounted with the waving Tafa-luste, or black ostrich plume, curving cavalierly over the back of his head; his rifle is the only costly thing he has about him, and is a silver mounted one, which his friend Thompson made him a present of, and which he bought in New York for one hundred dollars.

---

*Which means the "Rising Sun" Hassé in Seminole is Sun.

In his character Oseola combines much of the gallantry, cool courage, and sagacity of the white man, with the ferocity, savage daring and subtlety of the Indian. It was he who led on the bold and successful attack upon the vanguard and wagon train of Col. Warren,[21] near the Wacahouta.[22] He was observed by many at the Battle of Withlacoochee,[23] standing several paces in front of his men, taking cool aim with his rifle, and deliberately wiping it out after each discharge, and his clear voice was repeatedly heard, shouting to his followers the shrill yo-ho-ehèe, of the war gathering cry. He was present, when Gen. Gaines[24] was twice repulsed* in endeavoring to cross the same river, and vigorously attacked in an open pine barren, simultaneously from three different points—to his address is to be attributed the slight of hand feat and astonishing, *ruse de guerre*[25] which, almost in the very presence of an army of five thousand men, effected the safe retreat of the whole Indian force, by dispersing them into numerous small parties, so that when the invading army expected to meet and surround them, it found itself at fault—the enemy gone—and knew not which way to pursue them; and which concealed, as it were, in some magic retreat, their women and children, so that they could not be found, when it was supposed that they could not possibly escape—thus baffling the skill of three of our generals, and rendering the whole scheme for the reduction of the Indians, a total failure. He is allowed by all to be possessed of considerable military talent;

---

*This is perhaps too harsh an expression. Gen. Gaines was fired at, and returned the fire successfully, but did not cross the river, and fell back into his entrenchments.

in addition to his complete generalship and skill in the daring rapid and subtle evolutions of native warfare, he has evinced what scarcely any other Indian chief has ever done a considerable acquaintance with our tactics, and has succeeded in drilling his warriors to form line of battle, assume positions, fire by platoons, &c, which availed them much, when they happened to come into open combat, and put them more upon a par with us, than they used formerly to be, when they were without science, order or discipline. It was for some time credited by many, that he had received a thorough military education at West Point, which rumour arose from his having for a long time been in the habit of attending at the drills of the garrison at Tampa Bay, where he would practice with the soldiers their exercises, and by diligent seeking after information, and observation of military things, became very well versed in them. At that time, no one suspected that he concealed under his friendly gaze, a deep and mortal hatred to the whites, nor dreamt that at the very moment that they scoffed, abused, perhaps beat the insignificant half breed out of their company, or jokingly praised his proficiency in the drill and perhaps treated him to a dram, Powell smothered in his bosom secret hostility, and was maturing a plan which he was one day to put into Oseola execution; that the "Rising Sun" of the obscure, slumberous and peaceful Indian summer day, was waxing strong above the hazy atmosphere, and that shortly, forest and everglade would be hot and brighten under the beams of his fierce meridian and untempered rage. In this deep design of his preparing himself against a future event that he must have foreseen, we recognize the proof of no ordinary intellect, but of a great mind, steady in the pursuit of its purpose, and, grasping, not vainly, but with energy, the proper means to obtain it.

On other occasions, he has evinced the ferocious determination and sanguinary brutality of the savage—with his own hand he murdered the chief Charlie Omathla [Charley Emathla][26] (at a time that Omathla was security for his good conduct,) because he was friendly to the whites, and with the rifle, that his friend Thomson [Thompson] gave him, he pierced his dead body with more than one vindictive ball.

There is one instance in which he is reported to have acted nobly. In his engagement with Clinch at the Withlacoochee, he is said to have given particular directions to his men to be careful and not to shoot at a certain Lieut. G----; [John Graham][27] his wish was strictly observed, and the individual whose life he desired to save, was not once fired at or near, although he was foremost in the thickest of the fight. It appeared that Lieut. G---- and Powell had formerly been acquainted and friends, and for some service rendered and his having been kind to the "poor Indian," he was thus remembered.* Oseola does not pos-

---

*This anecdote of Oseola is inserted on the authority of the New York American whose authority is stated to be a brother of the lieutenant. The author does not however, think that the story is a probable one, and, as he has not seen or heard it confirmed from any other source, does not vouch for its authenticity; there may have been something misrelated or misunderstood; the fact may likely enough have occurred that the Indian bullets struck wide of Lieutenant G---- tho' he was foremost in the fight—the author has witnessed, and has heard of more than one Indian affray, in which similar occurrences have taken place; showers or bullets have been fired by the Indians, at a man within reach of shot, and not one has gone near him; but it is by no means so probable, that Powell, (granting that it was his desire to save Lieutenant G----'s life,) could have made known his wish to all of his men, and still less so, that he should have been obeyed is a matter so difficult to be performed, when it is naturally to be supposed,

sess those high *moral* traits which constitute, in our estimation, a great man among the Indians; he has not been able to avoid the contamination of the white man and the vices of the demi-civilized Indian, and he is intemperate and degraded—his manner and address are courteous and prepossessing, and he well knows how to assume all the pleasing traits of the friendly Indian. By his art, he made dupes of many, and Gen. Thompson could not be persuaded to relinquish the confidence he placed in him, until it was too late—he employed his address likewise, in gaining popularity among the warriors, and though he was not raised to the full command of a Chief until after the war broke out, neither did he inherit any title or power, yet he was always respected by them and considered a man of consequence, and his opinion was of much weight among them.

Gen. Thompson knew that the consent of Oseola would go a great way in effecting a peaceable execution Treaty, and he endeavored, by means of friendship which had existed between them, to prevail on him to acknowledge and to lend his great influence to induce the Seminoles to remove. Powell used much artifice and equivocation, and sought to evade the matter—he gave Thompson to understand that he was willing individually, to confirm the treaty, but said that his signature would be of no

---

the Indians would endeavor to kill all the white men they could. After all, the story may just as well as not, be a hoax, a burlesque upon the many extravagant things, which every day were afloat about the "great Seminole Chief," the new *rara avis*[28], whose fame, like the rising sun, after which he was called, had so suddenly sprung up at once into light, and attracted the eyes of every one. Such an extraordinary instance of friendship and forebearance, is not to be expected of the murderer of Omathla and Thomson.

.

account as he was not a chief but only a sub chief; some short time after, he appeared before Thompson in one of his sullen and moody fits, the effect in some measure of late inebriation, and in a paroxysm of passion, told him, that, *the country was theirs; that they did not want any Indian Agent, and that he (Thompson) had better be off,* threatening him with personal violence, in consequence of which Thompson had him arrested and confined in stocks, and with a chain, in the fort for three days; while he was a prisoner there he seemed to be a close observer of everything that went on in the garrison, such as mounting guard, &c., and made many shrewd enquiries and facetious remarks; he now seemed humbled, and his former gloomy, proud, and insolent manner softened down into good humour, friendly protestations, and fair promises; he told Thompson that if he would release him, he would sign the treaty. The agent had him set at liberty, and he performed his promise and signed the treaty. After this, he curried much favor with the Agent and the officers at Camp King, being of service to them by bringing to punishment criminals and desperate vagabonds of the Mikasauky [Miccosukee, Mikasuki] tribe, the worst tribe of the Seminoles, (who not many years before, had committed open hostilities in Florida) performing many feats of courage, and in this way he gained their entire confidence. But all this while, he was throwing dust in their eyes and secretly plotting with that very tribe. In July a ball play was got up between Osceola's town and that of Catsha-Tustenagge,-Hajo* the Mad Tiger

---

*Catsha, a Panther, called vulgarly in America, Tiger. Tustenagge a War Leader. Hajo, crazy or mad.

Chieftain of the Mikasaukies, and the Commandant at Camp King appointed a convenient place for it to be held in the purlieus of the Camp and made up a lot of settler's wares to the value of about thirty dollars, which was to be made a present to the winning party. At the appointed hour of midday, Oseola and his young men made their appearance, rushing along at great speed and whooping dreadfully, their bodies naked and painted frightfully after their manner, looking like so many demons let loose from the infernal region; they were making their course straight for the Camp, which became alarmed at beholding so wild an array and onset, and a messenger was dispatched to meet them and tell them to pass by a different way, but notwithstanding, the greater portion of them rushed through the Camp in so menacing and warlike a manner that the men were ordered to stand to arms, in case there might be a meditated treachery. Catsha Tustenagge did not immediately arrive, as his town was thirty miles distant, but he soon after made his appearance in similar style, and the two parties rushed to meet each other in the animating and manly contest of the Pokitcha. Oseola's town was the conqueror and they separated, without Oseola's claiming the goods; two or three days elapsed, and he did not demand them; this indifference to articles usually prized and coveted by Indians, somewhat surprised the Camp, and he was at length asked why he did not take them away. Oseola answered that he did not seek to brag over Catsha who had come such a long distance to play with him, but that he wanted to be generous to his brother and to make him a present; that his brother was very poor, and he, and his young men had not wherewithal to subsist, as the Mikasaukies were prohibited from buying powder and lead on account of their misdeeds, and their rifles were empty and they could not hunt; he requested, therefore, that the present might be made in powder and lead, that he might let Catsha have enough for his wants.

During the course of the summer, the chiefs were laying up stores of ammunition; they were supplied largely by the Spaniards, from the West India islands, and by unprincipled and unsuspicious traders; from Indian Key, St. Marks, and St. Augustine. At Volusia, on the St. John's, a short distance from the Indian reserve, they procured a great quantity from a trader, who lived there—he was detected once or twice, by Gen. Thompson, who threatened to break up his store, which at last he did. In the midst of his artifices, and when Gen. Thompson still entertained a perfect confidence in him, Oseola suddenly threw off the mask of friendship. His first open act of hostility, was the murder of Charlie Omathla*—this friendly chief, was surprised and assassinated as he was on his return from Camp King, accompanied by his two daughters— he then put himself at the head of the Mikasaukies, who were glad to have a chieftain whom they knew to be both artful and bold, and he compelled, through fear, many of the relatives of Charlie Omathla to join him—the next act of hostility, in which he appeared at the time, was

---

*Or Emartla, which signifies, one who goes before, or a leader in consequence of this murder, Holase Emartla, the brother of Charlie, with some of the clan, took up arms against Powell, and the hostile Seminoles, and were afterwards with Gen. Call in his expedition.

the massacre of Gen. Thompson. The agent had been warned more than once that his life was in danger, and advised by his friends, not to trust himself out of the fort, but he still was obstinate in his belief that the Indians intended no harm, and he apprehended no danger from them. On Monday, the 28th December, as Erastus Rogers the sutler, with his clerks, were dining at his house, which was about 250 yards from Camp King, and as Gen. Thompson and Lieut. Constantine Smith[29] were walking out nearby, a party of savages crawled up within a few feet of the road, unobserved, their bodies being naked, and painted red, so as to resemble the low scrubby oak leaves, at that season of the year. They fell upon Thompson and Smith, whom they immediately shot and scalped; they then attacked the house, fired at least a hundred balls at it, and then rushed into it, Powell being at their head. Rogers and his clerks had run out, and endeavored to make their escape into a hammock nearby; looking around, and seeing no one in the room, the Indians immediately left the house, and Rogers and the others, were detected before they could escape, and killed. This daring act was perpetrated within sight of the garrison, and within the range of the, two six pounders, with which the picquet was fortified, but notwithstanding, the Indians escaped without a shot being fired at them, or any pursuit being made. Many of the garrisons were at the time sick, and the rest were outside the picquet ditching, and had not their arms immediately near them—the six pounders were not fired in consequence of the interruption of a building, which stood in front of the small gate through wince they might have been used, and the large gate was on the opposite side of the picquet, and before the guns could be removed, the Indians had made off. There were fifteen bullets found in the body of Gen. Thompson, and sixteen in that of Rogers; the savages had taken off their scalps with the whole of the hair, and beat in and mangled their heads horribly. This is not the first instance upon record, in which agents or others, having to do with this treacherous race, have fallen sacrifices to their credulity, and faith in Indian friendship. Gen. Thompson had been always treated by them with a friendliness bordering on affection, but so deep is the Indian's love of country, so rooted in his soul his attachment to the soil of his fathers, and the ancient landmarks of his hunting grounds, that this master sentiment, will conquer the dearest interests of the heart.

This event happened some little time after the Indians had come to open hostilities with the whites; as early as the 1st December, information had been received at St. Augustine, that they had sent their women and children into the interior, and were making preparations for an attack upon the whites. It was reported that 4 or 500 warriors had already embodied, in the vicinity of Camp King, and the United States troops stationed there, were esteemed altogether insufficient for the protection of the inhabitants. About the same time the murder of Charlie Omathla became known. The town was thrown into much consternation at these reports; some already began to remove their families in the first vessels which offered a conveyance. The defenseless state of St. Augustine, unprotected

by troops, and possessing an inefficient militia, badly organized, and almost unprovided with arms and ammunition,
struck all with alarm; and the military commandant, Gen.
Joseph Hernandez,[30] began to take measures for the defence of the town; the militia were mustered, and 500 stand
of arms sent for from Savannah.

On the 17th, thirty Indians attacked Col. Simmons'
house, on the Palatka road, about 8 miles from Miconopy—they rushed on the house with furious yells and vollies
of rifles; Simmons, J. Carr, and two others, who happened
to be in the house at the time, barred up the doors and de-
fended themselves until daylight, when the Indians went
off, driving away with them a drove of fat hogs out of the
pens. Intelligence of this having been brought to the head
quarters of the militia, near Fort Crum, Capt's. Sumerall
and Gibbon's companies were immediately despatched at
20 minutes notice, accompanied by Carr as guide, to pursue and destroy the marauders, wherever they might be
found.

Capt. [Gabriel] Priest's plantation at Wacahouta was at
the same time devastated—his son wounded, his buildings,
one hundred bushels of corn, and all his cotton, burnt. The
savages got all his horses except five, and drove off 21 fine
fat hogs, which were in pen, ready for slaughter. The inhabitants everywhere in the neighborhood deserted their houses, and fled, congregating together into temporary stockades,
for protection. At Newnansville* the residents and those
who had come there for refuge, became so alarmed that upwards of 240 women and children were

*Newnansville is 60 to 65 miles west of Picolata.

engaged in endeavoring to throw up entrenchments for their
defence against the savage enemy, and while they were at work,
they were guarded by none but old men and boys; others took
possession of the court house as a fort, and the jail was used as a
blockhouse. At Fort Crum, 200 persons in a short time had collected, to embody against the enemy, and more afterwards
joined them; at this post Col. Warren soon found himself at the
head of 150 mounted volunteers. Receiving orders from Gen.
Clinch to scour the country about the district where the late
depredations had been committed, he, on the 18th inst. took up
the line of march, from Fort Crum, and proceeded to scour
out the Wacahouta* and adjacent hammocks. As the baggage
would be an encumbrance, he sent it on before him, with an escort, by the direct route to Wetumky, via Miconopy. On arriving at the Kanopaha prairie, Col. Warren took Captains
M'Lemore[31] and Lancaster's companies and pursued the trail;
they passed the house of Benj. Warren, which they found in
flames, and came up with the baggage train which had been
attacked and set on fire; about eighty Indians in ambush had
waylaid the wagons as they passed over the prairie; they suffered the guard to pass on, and then fell on and captured the
three wagons; the officer in command of the baggage train, and the
escort, escaped to Miconopy. The Indians had taken out the ammunition and burnt two of the wagons, when Dr. M'Lemore came
up with thirty men, attacked them, and retook the remaining wagon; the Indians then retired

*Corrupted from Wauca-hutche, and that from Wauca-hatche, a cow pen or
pasture; it is south west of Miconopy.

into a hammock. Dr. M'Lemore had two horses shot under him, and on foot, with sword in hand, he called to his men to follow him to the charge, but only twelve had courage to do so; he was therefore compelled to make good his own retreat, with the wagon and four men wounded. It was not ascertained how many of the Indians were slain in this affair. The Floridians had one sergeant and seven privates killed, and six wounded, one of them mortally, five horses killed and six wounded. Several papers of consequence, such as orders, reports, &c., were lost likewise, and ammunition, surgical instruments, &c., some of which were afterwards recovered.*

On the 20th, (Sunday) a portion of the Florida militia, under Gen. Call,[32] Cols. Parish[33] and Warren, and Lieut. Col. Mills,[34] marched by the place of action, gathering up on their way the remains of the baggage that had not been carried away by the Indians. As they were continuing farther on, the advance guard under Geo. Fisher, came upon a party of the enemy, who were burning the house of a Mr. Hagan; a brisk firing commenced with the guard, but the whole force soon arriving at the spot, the Indians fled into a hammock or thick scrub, surrounding a small grassy pond. Gen. Call ordered a part of the force to surround the hammock, while Cols. Parish and Read[35] rushed in the scrub, at the head of a detachment, and a desperate fight ensued; it was maintained with fierce spirit on the part of the Indians, who made the thicket resound

---

*This first affair with the Indians, which is known as the "battle of Black point," took place three miles across the Alachua prairie, south of Tarver's plantation, which is six miles north east of Miconopy.

with their savage yells, and kept up a continual fire by platoons, while the brave Floridians charged through the scrub* with much gallantry. Four of their number were severely wounded, among whom was Capt. Lancaster; he had stepped upon the trunk of a tree that had been blown down, and while he was looking about for an Indian, whom he knew to be hiding somewhere near him, his foe shot him from behind the roots of the tree, and wounded him in the neck; Mr. Curry, of Mandarin, coming up immediately, shot the Indian dead. Of those of the Indians who were surrounded, all were killed except four. The action lasted an hour.

---

*The terms scrub and hammock occur so frequently in the description of Indian battles in Florida, that they demand a note of explanation. What is called "scrub" in Florida, and in the southern states, is a barren tract of land, covered with tough stunted thickets; of scrubby oak, dwarf pine, myrtle, prickly pear, &c.

Hammock, according to Webster, is the proper orthography of hammock. He supposes it to be an Indian word—if it is, it must be from the language of the ancient Indians of Florida. The Seminole word for what we understand as hammock, is ett-say-cha (Dr. Simmons has Pilaklikaha for "scattered hammocks")—Quere, whether Tomoka, the name of a river abounding with hammocks, may not originally have been spelt Homoka. The Encyclopedia puts it as a sea term for conical mounds or hillocks, overgrown with trees &c: so Webster defines it; from which it would appear that it is more properly derived from hammock, the suspended beds used at sea (Spanish humaca), and applied first by Spanish seamen; as the soil is, as it were, suspended, or raised out of marshy, swampy tracts or savannas. The term is, however, very loosely applied, and in the mention of Indian fights, hammock is used generally for any thick wooded place. Pickering's Vocabulary has neither scrub nor hammock.

CHAPTER II.

*Destruction of plantations on the coast of Mosquito, south of St. Augustine, by
Philip and his bands; remark on the slave population; their fidelity and attachment to their masters; massacre of Mr. Woodruff at Volusia; alarm
at St. Augustine; measures for defence; distress and scarcity of provision; coincidence of the Seminole war with the Yemassee war in Carolina; Volunteers from Savannah arrive at Picolata; the progress of the Indians unchecked; delay of assistance from the Government; defect of the army; negligence, of the department of war; Gen. Clinch waits for a reinforcement,
and for Gen. Call to join him, in order to march against the Indians.*

By the end of the month, the Indians had overrun and destroyed
nearly all the plantations to the southward of St. Augustine, as
far as New Smyrna. All the principal houses and sugar mills at
that settlement, and at Mosquito, were burnt—the plantations of
Dunham, Cruger, De Peyster, Hunter, Dummitt, Anderson, Wil-
liams and Heriot[36] were ravaged—the sugar mills burnt, and
with one or two exceptions, every dwelling house. At Col. Dummitt's place, they drove out stock, rifled the house of all that was
valuable, and set it on fire; but from some cause, it did not burn.
They then crossed over to the light house, broke the lantern,
and destroyed everything they could lay their hands on. In some
of these devastations at Tomoka, not more than thirteen Indians
were concerned. These bands were headed by a chieftain called
Phillip, and an active smart negro, known by the name of John
Caesar. Philip was married

to a sister of Miconopy, and is the son of old Philip;[37] he formerly lived at Wacahouta, but now lives at Tohopeke-like [Toho-
pekaliga],* a town situated not very far from the head waters of
the St. John's, upon an Island surrounded by deep water in a
large lake. It derives its name from the circumstance of its being
a fine cattle country, where cow-pens are stationary, and not flying or transient.** This band consists of between 100 and 150
warriors, and was joined by a small party of Uchees, who formerly had a settlement about Spring Garden.[38] They are the
most savage and mischievous set among the Seminoles—noted
for their destructions in Mosquito, and hence, they have been
called the Mosquito Indians. From some cause or other, they do
not act in connexion and concert with Oseola and the rest of the
Seminoles, but take every opportunity, by themselves, to do all
the harm they can.

The inhabitants fled to the plantations of Darley and Bulow,[39]*** where a small force from St. Augustine, late from Picolata, under Major Putnam,[40] was stationed. The negroes generally
fled for protection, or were sent to St. Augustine; some were killed,
and others were carried off by the Indians, or voluntarily
joined them. It is a fact worthy of remark, and one which attests
the mild character of slavery in the southern States, and the affection of the negro for his master. that few were known positively to
have joined and acted with the Indians, while it is

---

*Tohopeke-like is 150 miles by the accessible route from St Augustine, 80
from Spring Garden and about the same distance east of Pilaklikaha.
**From *Tohopeke* a pen, and *like* sitting down.
***40 miles from St Augustine.

asserted on good authority, that many were either taken prisoners, or forced against their will, at the edge of the tomahawk, to go with them; and in one or two instances their families were barbarously butchered, which proves that compulsion was used; and that fear, not friendship and concert, was the cause of many not coming in to their masters. On the other hand, had they been discontented with their lot, and disposed to unite with the enemy, there were strong inducements for them to change their situation, and there was a favorable opportunity for them to do so. In parts of Florida there are still many Indian negroes, or slaves of Indians* who live pretty much like free negroes in settlements by themselves, spending much of their time in hunting, &c; they can scarcely be said to be slaves, having so much freedom, and they are indulgently treated by their masters. They are many of them runaways and refugees. In the late war with Great Britain, 400 of them were embodied in arms under one Col. Woodbine,[41] who received a commission from one of the governors of the West India Islands, and the Indians themselves were kept in awe by them, and found themselves in danger of being subjected to a dulocracy. It was to be feared that the dangerous example of the enticing independence enjoyed by these negroes, their corrupting communication with the slaves of the planter,

---

*Miconopy possesses upwards of a hundred negro slaves; they do no work except to make him a little corn, and he is not apparently the richer for them than any other Indian, and lives in much the same style as the poorest among them. Some of these negroes were purchased with cattle of which the Seminoles possess vast herds, and very fine; one of their chiefs formerly used to sell annually 1000 head of steers.

and their actual league with hostile Indians might exert an evil influence upon this property in Florida, but the event has shown that a large majority of our slaves preferred to remain with their masters in the happy and secure state of servitude to which they had been accustomed, rather than to seek a better one in a visionary and uncertain independence, and exemption from toil, in which they would still be subject to dominion of another sort—to the lawless caprices and cruel power of some savage tyrant, to cares and privations, and numberless other ills.

Their own conduct, in many instances, spoke for their fidelity; many fought by the side of their masters, and were willing rather to die in their defence, than desert them for the sake of life and lazy liberty, under Indian owners; their zeal and exertions in saving the property of their masters was in most instances astonishing, and gave proofs of the most marked and singular affection. Of their own accord, and at the risk of their lives, they remained on the plantations, working all day and half the night, in removing and thatching the corn, &c. in some safe place; the driver of Mr. Anderson used much forethought in stoving in the boats of the plantation that he could not save, so that the Indians might not cross the river; and the slaves of another gentleman, with that attentive love which is minute even to trifles, carried a favorite little boat of their master seven miles over land on their shoulders, with two women in it.

On the 26th, Mr. Henry Woodruff a respectable planter at Volusia, near Spring Garden, on the St. John's was killed; he was riding along on his horse, with his servant following on a mule; the servant was fired on and wounded in the thigh. At the same instant, Mr. Woodruff was shot down, and fell from his horse. The servant succeeded in making his escape on his master's horse; Spring Garden, higher up on the St. Johns, was left undisturbed some time longer. Mr. Forrester, who had an interest there, left the place as soon as he heard of the disaster at Volusia, and that the Indians were in the neighborhood, and put ten muskets in the hands of his negroes, requesting them to defend it until he could join some force and return to act against the enemy.

At St. Augustine, the inhabitants were becoming daily more and more alarmed. At a time when the enemies were upwards of a hundred miles from the town, and not known to be any nearer, vague rumors, the most extraordinary reports of the numbers, successes and progress of the Indians, were constantly afloat, and the minds of the citizens were kept in perpetual agitation. The little city already wore the appearance of a place upon the eve of an attack or siege—men running about, and parading with military buttons in their hats, to supply the want of uniforms; without organization, plan, or concert; some mounting guard in the old Spanish fort;* some patrolling, and others, in parties of from twenty to fifty, despatched in various directions, separated many miles from each other, to reconnoitre the country around, to look for trails and procure intelligence. A corps of St. Augustine Guards, under Major Putnam, marched to scour the country at Mosquito,

*Fort St. Mark—there was no ordinance in the fort.

and were directed to go from thence to Volusia, to guard the passes of the St. John's at that Point; another company was stationed at Picolata, and a third went to scout between that place and Volusia. Out of 240 men, and about 60 veterans, or alarm men, composing the militia, nearly ninety were employed in this way and the remainder, some of them old men, were harassed with patrolling and keeping guard every third night at least. There were some who esteemed absolutely necessary all these military movements, and saw the propriety of keeping out scouts daily, while others thought them only productive of bustle, confusion, and increased alarm, without any advantage. They blamed the commandant for sending so many men out of the town, and leaving all the duty of guarding it to a few. Picquets were afterwards placed over the bridge, and outside of the gates, as well as in the Fort, and this measure gave more satisfaction. During this agitation and tumult, business was at a low ebb, except among military contractors, who were preparing to make as much as they could out of the government. As the Indians made farther progress in their devastation, and approached nearer, matters grew worse, and the situation of the town was now, in reality, alarming and distressing. Numbers of the adjoining inhabitants and negroes had been driven into it for protection, and the want of provisions began, not only to be apprehended, but actually felt—horses and companies were to be fed, and depended chiefly upon the town for their supplies, as the resources of the country were cut off. The Indians had destroyed most of the corn on the plantations, and what remained, could with difficulty be brought in—they had driven off stock of every description, and what could be found, was procured at much hazard, and could not be kept away from their range any length of time—butchers and fishermen were employed nearly all their time in keeping guard; and common stores, such as hard bread and pork, were not to be had. To mend the matter, there was but one sloop in, the trade with St Augustine. and Charleston, and her trips were usually long, so that unless speedy relief was afforded by Savannah or Charleston, the most dreadful consequences would ensue. All this while no communication could be kept up with Gen. Clinch at Camp King; no one would venture to take the mail; and important despatches, which should have been forwarded immediately, were prevented from being sent.

One cannot help being struck with the remarkable coincidence in some respects between the present Seminole War in Florida, with that which occurred in Carolina with the Yemassees, 120 years ago. East Florida was the original possession of the ancient Yemassees, who also owned a portion of Carolina, and the fierce and warlike spirit of that powerful tribe, seems to have sprung up from their graves, to animate the souls of their conquerors; some few drops of their blood yet exist in the veins of the Seminoles, and the language of the latter has borrowed many of their words.* In both instances,

---

*The name Seminole means wanderers, or wild people.

**They emigrated from the main body of the Creeks about one hundred years ago, *[continued next page]*

***It is worthy of remark as to this term by which the Seminoles designate themselves, that at the present day they contra-distinguish the Creeks by the appellation "Taloph-ulke"—people living in towns or having an established home—*Talopha* means town and *ulke* a tribe.

love of country and hatred of the white man were the remote and abiding cause of hostilities. In both, the Spaniards were concerned, and aided the Indians, by furnishing them ammunition; for they chiefly supplied the quantities of powder which the Seminoles have so profusely expended, without exhausting; and it is now generally believed, that they have encouraged the carrying away of negroes from Florida, as they

---

*[continued from previous page]** roving about, as Indian tribes are fond of doing, in search of new hunting grounds and wild adventure. They entered Florida, enticed by the- pleasantness of a country, abounding in all manner of vegetable productions, grateful to their tastes and lazy habits; affording fine hunting grounds, and covered with beautiful lakes and shady groves; and there they encountered the Yemassees with whom they had some hard fought battles, and who were finally exterminated, and the scattered remnant of them made captives by the Seminoles. Bartram[42] supposes that some of them escaped and survived a considerable time, and relates a tradition of their enemies the Creeks—that a beautiful race of Indians, whose women they called "daughters of the Sun" resided amidst the recesses of the Oke-fanokee wilderness, where they enjoyed perpetual felicity in ever blooming islands, inaccessible to human approach—this terrestrial paradise situated in a beautiful lake, they related, had been seen by some of their enterprising hunters, who being lost in inextricable swamps and bogs, were on the point of perishing, but received unexpected relief from these beautiful women, who kindly gave them such provisions as they had with them—fruit, oranges, dates, &c; but enjoined them to fly for safety to their own country, as their husbands were fierce men, and cruel to strangers. It is probable he imagines that this fable took its rise from a fugitive remnant of the Yemassees, who found a refuge in this swamp, and were perhaps after a lapse of time, accidentally seen by some of the hunters of the Creek nation. Simmons,[43] in his notes of Florida, says, "the Ocklewahaw tribe of Seminoles are thought to be descendants of the Yemassees, as they are blacker than the other tribes, and the Yemassees are said to have been remarkably dark complexioned. King Payne, the grandfather of Miconopy, the present governor, married his Yemassee slave, and his son, chief Payne, uncle to Miconopy, bore strong marks of his dark descent."

*Though there is no positive certainty of this date, in is inferred from traditions among them, from the connexion of their history with that of the Yemassees, and also from the following talk, which their chiefs lately sent, to the American Government, in which there is much of that beautiful simplicity which is the characteristic of Indian oratory—"An hundred summers have seen the Seminole warrior reposing undisturbed under the shade of his Live Oak, and the Suns of an hundred winters have risen on his ardent pursuit of the Buck and the Bear, with none to question his bounds, or dispute his range."

formerly did from Carolina, and there is no doubt that the Indians have sold some of them to the Spaniards for ammunition. Though the proportion of whites to Indians in the whole territory, is far greater than it was in Carolina, yet the two countries bear some resemblance in point of settlement—a great portion of Florida being unsettled, as was the case with South Carolina. In both wars, the "Bloody Stick" was sent to the Creeks, and correspondence carried on with other tribes.* The Indians commenced and carried on their depredations and massacres from a similar point, south-westwardly and southwardly of the town, and at about the same distance. The settlements on the St. Johns and Alachua were laid waste in the first instance, as were Pocotaligo and St. Bartholomews. All the settlements near the coast, from Mosquito to Matanzas, were burned and destroyed, until the savages threatened St. Augustine from Picolata** and St. Josephs, as they did Charleston from Stono and Goosecreek. In both instances the inhabitants flocked to the town," they who came in brought such different accounts of the number and strength of the Indians, that the citizens were doubtful of their safety."*** In Charleston, they sent to Virginia for assistance, as they did from St. Augustine to Charleston; "the men in it were obliged to watch every third night****; there was, perhaps, the same relative estimation of the Indian and white force. In Charleston, there were 1200 militia, and the

---

*Gen. Scott is of opinion, that the report of their having sent a war belt to the Winnebagoes is not unfounded.
**Picolata was the highest point on the St. Johns unabandoned by the inhabitants.
***Ramsay's History of South Carolina.
****do do [ditto].

Indians were computed at, about 7000; in St. Augustine., they numbered between 2 and 300 militia, and they estimated the Indian warriors, together with negroes along with them, to amount to 1500 or 2000. Farther than these enumerated particulars, the parallel ceases; and the two cases are almost diametrically opposite. Our brave ancestors contended against such odds with their single forces, and in a very short time, not only drove the enemy from their walls, but chased them far from their own homes, and the "Indian land," over the Savannah River, and thus rid themselves at once of their foe. On the other hand, the Floridians were not only superior in number to the Indians throughout the territory, but were assisted by an United States regular army, alone equal to that of the enemy, besides troops from three or four States. Notwithstanding which overawing force, the Seminole, so far from being crushed in his lair, or driven to sue for peace, has, after five months hard fighting, grown only the bolder; and has carried the torch and scalping knife still farther into the more populous parts of the territory.

On the 31st of the month, a company of forty volunteers, from Savannah, arrived at Picolata to garrison the Fort at that place. This was considered an important post, as there were large stores of provisions and munitions of war there, which the Indians would have sought to take possession of; and the relief was timely, as it enabled the force which had been sent from St. Augustine there, to leave for Mosquito, where the ravages of the Indians called for every exertion to check their ruinous career.

Hitherto, the savage enemy had advanced upon the bloody war path with triumph, and without molestation; spreading desolation around, stopping only to bivouac and carouse in the rich fields and well stocked farmstead of the planter, or to revel around their midnight fires and the flames of burning dwellings, over the scalps and plunder they had taken. With the exception of one encounter, in which some blood was shed on both sides, and the punishment which was inflicted on the daring party that set fire to the baggage train, they had, as yet, met with no check—on the contrary, they were becoming more and more emboldened, as they beheld the scattered and panic-stricken whites flying everywhere before them, and saw flame after flame reddening the sky, as each marauding band applied the torch to some devoted sugar mill or villa; and by these sad and lurid beacons, made known to each other their several positions, and, at the same time, to the unfortunate planters, their several losses. About this time, however, they met with a severe retribution, and had to acknowledge, to their cost, the superior prowess of the white man. As this event was preceded by another of equal importance, and if anything, more disastrous to the Americans, the reader will find it mentioned in a subsequent chapter.

From the commencement of hostilities until the present period, the arm of Government, whose agency in the concerns of the Indians was the cause of their outbreak upon the innocent inhabitants of the Territory, had not been raised one jot to repress their fury.—A small force, as we have previously stated,

had been ordered on to Camp King, with the view of overawing the Seminoles into a compliance with the terms of the treaty;—but government, deceived by the misrepresentations of
the Indian Agent, who expressed confidence in the friendship
of the Indians, was not fully apprised of the storm that was
brewing, and miscalculated the power of the enemy. The report of the officer appointed so act in conjunction with Gen.
Thompson, for the emigration of the Indians, which was rendered to Government in Sept. 1835, estimated the population
of the Seminoles, inclusive of negroes, not to exceed 3000, of
which 1600 were females. This census was taken at a time,
when provision was to be made for the necessary articles
with which the Indians were to be furnished; it is supposed,
therefore, that they were interested in rendering in their full
number. But on the other hand, there was a counter interest
on the part of the Government, through its agents, to save
money to the coffers, and to make their numbers the least possible. Be this as it may, it is asserted by an official authority,*
that as a division of opinion was known to exist among the
Indians, it was to be concluded that the force of the hostile
party could not amount to more than 300 warriors. So far,
the War Department seems exonerated from blame, by the
misrepresentations of its agents. On the 8th October, 1835,
Gen. Clinch informed the Adjutant General that he was still
under apprehensions that force must be used to remove the
Indians; and suggested the employment of 150 mounted militia
for this purpose, in addition to a cutter,

---

*Washington Globe, 30th January.

and the force under Maj. Dade,[44] at Key West. This application was rejected, on the ground that the President had no authority to call the militia into the service, unless actual hostilities were committed, and that the regular force was fully competent to remove the Indians. Gen. Clinch was at this time notified that fourteen companies were at his disposal for this purpose, and for the protection of the territory. Ten of these had been placed under his command in Febr'y.; two more on the 15th October, and the other two on the 21st. It would appear that this force was amply sufficient, and from this representation, that all due diligence had been used to prepare against hostilities; but it remains to be considered, in what manner these troops were appropriated for the protection of Florida; and here, the error and fault of the government lay. In its improvidence and niggardness, it neglected to prepare beforehand for the crisis, and at the moment of alarm, before actual hostilities had commenced, to throw, as it should have done, a sufficient number of troops into the territory, concentrated at the point of danger. For this faulty omission of duty, we are to look to the imperfection of the army system, as well as to the negligence of the administration. It is impossible that of so small an army as we maintain, scattered over so immense a territory, that any adequate portion can be concentrated speedily enough at any point of danger; and unless a sufficient force should happen to be at the spot when hostilities commence—the country, especially in an Indian war, must suffer a great deal. A fortnight and more must elapse before troops, distant near a, thousand miles, can arrive; and if a few should chance to be nearer, their duty compels them to do the best they can; and rushing to the seat of war, brave troops encounter unequal odds, and for want of timely aid, are cut off and destroyed. In the mean time, important posts in other far districts, are evacuated and left unprotected, and before the scattered elements of the national defence can be brought to bear upon the point of action, it is found necessary to call out the militia, and the government undergoes as much expense as might maintain a large addition to the army, if, together with the expense and waste incurred in the employment of militia, the destruction of property, (which, in a case like the present, should of right be the loss of the government) and the diminution of the revenue of the country be taken into the estimate.*

Of the fourteen companies, placed at the disposal of Gen. Clinch, in October, none were under his actual command at the time when he most needed them. Some were in Louisiana, and did not arrive at Tampa Bay until near the end of December, more than two months after Gen. Clinch had written to inform that the Indians must be removed by force, and a month after, he again stated, that the Seminoles were determined upon mischief. After arriving at Tampa Bay, these detached companies had to march a distance of a hundred miles through the heart of the Indian country, to join him.

The imperfection of the army system mitigates, but it does not entirely exonerate from blame, the head of the department, to whose exclusive care was entrusted the management

---

*See appendix, Note A.

of the Indians, and whose duty it was to protect the inhabitants. It cannot be denied that there was tardiness and neglect in anticipating the evil. The official alluded to before, excuses this want of promptness, inasmuch as that because the Indians were not to remove before January, hostilities were not to be expected until the time of actual embarkment—a lame supposition—for what enemy, especially, what Indian enemy, would wait until the last unfavorable moment to take up arms, when their object would be to gain an advantage, and do all the harm they could, while their opponent was unprepared. It asserts that the first report of actual hostilities was received at the Adjutant General's office on the 6th of January, in a letter of Gen. Clinch, of 16th December, and that on the 8th, a request was made of the Governors of South Carolina, Georgia, and Alabama for troops—but even after this, there was very little celebrity in the operations carrying on. The consequences of waiting until actual hostilities had commenced should have been known—the department was aware of the length of time that must elapse before communications could be received and transmitted—of the difficulty of a speedy concentration of troops; and it was not enough that 14 companies were placed nominally, as it were, under the command of Gen. Clinch, but they should instantly, upon his advices of October and November, have been ordered to report themselves to him at Camp King—the proper officers should not have remained in ignorance of the force of the Indians and of their capacity to do mischief, and possessed with an unfortunate and blind confidence in the valor of a handful of regulars, and of their superiority over a foe whom they had been accustomed to look upon with contempt, or to regard with pity, rather than with fear. Hence it was, that after intelligence upon intelligence, came daily, of the distressed state of the territory and of the formidable embodiment of the savages, there appeared a perfect callousness and indifference on the part of the government to the safety of its citizens, and an utter paraliztion of the federal arm.

The commander of the southern station of the army, delayed to send reinforcements, under the erroneous impression that the force under Gen. Clinch, in conjunction with the militia of Florida, was amply sufficient to put down the Indians; and it was not, until nearly all the havoc was committed, that slowly, and by driblets, the United States troops began to make their appearance in the territory. During the interval, the militia had to bear the whole brunt of the war—the regular force was stationary, and Gen. Clinch had not moved a step from Camp King, where he was employing the best means he could for the protection of the frontier, without hazarding the few troops he had with him—dividing his force between Camp King and Fort Drane—and he waited for a reinforcement for Gen. Call to unite with him, to march into the enemy's country.

CHAPTER III.

*A reinforcement is despatched from Tampa Bay to Gen. Clinch; Massacre
of Major Dade's detachment; Battle of Withlacoochee.*

Through the means of runners of the friendly Indians, a communication had been carried on between Generals Thompson
and Clinch at Camp King, and Major Belton,[45] at Tampa. Bay. In
the letters which were sent, care was taken to state facts and
numbers in French, so that in case the couriers were intercepted,
the Indians might not be informed, through their negro interpret-
ers, most of whom speak English and Spanish, but not French, of
any contemplated movement. In pursuance of the instructions of
Gen. Clinch, Major Belton despatched a detachment of one hundred and two men, consisting of Brevet-Maj. Dade's company of
Infantry, Capt. Fraser's[46] company of 3d, and Capt. Gardner's[47]
of 2d Artillery, from Fort Brooke*, to join Gen. Clinch at the
Withlacoochee River. Maj. Dade took with him provision for ten
days, a light ox wagon, and a six pounder. The first night, he
halted at Little Hillsboro' river, 7 miles from Fort Brooke; the
next day, he made a halt near the bridge, on the Big Hillsboro',
and at 11 o'clock that night, was joined by a gallant volunteer of
the name of Jewell, who rode upon an express from Fort
Brooke. He informed Maj. Dade that Major Belton was making
every exertion to push on 1300 rations and all the ammunition
that could be spared, and also that the bridge on the Hillsboro'
had been burnt by the; Indians. On the 27th, Major Dade was
supposed, as well as his route can be traced, to have got to the big
Withlacochee, where he

---

*At Tampa.

entrenched himself that night, as he did each night where he stopped. The next morning, at 10 o'clock, while in column of route, four miles from the halt, north of the Withlacoochee, the Detachment were suddenly attacked from an ambush of pine trees, palmetto bushes, and grass; they received several rounds before an Indian could be seen. From the extent of ground which the fire of the enemy covered, they were supposed to be in light infantry extension, but suddenly, they rose up in a swarm, that showed them between the files. There were at least 800; about 100 of whom were well mounted on horses, naked, and painted in the most hideous manner. Among them were many negroes.—The unequal contest was maintained for the space of an hour; during which the Indians fired volley upon volley, cutting down soldier after soldier, until not more than 30 or 40 of the brave hundred remained alive. For a short time, the Indians drew off a little, and there was a pause in the action, during which the survivors, most of whom were wounded, felled some trees in a manner so as to form a triangular kind of breastwork of logs, and behind this defence, continued the contest, until, with the exception of three, who escaped, every officer and man of them were slaughtered. Maj. Dade and his horse were killed at the first onset, and an interpreter, named Louis. Capt. Fraser was in the advance guard, and also fell among the first; Lieut. Mudge,[48] of the 3d Artillery, received his mortal wound at the first fire; Lieut. Kean [Keais],[49] 3d Artillery, had both arms broken at the first fire, and was finally tomahawked by a Negro; Lieut. Henderson[50] had his left arm broken at the first fire, and after that discharged 30 or 40 shots from a musket, at the assailants. Capt. Gardner was wounded at the second attack; after he fell, towards the last of the contest, Lieut. Basinger,[51] (3d Artillery,) remarked, "I am the only officer left, and boys, we will do the best we can." He was shortly after wounded, and receiving several other wounds, he was crawling away, nearly dying, into a place of concealment, when he was discovered by an Indian Negro, and barbarously tomahawked and butchered.—Dr. Gatlin[52] was not wounded, and did not fall until after the second attack. He placed himself behind the breastwork, with two double barrel guns, and remarked, that he had four barrels for them. This was the only instance in the course of this war, up to the period when this sketch terminates, in which the Indians, confident in their superior number, left their hiding places, and rushed into close conflict with the whites. The sanguinary fight was maintained hand to hand, after the manner of the ancient Greek and Roman warfare. The two foes clinched in mortal strife—the Americans clubbed their muskets, and used their bayonets and knives—the Indians their tomahawks and knives, and muskets, which they wrenched from the gripe of the slain. The six pounder had been used, and 30 or 40 rounds fired from it; but the heavy cross fire of the Indians cut down the Artillerists as fast as they manned it, and eventually, the carriage was burnt, and the gun sunk in a swamp. After the massacre was consummated, the savages rejoiced over their triumph, after their usual mode, by dancing the war dance around the bodies of the slain; but, contrary to their usual practice, they did not themselves take the scalps of their victims, but left this to be done by the Negroes, who, outvying their savage masters in hellish cruelty, also barbarously pierced the throats of all whose cries and groans gave token of lingering life. After the fatal tragedy, a dog belonging to Capt. Gardner, returned to Tampa Bay and gave the first ominous tidings of the sad event. On the 29th, one man arrived at Fort Brooke, from the battle ground, who brought the intelligence, and the day after, another came in, severely wounded—the first related that he was in the act of being strangled, but he bought his life for six dollars, and in his enemy, recognized an Indian whose hatchet he had helved a few days previous—the other brought a note from Capt. Fraser to Maj. Mountford [Mountfort],[53] who was expected with a detachment to join Maj. Dade, on the route. The note was fastened in a cleft stick and stuck in a creek—dated the 27th, and stated that they were beset every night, and pushing on as fast as they could. Another wounded man soon after came in.[54]

Jumper headed the Indians on this occasion. and was the hero of this sanguinary triumph, which was a meet sacrifice to the fierce and vindictive soul of this haughty and determined chief. Miconopy, the head chief or Mico, was also present, but does not seem to have been at all prominent. He was said to have fired but one rifle during the war, and on this occasion, was presented the alternative, to fight or die; whereupon, he shot at and killed Maj. Dade.—After the massacre, he immediately retired to his town,* and he does not appear subsequently very conspicuous upon the theatre of events.**

When six weeks after, Maj. Gen. Gaines, with his army, passed by the scene of this fatal rencontre, everything had remained undisturbed, and in the same position in which it must have been on the day after the battle. There was a preciseness and truth in the picture of this field of the dead, which was striking and appalling in the highest degree, and brought to mind the fable of the Enchanted Eastern City, whose inhabitants were suddenly turned into stone, and in death presented the startling similitude of life. First, the army met with broken and scattered boxes and belts, strewed over the ground—next, a cart was seen with two oxen lying dead beside it, with their yokes on, and seemingly as though they had fallen asleep there; a little farther, the skeleton of two horses and that of a dog, and then they came to a small enclosure—a few logs, which seemed to have been hastily flung down, to make a rude and vain defence-work.

---

*Pilacklikaha which means 'the scattered hammocks.' Jumper resided there also.

**Miconopy was in favor of the Seminoles removing, and had always been considered friendly—he is not much respected by his warriors—he is not so old a man as he is represented to be, and is not much over 50 years of age— Dr. Simmons, in his notes, renders the meaning of Miconopy 'young chief.' The following account of the origin of the name was given [to] me by one who had resided among the Indians. Miconopy means 'a king upon a king,' or 'twice a governor'—his previous name—a kind of nickname which the Indians are fond of calling one another by, and which is given on account of any remarkable circumstance in the private life of an individual, and is not to be founded with the war-title, was Sintchakke, by which is to be understood 'a frequenter of the pond,' as there is a certain pond, where the young chief was always to be found driving up cattle; as at that time he was a prince possessed of a considerable share of authority, and was sometimes called Mico, when his uncle King Payne died, and he inherited his title and property (which among the Seminoles does not descent linealy to sons, but to nephews, the sister's sons) he received the name of Miconopy, as one who united two titles, or a present dignity unto a former one.

Here a remarkable sight, and one that thrilled them to the soul, met their eyes. Within, along the north and west faces of this little breastwork were about thirty bodies, mostly mere skeletons, but clad in clothing; nearly all were lying exactly in the position in which they must have lain during the fight—their heads stooping to the logs over which they had fired, and their bodies stretched, with singular regularity, parallel to each other—they had kept their posts to the last—until they were shot dead—and the Indians had not disturbed them, except by taking off the scalps of most of them, thereby rendering their aspects still more grim and horrible—they had taken their arms, some of their belts, and what ammunition they had in their cartridge boxes, but it was remarkable that money to the amount of 5 and 10 dollars, and some jewelry that they had with them, had been left untouched. A little way from the breastwork were found other bodies, laying along the road, generally behind trees, which they had resorted to as covers from the enemy's fire, and about 200 yards farther; were a number of bodies in the middle of the road, which were evidently the advanced guard in the rear of which was the body of Maj. Dade, and a little to the right, that of Capt. Fraser. As many of the personal friends of Maj. Dades command were present with Gen. Gaines every officer slain was satisfactorily identified, and all the men accounted for. They were all interred and the six pounder which was recovered out of the swamp, placed in a vertical position at the head of their graves.

The history of Indian Wars, presents few instances of so disastrous a defeat, and it is unparalleled by any in our more modern annals. The battleground of the unfortunate Dade and his companions, will long hereafter be visited with feelings of deep interest and awe. When the swift waters of the Withlacoochee shall roll dark and mournfully by the graves of the red warriors, whose last defiance shall have died away in the echoes from its banks, and whose last blood shall have crimsoned its tide—when in hammock and prairie, shall be heard no longer the wild shout and glee of the fierce and once merry Seminole,* but the woodman's axe and the voice of civilization shall mingle with the peaceful tuneful notes of the groves, the future lingerer at this spot, will fancy himself surrounded by the bloody eight hundred: he will hear their shrill onset-cry, and see the woods thicken before him with the savage hordes, and behold that band of the elite and brave in the midst of the howling wilderness, struggling against their overwhelming odds behind a miserable barrier of low logs, until one by one they are shot down; then will he see the dreadful rush of those red fiends, the battle's last terrible strife, and the horrible carnage—the whirl of the deep buried tomahawk—the ghastly gash of the knife—the violent pressure of the strong upon the weak— and the upraised arms, the savagely-elate front, and the horrid maze of the war dance: the woods around will echo dying groans and piercing yells, and savage mirth, and then suddenly there will seem to him to be a pause—the forests will have resumed their primitive silence—an enchanted stillness will reign around, and he will fix his eyes

---

*See the picture Bartram gives of the happiness, gaiety, &c of the Seminole.

upon the skeleton spectres of the miserably slain, arrayed still in death for the fight; shuddering and stricken with awe, he will fly the spot, like the subject of some German superstition pursued by howling noises and strange and dire images, and the legend of the "FIELD OF THE DEAD" will be told![55]

BATTLE OF THE WITHLACOOCHEE.

Having formed a junction with Gen. Call, Gen. Clinch marched on the 29th from Fort Drane with an army consisting of 212 regulars, and 550 volunteer militia under Gen. Call; and on the morning of the 31st, by daylight, he arrived at the Withlacoochee river.* The river was high, and instead of finding a ford, as the guides had reported, they met with a deep and rapid stream; they commenced swimming over the horses, and one man was sent over for a canoe that was discovered on the opposite bank. The regular troops crossed over first, seven at a time, in the canoe, and as they landed, marched and occupied a position about 400 yards from the river, where they remained for two hours undisturbed; by mid-day fifty of the militia had crossed over, and Gen. Call was engaged in constructing rafts

---

*The Indian meaning of the Withlacoochee or Ouithlacochee, the author was informed by an interpreter is "little Creek"—hutchee or uchee is the word for a Creek but to one little versed in the language the meaning of the preceding word or words is puzzling—in the author's Vocabulary, or in those he has seen, there is no term similar for little, and the adjective is added, not prefixed in the Indian language as 'Tustenagge-Cluccko' a 'great warrior'— 'Cluccko'--'big' as it is spelt by Bartram and others, is pronounced Thluccko. 'Wee-wa' is 'water,' in composition, 'wee;' as 'wee luste,' 'black water; 'weehatke, white water' therefore Wee-thluccko-hutchee would mean the "big water creek," and pronounced rapidly, would very nearly with a slight change be Withlacoochee—this may be possibly its meaning, having reference either to the nature of the river, which is deep, but narrow like a creek, and wide at the mouth, or to its rise near the 'Big Swamp.'

to put the rest over more speedily, when they heard the fire of the sentinels on the other side in front of the regulars, and immediately after knew by the volleys, that they were engaged with a large number of Indians.

The Indians were stealing down the hammock to the river, for the purpose of preventing the crossing of the volunteers, when the sentinels discovered them—gave the alarm by firing; and retreated to their lines. Col. Fanning,[56] who was in command of the regulars, immediately led them to the charge upon the hammock, and received a tremendous fire—at the same time, the Indians on one flank leapt from their hiding places behind the trees and bushes, and formed boldly into line, with their chief, Powell, at their head; Col. Fanning returned their fire, and did considerable execution among them, which caused them to break and to take to their coverts again—he then instantly charged into the hammock. At this time, Gen. Clinch, who had been at the river side, superintending the constructions of the rafts, rode up, and about 25 of the militia, also came up to the scene of action. Cols. Warren and Mills, who were with the volunteers, that had crossed the river, had immediately on hearing the alarm, extended their line from the river, out through the swamp, to the pine barren, and had received orders to remain stationary in that position, and prevent the enemy from entering their lines; the volunteers beheld the regulars on their right in advance, hotly engaged with three or four hundred Indians, and Cols. Warren and Mills, after much solicitation on their part, assumed the responsibility, and Col. Warren and Major Cooper led the right to the left of the regulars, while Col. Mills held his position on the left of the line; in the mean time Gen. Call, after having used every exertion to get the rest of the militia over the river, and to arrange those that were still on that side, ready in case of an attack, crossed over, and by his coolness and judgment, aided much the protection, which this disposition of the militia gave to the flank of the regulars; the hammock was then charged, and after ten minutes more of sharp fighting, the Indians were compelled to retreat, and dispersed.

In this battle, the Indians displayed more than their wonted courage and coolness, and fought with much fierceness and determination—at one time, they advanced out from the hammock openly, and fired by platoons like regular soldiery, receiving a destructive fire in return—at another, they adopted their usual cautious mode of fighting, and concealed themselves so effectually in the woods, that the American were obliged to wait and watch their opportunity to fire a volley upon them through the opening, wherever they saw the flash or heard the report of their rifles, and in the mean while, were exposed to their rapid fire. Nothing but the boldness and success of a charge, made them give ground, and saved the Americans from great loss, and perhaps defeat. There were many circumstances and reasons which caused the Indians to make, and led the Americans to expect a bold stand and a desperate contest at the Withlacoochee; there in the midst of their native fastnesses, surrounded by swamps and hammocks, in the heart of the nation where most of their towns were situated; within a short distance of their chief Oseola's town*, where their women and children were assembled, and headed by that bold and subtle warrior, the main body of the Indians were known to be assembled, and informed by their scouts, of the approach of the army, they had chosen the most favorable ground, and waited in ambush near the ford, determined to dispute the passage of the invaders. The engagement lasted more than an hour, during which time they kept up a constant heavy fire, and a dreadful yelling; and when at last, they were forced to retreat, the chief Oseola was distinctly seen, waving his hand, and his shrill voice repeatedly heard, calling to them to return, and renew the fight but they had probably suffered too severely, and had dispersed in the woods. The slaughter must have been great among them, as the bushes and branches where they stood concealed, were cut up with shot, and 1000 rounds of ball and buck shot had been fired by the regulars; forty Indians were found dead, but they must have carried off many more. A small body fired upon the volunteers on the bank of the river; the fire was returned, and three Indians killed. The loss on the part of the Americans was severer than in many other more important Indian battles. Out of 227 men in battle, there were, of the regulars, 4 killed, and 56 wounded, and of the volunteers 7 wounded; many had their clothes shot through, many horses were killed and wounded. Gen. Clinch received a ball through his cap, and one through

---

*Before the war, Oseola lived at the Big Swamp, near Camp King—he afterwards retired to the Long Swamp, about 12 miles to the south-west.

his jacket sleeve, and his horse was shot in 2 places, his aid de camp, Maj. Lytle,[57] had his horse shot under him; Col. Fanning's horse was shot in two places; Col. Warren of the militia received a severe shot in the breast, & had his horse wounded; Capt. W. Graham[58] and Lt. C. Graham,[59] of the regulars, were severely wounded; the latter, being in command of his company, and having fallen wounded, Serj. Johnson, altho' severely wounded, immediately headed the comp'y & led it gallantly to the charge; Lt. Ridgely[60] and Dr. Clarke were also wounded, and the horse of the latter shot under him. The large portion of wounded is to be attributed partly to the want of skill in the Indians, in loading & firing at too great a distance, or in too much haste, & partly to the badness of their powder. There are several accounts of Indian fights, in which our loss in killed & wounded has been nearly proportionate, & at a safe estimate, the average result of Indian rifle shots in ordinary skirmishes and engagements, maybe said to be the killed to the wounded as 1 to 9 or 10, while our muskets usually kill 1 out of 3.

The position of our troops was unfavorable, while the Indians had selected theirs with a great deal of skill. The field in which the regulars were drawn up was in the form of a horse shoe, with a belt of hammock nearly surrounding it, from which the enemy were enabled to keep up a cross-fire, and attempted to outflank the army.

Under the direction of two such chiefs as Jumper and Powell, the Seminoles had displayed great tact in the disposition of their forces and a celerity of movement which appeared wonderful, and which to one unacquainted with their habits and mode of warfare, would have seemed almost a supernatural omnipresence at the same time that bands of them were committing havoc about Mosquito, and near St. Augustine., and were threatening the extreme southern point of the peninsula—while their tracks were fresh near Picolata and Miconopy—they had in the course of three days, in another quarter, promoted three very important events. On the very same day that Thompson was slain at Camp King, by Powell, Dade's command was massacred near the Withlacoochee by Jumper, and on the morning of the third day after, the battle of Withlacoochee took place. Oseola, it has been seen, led them on this occasion; he was distinguished by several, having on a uniform coat of our army, occupying a conspicuous station, where he could observe the movements of the army; at one time, heading his men boldly in the advance, but chiefly using his rifle like the rest, behind a tree, which he shot, and wiped out now and then with great coolness, but with which he did not prove himself as good a shot as he is said to be; or he alone ought to have killed more than were killed. The tree behind which he stood was stripped of its bark, and torn all over with the shots which were fired at him. For some time after the battle, he was not heard of, and it was supposed that he was either severely wounded, or killed; but he was only wounded in the hand. An impression got abroad after the battle, that the Creeks were making cause with the Seminoles, as during the contest, their ranks were observed to be reinforced, and many Indians, with packs on their backs, who were recognized as Creeks, were seen coming up through the woods to the action.

As it was late in the day when the battle terminated, and there was no good and secure ground for an encampment nearby, Gen. Clinch determined to recross the Withlacoochee, and retire to his former position, which he effected safely and in good order, and reached Camp Langsyne* on the 2d January. Had this victory been followed up, and had the army continued its march upon the Indian towns, a powerful impression might have been made upon the enemy; and it is probable, they might have been brought to sue for peace. Their leader might have been taken or slain, or their women and children been surrounded—in either of which cases, the war, if not then, would sooner have been put an end to. But want of provisions, of which they had barely sufficient to last them until their return, compelled Gen. Clinch to retrace his steps, and the term of service of the militia, who had volunteered for a month just then expiring, Gen. Call, with the volunteers from Middle Florida, and Cols. Warren and Mills, with those from East Florida, set off upon their return home.**

---

*Camp Langsyne and Fort Drane are at Gen. Clinch's plantation, 20 miles from Camp King, and 10 from Miconopy.
**Clinch's battle ground on the Withlacoochee is 25 miles south of Camp Smith, which is about 6 miles west of Fort Drane.

CHAPTER IV.

State of the Territory; In the almost undisputed possession of the Indians; They continue to commit depredations, &c., and fall upon the settlements in South Florida; Massacre of Mr. Cooley's family; the inhabitant take refuge at Indian Key and Key West; alarm at Indian Key; extent of territory overrun by the enemy; Battle of Dunn Lawton; Creeks hostile; Gov. Schley orders out the Militia; a more serious war apprehended.

JANUARY.—The situation of Florida, was at this time, in the highest degree alarming; the whole of East Florida was in imminent danger. The militia under Gen. Call were disbanded, and Gen. Clinch was compelled to wait at his former position, hemmed in by the Indians, and cut off from all communication with Tampa Bay, at which place, should any troops arrive, they would be of no use, or if they attempted to come to his assistance, would run the hazard of being cutoff as Dade's detachment was. From the 14 companies that had been reported by the Secretary of War, some time since, for the service, no assistance had been yet received. In the mean while, Gen. Call was making preparations, for a draught of 1500 militia, to proceed to the assistance of Gen. Clinch, and co-operate with him in a regular campaign against the enemy.

The country being thus left in the almost undisputed possession of the Indians, they continued their havoc upon the plantations, carrying off negroes, and murdering settlers or travelers wherever they chanced to meet with them.—Spring Garden, a valuable plantation, owned by

Col. Rees and Mr. Forrester, was utterly destroyed, and 160 negroes carried off, so that, it was now supposed that they had in
their possession between 3 and 400 of the planter's slaves.
They burnt the storehouses of Rogers, who been killed with
Gen. Thompson, near Camp King, and fired a few shots at
the Camp, which were returned. A man was murdered, and
his house burnt 5 miles from Picolata, on the road to St. Augustine., and the stage driver would not return with the mails
to St. Augustine, having seen tracks on the way. At the same
time that signs of them were seen as far north as on the road
between Jacksonville and St. Augustine, large body carried
their depredations to the southern extremity of the Territory, and fell upon the settlements at New River and Cape
Florida. On the fourth of the month, (Jan.) some of the
inhabitants in the neighborhood of New River, were alarmed
at observing a party of Indians surrounding the house of Wm.
Cooley,[61] in which a quantity of materials from a wreck had
been stored, and carrying away portions of the goods, and at
hearing at the saw time several rifle reports. It was soon afterwards ascertained that the whole family of Cooley had been
massacred. He was absent at the time, and when he returned,
a shocking sight met his eyes; he first encountered the mangled
body of Flinton, a teacher in his family who had been killed
with an axe; nearby were the bodies of his two eldest children, who had been shot through the heart. The little girl
still held in her hands the book from which she had been
getting her lesson, and that of the boy was close by his side;
a hundred yards farther,

a more affecting sight still, awaited him; there lay the corpse of his beloved wife, with her infant in her arms—one ball had pierced the heart of the mother, and broken the arm of the infant. All his houses had been burnt except one in which a quantity of Conti, or Arrow Root,* was kept, with the machinery for preparing it. As this root forms one of the chief articles of Indian subsistence, they took care to preserve it, and probably intended to carry it away.

The massacre of Mr. Cooley's innocent family, was one of those atrocious enormities which swell the catalogue of Indian cruelties, and distinguish the wholesale bloody-mindedness of the savage. He had lived many years among them; associated with them; had always treated them with the utmost kindness and hospitality; his house was open to them;—they frequently sat at his table, and in token of his friendship towards them, he had named two of his little sons after two of their distinguished chiefs. Violently outraging the respect and regard they owed him, these brutal wretches, with the fury of fiends, without compunction or remorse, invaded in his absence his happy home, and made

---

*Manioc or the Herbe-au-Fleche, so called by the French; by us Arrow Root, botanically Zamia, a genus indigenous to India, the Cape of Good Hope, New Holland, and Tropical America—of which this species, Zamia integrifolia, (Pursh), pumila, (Bartram), is a native of Florida, where it grows in great abundance; but its principal habitat is in the pine barrens between New River and Cape Florida, and about Cape Sable; it grows in tufts or clumps, has beautiful deep green leaves like a fern, and a strobile disclosing large coral red berries; the roots are large, generally of the size of a beet, sometimes larger, and of the consistency of parsnips. To prepare them for food, they are first peeled or the skin scraped off; they are then washed, after that grated fine, and reduced to a pulpy substance, then after an immersion in water for some time, and the noxious quality of the juice having been expressed, the farina is drawn from the Lixivium and made into cakes or bread, such as is known by the common Indian name of Tuckahoe, but this kind is called by the Florida Indians Sewoapo, and they call the plant Contihatke, or White Root. The women are employed in preparing this food, and Mr. Cooley was in the habit of hiring them to aid him in the manufacturing of it.

of it a desolation!—Without chivalry or pity, they slew the weak mother and her unoffending children, and the only mercy they had, or what their savage nature at least, esteemed as such, was not to scalp them; as if to pay some veneration to the re-membrance of past friendship, they refrained from this barba-rous consummation of their dire revenge—but to the teacher they did not extend the same savage courtesy, and he was scalped.

The news of this outrage soon spread among the scattered inhabitants in the neighborhood between New River and the Cape—to the number of sixty, they gathered on the premises of the lighthouse, but when they had assembled they found themselves without ammunition, provisions, or water, and con-cluded that it was best to leave the place if they could, before the enemy came upon them—they fortunately discovered a vessel in sight, and having made signal of distress, were taken and carried to Indian Key—another boat which had been des-patched to their assistance from the Key, arriving shortly after, before the lighthouse, saw the Indians in possession of it.

Some of the inhabitants underwent great sufferings in their hasty flight—helpless females were compelled to run twelve or more miles through the woods, and when they reached the Cape, they were in the most pitiable state, scarcely any clothes upon them, their limbs lacerated with the rude branches of the forest, and with sharp palmet-toes, and they were so exhausted that they could not walk for some days after; the inhabitants from all the other Keys, took refuge at Key West.

At Indian Key there was much alarm; they were daily in expectation of being attacked; there were no troops there; and the only cutter which was on the coast had left for Mobile. All the militia, which constituted but a small force, was called out.

Not long before their appearance at New River, several Indians in boats had come to the Key for the purpose of trading, as they said, and they did not seem to know anything of the late murders and outrages, which had been committed. They were ordered off, and appeared to have left the neighbourhood. It afterwards generally believed that they were the same party who murdered Mr. Cooley's family. They went to the Key to procure powder and lead, which, with great audacity, they demanded at the stores, as they had been in the habit of doing; as though their intercourse was still friendly, and they were preparing for the hunting season, instead of a massacre of the inhabitants.

Parties of them had collected at Cape Sable and New River to the number of 2 or 300. The keeper of the Cape Florida Light was compelled to fly with his family, and the light being discontinued, many vessels that were in the habit of making their course for it were in danger of being wrecked.

The whole intermediate Southern country as far north as Bulow's, forty miles from St. Augustine., was in their possession; towards the west they had advanced as far Picolata on the St. John's, and they had ravaged the whole country between Whitesville on Black Creek, Alligator, and the Suwannee, making an extensive and exposed frontier. The situation of the inhabitants of the frontier was lamentable—it was heart-rending to behold women and children, excited by their fears almost to frenzy, clasping the knees of the officers and soldiers, and entreating them not to go away and leave them to the merciless Indian rifle and scalping knife. We have mentioned that Maj. Putnam at the head of the St. Augustine guards, a company composed of gallant and spirited young men of the town, was stationed at Musquito to protect the plantations in the neighbourhood that were still unharmed; to save whatever could be saved on those that had not been totally destroyed, and to intercept the Indians in their progress towards the city. He was joined at that station by a few mounted volunteers of Mosquito. A smoke having been observed in the direction of Dunn Lawton, Mrs. Anderson's plantation on the Halifax river, the company, which amounted to 40, proceeded thither on the 17th; on the way, Maj. Putnam was informed by a negro that the Indians had burnt the place—it was night when the company arrived there, and the buildings were then burning; they were quartered in two negro houses, and at daylight the next morning commenced to carry away the provisions that could be saved; they had not long been engaged in this, before two Indians were seen approaching by Messrs. Anderson and Dummitt, who were keeping guard; these gentlemen fired on them, one of the Indians fell, and the other was wounded. Mr. Dummitt ran to the fallen one and as he was stooping over him, there was a report of rifles, and he received a wound in the back of his neck; a large body of Indians immediately after rushed out of a scrub, about musket shot distance, and commenced a furious attack. The company, sheltered behind the fragments and walls of the burnt buildings, returned their fire warmly; the Indians were more exposed being in a field, but their numbers gave them confidence—they amounted it was supposed, to upwards of 150.

Maj. Putnam's company, though so inferior in number, kept them off for the space of an hour, during which the firing was sharp on both sides. The Indians, however, began to flank and surround them, and their situation was getting dangerous and desperate,—they were compelled to retreat to their boats. The Indians pursued and poured a destructive fire upon them as they were embarking—no time was to be lost, and in their haste to put off, and get into the boats, all the guns, with the exception of one, got wet. Their destruction seemed now inevitable— the water was shoal for some distance, and unless the Indians could be kept at bay, they would rush into the water, seize the boats, and massacre all whom their rifles did not kill. They did the best they could, and fired the single gun, though it was vain to expect that its discharges could avail them anything— they rather seemed a mockery. Singular to say, however, the solitary fire of this one musket kept the Indians effectually off and they were afraid to advance upon the dauntless little band, who succeeded in escaping, and getting to Bulow's, having lost but one of their number, and two negroes. Seventeen of the party were wounded, some mortally, during the retreat and embarkation; Capt. Dummitt was the only one wounded previous to the retreat—the unfortunate lad who was lost, was the son of Judge Gould, of St. Augustine; the boat to which he had repaired was behind hand, and in danger of being taken by the Indians; he was hotly pursued, and compelled to jump over board for safety—he swam to an Island opposite, and although he escaped a cruel death from the Indians, was drowned in attempting to farther his escape by crossing to the main. In the action, some of the party were wounded in three or four places, which would have been mortal, had not the bullets of the Indian rifles rebounded, inflicting only slight hurts; in this encounter 16 Indians were killed.

For fear of unnecessarily adding to the alarm which prevailed at St. Augustine., the commandant Gen. Hernandez did not for some time disclose the despatches of Maj. Putnum, which stated the particulars of the engagement, and that the Indians were every moment increasing in number and confidence, so that with many of his men wounded, he would not be able to hold out much longer against them, unless speedy assistance was lent him; whereupon a detachment of militia was despatched to his assistance. Rumours got abroad, and the mystery of the affair excited misgivings and apprehensions; in the mean, time, some negroes belonging to Dunn Lawton, bro't vague and exaggerated accounts to the town, of a battle having been fought; mothers, wives and sisters were thrown into the deepest consternation and affliction, each believed that she had lost a son, husband or brother; while it was impossible to allay their alarm until farther particulars were correctly ascertained.

To add to the alarm, which at this time prevailed generally throughout the territory, it became to be no longer doubtful that there was an understanding between the Seminoles and Creeks, which had been anticipated and feared. To what extent the Creeks were hostile, was not yet ascertained. On the 19th, it was rumored that 500 Indians, supposed to be Creeks, were encamped on the north side of the St. Mary's river in Georgia. It was farther stated that they had committed depredations, and that two men had been killed by a party of 40 or 50 in Baker county, and several others wounded. By the confession of a half-breed, a plot of some of the Creeks, supposed to be friendly, had been disclosed, to set fire to the town of Columbus, and to attack it during the confusion. A large portion of the Hitchitee and Uchee Tribes were found to be absent, and there was no doubt that they had gone into Florida, to join the Seminoles. Gov. Schley had ordered out troops, and was making every exertion to put the Georgia Frontier in a state of preparation.

Thus a more serious and complicated war began to threaten. The Creeks numbered about 7000 warriors, and were a powerful and warlike nation. It was to be apprehended, that if they took up arms, the Cherokees, who were known to be averse to removing,* would next catch the contagion; and the other tribes on our borders might take advantage of the opportunity to revive their ancient national hatred to the whites, and revenge themselves upon their natural enemy—so that many looked forward to the breaking out of a general Indian War. It would

---

*They were to remove in two years.

transcend the limits of this Sketch, to enter into views of the country at this time, or to hint at the nature of the two grand elements of the political warfare which was carrying on between the North and South; at the progress of the murky cloud which had gathered over men's minds, threatening to discharge its electric force over the Union; at the secret agencies which were at work, and the foul conspiracies which were on foot—it is enough to mention that these agitations contributed to the alarm which pervaded the Territory.

CHAPTER V.

Interest felt by the citizens of Charleston in the distress of Florida; meetings; resolutions; measures of relief; Volunteers; Georgia, Alabama and Louisiana send volunteers; measures of General Government; Gen. Gaines; naval assistance; Gen. Scott appointed to conduct a campaign.

All this while, the most lively interest and sympathy were felt by the citizens of Charleston in the sufferings and dangers of their fellow countrymen in Florida. This City, always celebrated for its humanity and chivalry, as well as its hospitality and refinement, was, on the present occasion, distinguished for the zealous exertions which it displayed in affording its prompt and generous assistance so soon as the disastrous situation of the Territory became known.

On the 31st December, a large meeting of the citizens was held for the purpose of devising measures of relief, and embodying volunteers to go to the assistance of their distressed brethren of Florida. A committee was appointed, and the chairman of the meeting was requested to communicate with the commanding officer of this station, and to inform him of the willingness of the citizens of Charleston to co-operate with him in any measures for the assistance of the people of Florida. 500 stand of arms, and ammunition, were immediately forwarded; but it I was not deemed necessary to send any volunteers, at this present time, as the commanding officer of the station gave it as his opinion that there were more than a sufficient number of troops, already in Florida, to subdue the Indians, and as no call had been made for troops by the ordinary authorities. On the 8th January, subscription lists were opened for money to furnish aid to the inhabitants who were driven from their homes, and suffering from want, and private donations of from 50 to $200 were received. On the 12th, a committee of gentlemen, in conjunction with Gen. Abraham Eustis,[62] of the army, at this station, chartered a steamboat, and sent on a large supply of provisions and a company of Regulars, under the command of Capt. Porter,[63] with a field piece. At that very time, Gen. Williams, aid-de-camp to Gen. Hernandez, arrived at Charleston, with despatches for Gen. Eustis, demanding assistance. He expressed his satisfaction at the timely aid that had been afforded, and deemed the measures of relief ample for the present.

At a public meeting, held at St. Augustine., on the 20th, the Mayor and Aldermen were directed to express, in behalf of the citizens, their warm thanks to the citizens of Charleston, for the assistance that had been rendered, and to request that a body of volunteers might be sent them, if it was only to relieve their old men from the fatigue of watching and guarding the city. Before this request was received, another large meeting was held in Charleston on the 21st, at which, after a luminous and eloquent report had been read,* the following, among other resolutions were adopted:

That the citizens should assume, either thro' their public authorities, or by voluntary contributions among themselves, the immediate payment of the expenses incurred in furnishing supplies. That a committee be appointed to confer with the City Council as to the best meant of organizing a system of immediate relief, and to open a correspondence with the department of war, informing the General Government of the steps taken, and of the voluntary assumption of the citizens of Charleston, of duties rightfully belonging to it; and that for all loans made by the city of Charleston, or by the citizens thereof, or from the Banks, they should look for ultimate repayment to the General Government, under its just obligations to the people of Florida.

That the committee be authorized to receive volunteers from the 4th Brigade.

On the 25th, accordingly, the following companies of Volunteers offered their services, and were accepted.

The Washington Volunteers, Capt. J.E.B. FINLEY.

Washington Light Infantry, Capt. [HENRY] RAVENEL

The German Fusileers, Capt. [W. H.] TIMROD.

A detachment of Hamburgh Volunteers also

---

*See Appendix, Note B.

the same day arrived and were accepted. These volunteers offered to remain in St. Augustine. for the term of one month, to defend the town; and they were not to go upon any expeditions into the interior against the Indians; as a regular campaign, which it was the part of the General Government to institute, would be necessary to ensure success, and this would shortly be prosecuted; an express from Washington having, the same day that the volunteers were accepted, left Charleston for headquarters with a requisition upon the Governor for a draft of 600 militia for three months service. Two other companies, besides those mentioned, likewise volunteered, and many individuals were anxious to join them, but the number was considered sufficient, and completed. On this occasion, many of the citizens who did not publicly evince their zealousness and liberality, were generous in private. An officer of one of the Banks, who held a commission in a volunteer company, was informed that his duties would be attended to, and his salary continued during his absence. A clerkship in an important house was dispensed with; the salary of the individual was continued, and the place kept for him until his return. A steamboat was offered to carry the volunteers gratuitously; and shop-keepers limited their prices on articles which were in demand. On the 27th, the City Council appropriated $10,000 for the relief of Florida.

The citizens of Savannah and Augusta evinced the same sympathy and enthusiasm. In addition to the volunteers, who some time before had promptly gone from the former city to defend Picolata, another company of riflemen and

100 volunteers left the same city for the same post, on the 27th of this month, and on the same day, the Richmond Blues, under Capt. F. [Francis] M. Robertson, a company of 100 men from Augusta left Savannah, a company of United States troops was also sent. Besides these volunteers, there were many enrolled at Mobile, and at New Orleans.

Though all this while there had been little or no aid received from the General Government, it will be proper here to mention what had been done on its part up to this time. Congress, on the 6th of January, passed a bill making an appropriation of $80,000 for the suppression of hostilities commenced by the Seminole Indians. On the 25th, a resolution was brought in calling upon the Secretary of War for information of what force would be requisite to prosecute the war.

On the 26th, the House unanimously passed a Bill making another appropriation of $500,000 which was read, and the next day passed in the Senate. At this late date, after the war had been raging nearly two months, during which Congress had been in session, there had been no official communication made to it of the cause of the war; all that was known was derived through gazettes and some of the communications of departments—all this while, only $80,000 had been appropriated. Accounts upon accounts arrived at the Capitol, of the state of affairs in Florida, and the Delegate importuned and urged, day after day, immediate relief, but other matters appeared to engross the attention of Congress, the Executive, and the heads of Departments. The whole country was at this time interested in two great subjects, the French war and the abolition petitions, and the grand electioneering vortex at the capitol seemed to have swallowed up all concern and commiseration for an insignificant Territory, which had no vote in the Presidential election.

On the 1st of February, Congress passed a resolution authorizing the President to cause rations to be distributed to the suffering fugitives from Indian hostilities in Florida.*

In addition to what has been remarked in a previous chapter, of the ineffectiveness of the 14 companies which had been appropriated, it may be necessary to state, that in connection with the movement from Tampa Bay, which resulted so unfortunately, there was another command, under Maj. Mountford [Mountfort], which would have joined Maj. Dade, had the transport in which the troops were, not gone up the wrong bay, and detained them until it was too late to form a junction. At this time (1st of January) the vessels which were to take the emigrating Indians, arrived at Tampa. Maj. Belton the commandant at that post, was active in furthering the defenses there and in forwarding immediate intelligence of the state of things; and he wrote to inform the Adj. Gen. that, owing to the combinations of the Indians in the interior, it was impracticable to keep open the communication between Tampa and Camp King, unless with a well appointed force of 1000 men.

On the 19th January, a Batallion, under command of Maj. Gates,[64] received orders from the War Department to proceed to Florida—two companies from Charleston and Savannah,

---

*See Appendix Note C.

it has been seen, went soon after. At the same time, large stores of provisions were ordered on from New York to Camp King, to be ready for a campaign. While preparations for this were making, and the regular troops were still inactive in Florida, Maj. Gen. Gaines, of the army, having heard on the 15th at New Orleans, where he was, of the massacre of Maj. Dade, thought it incumbent upon him, though he had not received any orders, to repair forthwith to the territory, which was in the department of his command, and promptly made a requisition upon the Gov. of Louisiana for troops. On the 3d of February, he embarked with an army of 1000 men, on his way to the scene of action. After having despatched from Baton Rouge to the Fort at Tampa, all necessary supplies, ordnance, Quarter master's stores, &c., he stopped at Pensacola, where he expected to procure the assistance of some vessels of war, to cruise along the coast and co-operate with the land troops, in cutting off the communication which was carried on between the Cuba Fishermen and traders of the West India Islands, and the Indians.

This was a very important service, as from the vast quantities of powder in the possession of the Indian Chiefs, it was supposed to have been obtained in this way. It was important also for other purposes. As early as the 14th of December, an express had been sent to Pensacola and Mobile from St. Augustine., for some small armed vessels to co-operate with the land forces and intercept the passage of the Indians in canoes through the rivers and inland channels.

Along the Keys especially, this mode of protection was the best that could be resorted to. About the middle of January, a cutter left New Orleans for St. Marks and Tampa Bay. On the 16th, the Frigate Constellation and a Sloop of War arrived in the waters of Key West. Having been informed of the destitute situation of the South of Florida, the naval commander acted promptly in compliance with the wishes of the residents of the coast, in coming to their assistance. Soon after this, another sloop and a cutter were sent on to be subject to the orders of Gen. Clinch.

On the 27th (January,) Maj. Gen. Winfield Scott[65] was appointed to conduct the campaign—he had previously left Washington for Florida on the 22nd. At this time, the War Department began to put forth more energy. A detachment of Dragoons was despatched on, and a general order was issued to several of the Southern Garrisons, to despatch a portion of their forces to the seat of War.

CHAPTER VI.

Gov. Eaton's Message—Col. Parish attacks a body of Indians—Daring conduct of 4 Indians—Oseola's communication to Gen. Clinch—natural difficulties of Florida—No country so advantageous to Indians—Remarks on the warfare with—Troops suffer from the Climate—Conclusion.

January 7.—After mentioning a few other events which took place in the course of this month, I shall conclude this sketch. On the 7th, Gov. Eaton[66] addressed his message to the legislative Council of Florida, which appeared before the public at the same time that the Battle of Withlacoochee was made known. After the usual remarks and congratulations upon the successes of agriculture, the plentiful harvests of the last year and the bountiful climate of Florida, his excellency proceeded to make some observations upon the criminal code and jury trials. The Indian War, which his Excellency called a "border War," and "an event," was next mentioned, and a revision of the Militia Laws recommended, which were very defective; an appeal having been made, and orders given twelve years ago, for the Colonels of Militia to return the rank and file of the territory, in order that legal application might be made for the quota of arms, to which the territory was entitled; but his Excellency remarked this had not been attended to; cotton crops had been too abundant, and prices so high that the cupidity of military men had been enlisted, instead of their attention, to the duties required of them. In the enjoyment of a prosperous peace none looked forward to the contingency of war; the people disliked musters; and if they did not actually refuse to attend and vote, (which had been in some instances actually the case,) they elected those who, like themselves, loathed restraint, and did not obey the law—public opinion being against it, penalties were not enforced. He recommended that the commanding general should have the power of appointing officers. The Legislative Council then passed a law authorizing the governor to draught a portion of the militia and to accept of volunteers. The Governor sent the adjutant General to Augusta, to procure arms and by the middle of the month, a brigade was put into the field.

On the 12th, Col. Parish, at the head of 200

volunteers, had a sharp encounter with a large body of Indians—the attack commenced with the advanced guard—Col. Parish hastened forward when he was attacked on both flanks by the enemy in ambush. The volunteers made an unsuccessful attempt to charge on horseback, after which they dismounted, and forming in good order, charged and routed the enemy, who took shelter in a thicket; night coming on, they did not pursue them, but the volunteers rested on their arms in the pine woods the whole night, expecting an attack, the Indians, however made off, having sustained some loss. Afterwards, Col. Parish marched to Powell's town, and destroyed it.

As an instance of the daring and desperation of the Seminoles, the following may be mentioned. As 600 militia were marching through Alachua, they were fired upon by four Indians; these audacious warriors were seen and pursued and all the four killed.

Since the engagement at the Withlacoochee, no intelligence had been received of the main body of the Indians. They appeared to have separated into bands, sufficiently large to oppose with confidence any forces the inhabitants might direct against them. Wherever they were met, they fought boldly and desperately, but invariably eluded pursuit and escaped into their fastnesses sustaining a trifling loss. They expressed repeatedly, that they would die before they would leave their country, and their chief Oseola sent a communication to Gen. Clinch, in which he used the following bold language, set forth in a style, concise, and characteristic; "You have guns, and so have we; you have powder, and lead, and so have we; you have men, and so have we; your men will fight, and so will ours, until the last drop of the Seminole's blood has moistened the dust of his hunting grounds." He daringly defied Gen. Clinch, and told him that as he had been idle so long, if he would give him a very little while longer to secure his position, he could maintain it for five years against the United States.

Without a well organized force, operating extensively, it appeared impracticable to make any impression upon so subtle an enemy. Indeed, so favorable is Florida for this guerilla warfare; so well adapted in every respect to the nature of the Indian, that, after the experience of the late unsuccessful campaign, and a more thorough knowledge of the country, military men have been obliged to acknowledge their errors; and that, even an overwhelming force, unless conducted with great energy, and so constituted as to combine military science with aptness to adopt the habits, and conform to the strategy of the enemy, may, so far from exterminating the Indians, only increase their confidence, by failing to effect anything. The ridiculous threat of Oseola has since been regarded as we may say, fulfilled—to use a vulgar adage, "the miss was as good as a mile"—and the disgrace to our arms, that a handful of Indians should still beard us, after five months of furious war, is as much as if it had been five years. The boast was by no means the mere foolish bravado of an Indian hajo, or Seminole Col. Wildfire; but Oseola knew well the peculiar advantages of the country, and his threat, which meant that the Seminoles could elude for that length of time the forces sent to expel them from the soil, will not seem so irrational, when we consider the character of their country.

This remarkable peninsula seems to have been intended by nature as the peculiar refuge place of the red man; as though, after having been hunted to this extreme point; to the verge of the ocean, he was here to find a strong hold and a vantage ground, where he might make his last stand. It is one vast forest castle, surrounded by moats, and guarded by difficult approaches—hammocks, morasses, scrubs and jungles, some too boggy, some too thick to enter, except by a few obscure paths, known only to the hunters—other portions of the country are of a nature that may be termed super-aquaterreous, or Polyhydrous, abounding in and flooded with water. Such is the character of the country, as it approaches the shores of the Gulf; that about the head of the St. Johns; and such are the far-famed Everglades.

The peninsula is regarded by some as a prodigious mound, or wing dam confining the waters of the Gulf of Mexico, which are elevated above those of the Atlantic, and preventing them from falling with irresistible weight into the latter, and the waters of the gulf pressing against that side of the peninsula, are supposed to be the cause of all this water. A more reasonable supposition, entertained by others, is, that as the rains flood this low country, which seems formerly to have been one lake, or but lately reclaimed from the ocean, the water, having no easy vent, takes some time to run off; and in dry seasons, many of these tracts are unflowed. At the head of the St. Johns, the peninsula consists of one immense basin, or marshy tract of land, which the Indians call "Hayuppo," and describe as a large marsh or open place. Over this inundated tract, they are acquainted with but one crossing place, where they are in the habit of driving their cattle. They state that it takes them three days to journey over it, and they are obliged to defend their horse's feet with wrappings of cow hide, against the sharp saw grass which covers the way.

The following account of that singular region known as the "Ever-glades," is given by Dr. Strobel, of Charleston:

"By the Everglades is meant an immense tract of country, lying in the middle of the Southern portion of the Peninsula. At certain seasons the whole of this region is laid under water, excepting the higher points of land, which constitute so many Islands; the extent of this lake, for so it may be called under such circumstances, is unknown. A captain of a wrecker told me that he entered it once at high water, and sailed in a fast boat, with a fair wind, for three days in a northerly direction, without being able to discover any bounds; another party started from New River, and sailed for two days, without reaching its westerly bounds. The Indians traverse these everglades in all points, with their canoes; the depth of the water varies at different places, and in different seasons; I have been told that in some places it is as deep as 10 or 12 feet; in shoaly parts, the bottom appeared to be covered with long rank grass, so thick in some places as to impede our canoes. The small islands or keys, appeared to be covered with Mangrove—others were nothing more than grass knolls; the shore appeared to be in some places fringed with cyprus. To the south, it extends nearly to cape Florida, whilst its northern boundary is still unknown; in the last direction it is supposed to terminate in lagoons and cyprus swamps. The descent from the shores to the middle of the Everglades being very gradual, in some places not more than two or three inches to the mile, a rise of six or eight inches will inundate the country for miles."

It is acknowledged on all hands, that, should the Indians escape into the Everglades, it would be a matter of extreme difficulty, if nor an impossibility to act against them; There would be no trails by which to follow them; the army would have to pursue them in small vessels and canoes, and would not know in what direction to steer, to find them in such a vast region, and the numerous hiding places would afford them safe retreats.

Another famous strong-hold, of which Oseola boasted, as a place impregnable by the white man, was the "cove of the Withlacoochee," a formidable swamp on that river.

Forty miles south west of 'Long Swamp,' the 'Big Hammock' commences, which is said to be forty in length by six and seven in width;* 40 miles south east of Tampa Bay, is another fortress, the celebrated 'Peas Creek,' the enchanted asylum of the women and children. The head of this creek was explored by a party of Col. Goodwynn's [Goodwyn's][67] horse during the campaign, but they discovered no trails. Col. Smith,[68] with

---

*Simmons.

some Louisiana volunteers, also went on an expedition, but to no purpose.

Of the country to the south of Tampa, Dr. Leitner,[69] who has recently travelled there, says "Term it a dreary succession of shelly bluffs, pine and mangrove forests, saw-palmetto tracts, hammocks, savannas, lakes, marshes, morasses, islands, lagoons, cypress ponds, and innumerable smaller or lesser tortuous and shoaly water courses, and you have the exact description of it.["]

Besides these, and many other such similar retreats, the numerous bayous, inlets, and creeks which intersect parts of the country, afford channels for speedy communication and escape from one covert to another; so that to follow successfully this wily and slippery foe, a General must not only make himself thoroughly acquainted with the country, but he must be provided with troops lightly armed and equipped; should have no encumbrance of baggage wagons; but convenient depots of provisions should be established; the soldiers should learn to tent like the Indians, under palmetto sheds; they should carry, at least, ten days provision in their havresacs, not all hard bread and weighty pork; but only a portion, and the rest some article of subsistence, which contains the greatest nutriment in the smallest space; meal prepared from corn parched in its milky state before it hardens and good beef, prepared after the French method, reduced to one sixth or seventh of it bulk, and containing nothing but the concentrated nutriment, have been recommended. A modicum of these victuals is said, upon good authority, to maintain a soldier. We know that the Indians set out upon long travels with nothing but a piece of bear's fat in their pouches, and that a single hard egg a day will sustain life a long time; they should have to accustom themselves also to live on the palmetto cabbage, and other wild fruits of the soil. Part of the force should consist of mounted men, the horses should if possible, be such as are manageable, accustomed to the tangled woods and boggy swamps. Part of these mounted troops should be armed with rifles and the rest with pistols and sabres, so that the Indians might be dislodged from the hammocks with the latter, assisted by the infantry, and cut off in their retreat by the former; artillery might be dispensed with, as it would encumber and delay the march. The Spaniards, under De Soto, had a field piece with them, but they found it more an annoyance than an advantage to them—celerity of movement is indispensable, in order to defeat these Indians. The march of the army should not be slow and unwieldy, like that of the Gopher, to which the Seminoles ridiculing it, compared the army of the late campaign, but it should rival in speed and activity the Seminole himself, who, as his beautiful language expresses it, "swims the streams, and leaps over the logs of the wide forest, and is like the Whooping Crane, that makes its nest at night, far from the spot where it dashed the dew from the grass and the flower in the morning." The enemy should be followed up indefatigably through the hammocks and the swamps, from hiding place to hiding place, while the trail is warm—at night, he should not be allowed to pull off his moccasins, and the first gleam of day should shine upon bayonets, bristling around their camps; they should be foiled by counter ambushes, and counter stratagems; the constant employment of small armed vessels up then rivers inlets would be necessary, and a decisive effort should be made to attack their towns and surround their women and children, which would bring them to what has been found so difficult, a general engagement. It is a difficult matter to starve into conditions an enemy possessed of such resources as the Seminoles are; their growing crops of corn, &c. may be destroyed; their cattle may be killed; but they can live just as well without these in the woods. The forests of the cabbage tree furnish them, at every step with their wholesome vegetable fruit; from the centre of the stem of the saw-palmetto, which covers thousands of acres, they procure a flour which they mix with that of the China briar and arrow root, and make a palatable food of; the Conti, or arrow root, has been already described; its locale is more confined, and as they resort to certain places where it is to be found in the greatest abundance, they perhaps might be cut off from this resource, but then a cordon of many troops would have to be kept at these places constantly for this purpose. Ah-hah, or Indian potatoe, serves them with another kind of provision, and the Heh-lah, and several other roots;* besides many fruits grow spontaneously in Florida; the orange trees were nearly all killed by the last severe winter; they used to roast the oranges and lived much on them; they also gather quantities of hickory and other nuts of which they are fond; they have been known to encamp a long time in the swamps

---

*See Catalogue of Plants.

with none other than these wild provisions; they have plenty of venison, wild turkeys, and other game; the rivers and Keys supply them with an abundance of fish, turtles, and oysters; and the sand hills and pine barrens, with the rich and much prized meat of the Gopher, or land Tortoise.

From the facilities of water transportation, Florida cannot be pronounced a decidedly unfavorable country for military operations, speaking in a general military sense; but there cannot be a more miserable country for land transportation, and for troops to march through and manoeuvre.

With regard to its healthiness or unhealthiness, it has generally been considered healthy. Romans, Darby, Forbes, and other writers upon Florida, represent the climate to be temperate, the air pure and salubrious; the Peninsula is constantly refreshed by breezes from the Atlantic and Mexican seas; the dews are very heavy, especially on the coast; fogs are not frequent, except upon the St. John's river. The spring and summer, says Romans, are in general dry; the autumn very changeable; the beginning of winter, wet and stormy, but the latter part very dry and serene; from the end of September to the end of June, there is, perhaps not anywhere more delightful climate, but all July, August, and the most of September, are excessively hot. Flint says, "From June to October, the frequent rains and unremitting heat are apt to generate the fevers of a southern climate, especially in the vicinity of ponds and marshes; where fields are flooded for rice."

It is the general opinion that the rich,

timbered lands, such as those on the St. John's, the wet pine barrens, cypress swamps and ponds, and many of the plantations, are sickly in the summer and autumn, though some of the settlers maintain to the contrary, and others affirm that though they are not exempt from fevers in Florida, they are much milder than with us in Carolina, and do not occur as often. There is no doubt that in many parts of the territory, swamps, the luxuriant growth of rich lands, stagnant ponds, and marshes, generate disease, which the general salubrity of the air cannot counteract. In other parts the country is more open, the ponds are clear, and freshened by springs and rivulets, the air is much drier. The army, during its march to Tampa, in April, when the weather was very warm, left some pieces of beef hanging up, and on its return some time after, it was perfectly sound. The existence of heavy dews does not of itself prove unhealthiness, for the dews are no where heavier than at St. Augustine, and all testimonies concur in pronouncing that town the Montpelier of America. It does not require many facts to prove that troops suffer a great deal from sickness in marching through Florida. Cardena asserts in his history, that the troops who arrived in Spain from Florida in 1569, were healthy and strong, but he attributes the fact to the use of sassafras, and not to the nature of the country, for he continues, that each soldier carried about with him a piece of sassafras in his pocket, which he would exhibit and say: "this is the tree which we have brought to cure us, if we should be taken ill, as was done in Florida."

In Pamphilo de Narvaez's expedition into

Florida, who landed somewhere on the Eastern Coast, and marched first north to the country called Apalachee, and then south to Aute, or St. Marks, he lost from encounters with the natives, hardships and sickness, one third of his troops, and of the survivors a great many were ill, and disease was spreading rapidly among them.

Of the thousand cavaliers under Hernando de Soto, but very few returned home, more having perished by diseases contracted in wading through morasses and lagoons, breast high in many places, than were slain by the Indians.

When Ribault was sent out from France to supersede Laudonnier [Laudonniére] as Governor of Florida, he arrived at Fort Caroline, which Laudonniére had built on the river May, now the St. John's, in the month of August; he took from the fort the best troops to go against the Spaniards, and left Laudonniére, and 80 souls sick in the fort, who were afterwards set on and massacred by the Spaniards.

In Gen. Oglethorpe's unfortunate expedition against St. Augustine in May, the Carolinians suffered much from the effects of the climate and disease. The Historian of South Carolina says: "The Carolina troops, enfeebled by the heat, despairing of success, and fatigued in fruitless efforts, marched away in large bodies; the General was sick of a fever, his regiment exhausted with fatigue, and rendered unfit for action by disease."

The same troops, in the late campaign, it is known, suffered very severely; more than one half were at different times disabled by sickness, most of which was the measles, it is true, but fatal disorders were superinduced by marching through wet wilderness, standing in water knee high by the hour, and wading creeks and swamps waist deep, laboring in the hot sun to drag the heavy wagons over these morasses, where the horses sunk up to their hams and had themselves to be dragged out—moreover, some cases of malignant bilious fever occurred among the garrison at Volusia, on the St. John's, towards the beginning of May. In Williamson's expedition against the Cherokees, in the healthy upper country of South Carolina and Georgia, in October, 1776, out of an army of 2000 men, not one died from disease; and only one man was disabled for a few days by sickness, notwithstanding the fatigue and the natural difficulties of the country were immense; pathless mountains and rugged acclivities had to be surmounded, and the army seldom marched more than 5 or 6 miles a day.

————

The object of these pages being completed which was to present to the reader in the most approved form, a review as he will term it, of the events of this Indian war prior to the campaign, which is considered not out of place as an introduction to the other parts of this work, though it would properly belong to another design—the author concludes this sketch and leaves it to a future time, or to others better qualified to resume, if the task be thought worthy, the thread of the history of the Indian war in the South to which this slender filament may assist.

APPENDIX.

Note A. The army, which, at this time, did not exceed six thousand men, and consisted of only 13 regiments, forty or fifty men in a company, has since been increased to an establishment more suited to the need of the country. Two additional regiments of dragoons have been created, and a bill has at the time I write, just passed the Senate, making an addition to each company of Artillery of 27 privates; and to each of infantry thirty privates; it amends the Quarter-master's department, which was very defective, by the creation of a quarter master sergeant to each company. The President, by a previous act, was authorised to raise a provisional army of ten thousand volunteers, for the exclusive protection of the country against Indian hostilities; there being a necessity to keep up a large force on our frontiers, to act at any time, if required, against the large number of Indians which are collected upon our western borders.

We are proving the effects of the present policy of the government, in removing the Indians from their soil, and from the influences of civilization, and assembling hordes of them together, by themselves, where they will resume their wild habits, and only give us future additional trouble, by their wars among themselves; which we are bound, by our treaties with them to take part in, and by their hostilities against us.

31,348 have been already removed, and there remains to be yet removed 72,181; total 103,529; besides there are of native tribes upon our borders, 150,341; making an aggregate of 253,870 Indians, which will be collected west of the Mississippi.

The extent and boundaries of the Territory assigned them is thus stated in a recent account. It is bounded on the east by the territorial line of

Arkansas, and the State line of Mississippi; on the South by the Red River, which is the dividing line between the United States and Mexican territory; the western line is not permanently established, but is contemplated as parallel of longitude 300 miles west of the East boundary line. The north line is also undetermined, but is designed to extend the Territory north until it strikes the river Platte.

If extended as far as the 46th degree of north latitude it will be 800 miles long, and 300 wide.

The government of the United States in the relations it maintains with the Indians, and in removing them into this region, acts with a sincere view to their benefit, but the more we consider this system the less we can reconcile it with the liberal and humane one advocated and maintained by Washington, Adams and Jefferson, which was to civilize and adopt them among us. Our present policy is visionary in the extreme, and perfectly suicidal; we wish to reclaim them from their wild and barbarous habits, to humanize them, and to unite in the bonds of peace, into one enlightened and happy society like ourselves, all the ragged remnants of the tribes of America; but at the very outset we deprive them of the fundamental principle of civilization: attachment to home and to the soil; and by sending them to a new country, barren of any local associations, with no far-remembered and consecrated stream, or hill, no ancient town or field, no monuments of the beloved time-honored dead—a strange land which they know not of, wot not of; we tear from their bosoms those softening ties, and set up in their hearts discontent, a gloomy feeling of exile, and a restless and roving disposition—we let them loose among other strange and fierce tribes, thus discontented and desperate, and like so many ferocious wild beasts, conquered and caged together, they vent their rag upon one another—we place them exactly in the situation the best that could be devised to reduce them into a state of primitive savageness and barbarism—

their propensity to war is fomented, and their progress to civilization retarded, by bringing one strange tribe in contact with another, whose instinct it is, like that of fighting fowls, to feel an aversion to one another. I, not long ago, was handed by a gentleman of Georgia, a letter from a distinguished Cherokee, who had gone on a tour of inspection to the Arkansas; the letter was written in very good English, and with much force, and piquancy of expression—he gave an unfavorable account of the country, and among other things, dwelt much upon the disagreeable and strange people whom he met with; he happened to came across some Delawares—"I was told," said he, "that these were my brethren—my brethren! I cannot believe it—is it possible that these ugly looking people can be of the same flesh and blood as we Cherokees? I will describe them to you; they have big yellow heads like pumpkins, out of which their eyes stick like pewter bullets; I think they must be nearer relations to our kind Father Jackson than to us."

We treat them as a nation, and by our formal embassies, and the talks we receive from them in exchange, at one time, flatter their national pride, and make them look upon themselves, as a superior distinct people, while at another, we show them that they are in reality stripped of all sovereignty, and degraded beneath our power; we assume over them the right to regulate their trade—to have free ingress into their country; we establish military posts and agencies among them; they acknowledge themselves under our protection, and an Indian who kills a white man, or a white man who kills an Indian are alike tried by our laws and courts, though the offence was committed in the Indian territory. Instead of seeking to assimilitate their manners in to ours, as the first necessary step to induce them to adopt our habits and become civilized, we do just the contrary, and estrange and distinguish them as much as possible from ourselves, by encouraging them to dress extravagantly and fancifully, in a style totally different from ours. When Great Britain sought to subdue unto civilization the fierce and warlike Highlanders, she prohibited the national costume, and endeavored to eradicate their peculiar customs and the Gaelic language, and not to keep alive the remembrance of their ancient dignity and sovereignty.* When the Sultan Mahmond was reforming the Turkish empire, one of the methods he adopted to break the indomitable spirit of the Janisaries, was to substitute the simple fer [fez] for the lordly turban, and to overset the soup kettle. While we thus degrade them, and taunt them with their nominal independence, leave them in full possession of their savage customs and manners, and isolate them from us, and from the ameliorating influence of our society, placing them in contact for the most part with savages; thus inducing them to hate our power, encouraging their savage pride, and enstranging them from our habits and manners; we send a few artisans, agriculturists and schoolmasters among them, to instruct them in the ways of civilization; with this limited influence, how can we expect success? Has it not been truly remarked, that where one savage adopts the custom of civilization, fifty civilized men enter into the savage state? Here [There] is no hope for the Indians as long they remain a distinct and separate nation, with habits and manners that do not conform to ours. Had the policy of Washington and Jefferson sustained a fair trial, can we doubt that in time it would have eventuated in the civilization and happiness of this unfortunate race, or at least of a considerable portion? Does it seem impossible that they might have gradually weaned from their rude and savage state, and from their notions of wild independence, have become agriculturists and tradesmen; have, we do not say immediately, but by degrees, as they

---

*I have repeated here from memory some of Judge Hall's remarks on this subject in his Sketches of the West.

progessed in civilization, been admitted to the privileges of citizens, and lived in peace and happiness under the broad and universal philanthropy of that government which welcomes to the enjoyment of its blessings, the pilgrims from every realm and people; all but the poor Indian? Why should he be excluded? Experience has shown that he is fully capable of a high state of improvement and civilization; the intellect of the Indian in his native wild state, has generally been remarked upon by travellors, as shrewd, evincing much common sense, active, and frequently comprehensive; few have underrated it, and in those instances in which they have, the subjects were unfavorable, either individually or they were peculiarly degraded by particular habits of extreme barbarism, their eloquence has been the theme of universal praise, and their ingenuity in mechanical arts, with which they are acquainted was such as to warrant skill and industry in other more important ones.

As far as the experiment has been tried, it was working admirably well; the Cherokees, Creeks, Choctaws, and some other tribes were becoming farmers, were learning how to make money, and treading the speediest path to civilization; by a statistical table we find that, more than ten years ago the Cherokee nation owned 1000 negro slaves; 7683 horses; 22,531 head of cattle; 46000 head of swine; 36 grist mills; 13 saw mills; 762 looms; 2486 spinning wheels; 192 wagons; 62 blacksmith shops; 2 tanyards; 1 powder mill; besides some public roads, ferries, turnpikes, taverns, and gold mines, all of which they attended to nearly the same as white men. They had 18 schools, and 313 scholars; an ingenious alphabet, consisting of 84 characters, was the invention of the famous Guess, almost a full blooded Cherokee, in which he succeeded after several attempts, merely by his own acute observation, and the force of native genius. They had a newspaper, printed partly in their own language, and spelling books, hymns, and the litany translated into it. They were making a still greater march towards a high state of intellectual and moral improvement; they had their written constitution modelled after ours, but at the same time adopted [adapted] with much wisdom to suit themselves; their legislative council, laws and circuit judges; but Georgia would not allow this imperium in imperio, and wisely; but when she extended her own laws over them, it should have been with moderation; she should gradually have made them citizens; intermarriage's would in time have incorporated them; they would have been respectable, and the future aristocrat might have founded his claims upon a pedigree traced to an ancient lord of the soil. It is very certain that the evil so cried up, which is supposed to present an insuperable obstacle to the amelioration of the Indian's condition while he remains among us; the introduction of spirituous liquors, and the uniform degradation which ensues, would diminish the more they became amalgamated into our society; it is an evil attendant upon the change their natures have to undergo, like a disease which affects a certain stage of the constitution, but vanishes as the constitution gradually assumes another state; it has been remarked, that the Indians who are most vicious and degraded from this cause, are the idle roving tribes, upon the borders of the settlements.

How much better would the money spent by government, in purchasing the land of the Seminoles, in paying them annuities in money, of which they do not know the use, which only encourages them to lead an idle life, and which they immediately exchange for whiskey and gun powder, the money spent in purchasing trinkets and articles of dress to gratify their tastes, and keep up in their minds, vain ideas of distinction; in expenses of emigration; in maintaining military posts among them, and the 5,000,000 *for the war*, have been expended in a vigorous system of improvement and assimilitation, in establishing among them farms & increasing the number of responsible agents among them, whose business it should be to prevent the introduction of spirits and powder among them; as much of the country they inhabit consists of watery wastes, and savannahs unfavorable to raising the sugar cane, cotton or grain, but is the finest in the world for raising cattle, their life would be chiefly pastoral, at least for some time, until the change to the more fixed habits of agriculture, could gradually take place. Having an abundance of meat to live on, they would thus, as the first stage towards civilization, be easily weaned from their erratic hunting habits; the deadly rifle, the possession of which excites to war, would then be no longer necessary to supply their wants, and they might be persuaded to go without it; they would have nothing to fear, in this respect from their neighbors, for they would be disarmed likewise, and besides, the faith of the government would be pledged to protect them. At this stage too, the bane of ardent spirits would sensibly begin to diminish, for it is an established fact, that hunger and want of occupation are the prime and powerful incentives to the indulgence of this vice.

Another important consideration, and one which causes us to be surprised at the folly of our system, is, that the country which lately has been the scene of bloodshed; on whose account so much treasure has been squandered, and to take which from the owners, we are prepared to squander still more, and to exterminate, if we cannot remove, the Seminoles, could not be turned to better advantage than by adopting the method we are advocating; the civilized Indians would make the best cattle raisers, the pastoral life suits them, and they are already acquainted with the nature and facilities of the country; at the same time their residence would not be incompatible with the cultivation of those parts of the territory which are available; they would readily part with certain portions of their land for money, which they would apply in increasing their stock, or in purchasing the necessaries and comforts of life, as these would begin to be appreciated by them. But however just may be the intentions of the government to the Indian; whatever the philanthropist may still urge in his favor; all that may be done or said, cannot preserve him from the rapacity and determined tyranny of the white man, and sooner or later, it seems, he must be devoted to destruction. We are reminded of the wolf and the lamb in the fable: The wolf accused the lamb of dirtying the water where he was drinking, the lamb answered 'that cannot be, because I am below the stream where you are drinking', 'no matter,' repeated the wolf, 'you did it six months ago;' 'that cannot be, because I was not then born;' 'it is all the same, your father or mother then it was,' said the wolf; 'I have no father or mother;' 'but you are vile, and thereupon deserve to die,' and he fell upon devoured the lamb.

———

Note B. This is the conclusion of the report.

"The country is for the most part a sterile waste, interspersed with hammocks; the white settlements are sparsely scattered on its face, and every facility thus afforded to the Indian mode of warfare. The Indians themselves, heretofore a conquered people, and from whose energy no danger was apprehended, have been profiting by the false security of the whites; gaining experience from past defeats, and putting into exercise their whole skill and resources, have on a sudden started up, a courageous and determined host. There is a discontent and desperation among them; a power of evil, working to destruction of all the civilized settlements; nor have these rude sons of the forest displayed any want of skill, or foresight; on the contrary they have manifested a wary dissimulation; a celerity of movement a courage in attacking, and a skill in retreating, subversive of our military plans; they have become so emboldened in success that they are preparing to break in upon the walled cities and the fortified camps.

"It must be obvious to every one, that any system

to be adopted in this emergency, should be a comprehensive one; operating at various points; leaguing simultaneously all the forces; and proceeding in one grand movement; eventuate in a prompt and decisive result. Whether the elements of such a system be within our power, you fellow-citizens can better determine; whether assistance will speedily be afforded by the General Government, remains to be seen; at present confusion seems to prevail both in the war and financial departments of the Government at Washington; a confusion which threatens utter ruin to the poor inhabitants of Florida; whatever you may resolve upon, it must not be disguised that great difficulties and dangers are to be encountered by any troops which may be sent into the territory. The Indians to be overcome must be persued through sandy wastes, untried paths, and tangled swamps; resolution, patience, and fortitude are required to accomplish the work."

————

Note C. A similar resolution is at this time pending to afford the same relief to the inhabitants of Alabama and Georgia, sufferers from Creek hostilities. In the debate which ensued on this resolution, Mr. Adams denominated these enactments, *the Scalping Knife and the Tomahawk Laws*; he objected to the principle that Congress should, in such cases, act upon feelings of mere charity and commiseration, and based the authority to apply money out of the Treasury, to these and similar purposes, which the constitution does not clearly recognize, upon the war-power, and the power to pass laws for the general welfare. The former power, as Mr. Adams says, is a tremendous one; therefore it is equally as dangerous as the latter; the general welfare, the war-power, a power to appropriate money for any charitable purpose, are just as liable to be abused, the between liberal constructions of the more important and high powers of our government, and the power to enact whatever may seem necessary from the general welfare; one such construction make precedent, and precedent finally makes law. It may be asserted that there has not been one, the most rigid construer of the constitution, who has not, at some time or other, in the course of his legislative life, aided unconsciously by his vote in establishing precedent, and insensibly acknowledged the doctrine of the general welfare; the law was one from which his constituents were to reap a benefit; he could see it clearly, constitutional under one or other of the provisions of the constitution, though others less interested, might not. Congress may at one time feel itself urged by paramount necessity, by philanthropy, to extend that liberal aid, which every government it would seem, in order to be respected, ought to be enabled to extend to its citizens, and even abroad; to pass scalping knife and tomahawk laws, fire laws, or earthquake laws, and the States perhaps would sanction the proceeding, but are these laws *strictly constitutional?* Are they not *dangerous precedents?* Might they not lead to the creation of a fund for the purpose of emancipation, or to the "saddling of the people of the United States with the insupportable burden of the whole system of the poor laws of England"? On the other hand, the framers of the Constitution knew the practicability of a more particular enumeration of the powers of the government, and after general cessions of power to the General Government, and reservations of power to the United States, left all dubious and unrenumerated exercises of authority, to be construed according to the terms, *for the common defence and general welfare*, which, at one and the same time enlarge and limit power; which do not, as some would have them to mean, enable Congress to enact any thing it pleases but give a larger scope to the grants of power, and refer to them, and this clause is checked by the reservations contained in the constitution, and its spirit throughout. The *spirit* of the constitution, therefore, is the test by which such doubtful exercises of power not strictly pertaining to any given power, but demanded for the good of the country are to be tried; we are never to lose sight of the fundamental principle, on which the spirit of the constitution rests; that the system of our government is a mixed one, of exclusive federal power, exclusive State power, and of both concurrently; the act to afford relief to sufferers from war, citizens of a State, falls under the last mentioned division; the State is bound to protect its citizens, but it is also incumbent upon the General Government to afford relief in such cases, as to it belongs the whole control of war and its consequences. Florida being a territory, was, of course, entitled to this aid; but the expediency of this measure, was questioned by some who were apprehensive, that it would prevent the inhabitants from making the defence they should against the Indians and encourage them to fly into forts to receive this relief and maintainance—a paltry supposition.

A VOCABULARY
OF THE
SEMINOLE LANGUAGE

The language of the Seminoles and that of the Creeks is the same, with the exception of some words which the former have borrowed from the Yemassees; a few Spanish, acquired by their own intercourse and that of the Yemassees, with the Spaniards, and some of the original invention; a few English words may also be found in it, as Alaha-Cheyna for the China Orange. The Uchees among them belong to a distinct tribe of Indians who speak altogether a different language. The reader who is curious to know something of the construction and idiom of the Indian language is referred to Adair, and later writers on the subject. I shall not pretend to more than a few remarks in explanation of my vocabulary. The authorities I have referred to are Creek words, excepting Simmons.

The Seminoles have not the R in their language; two or three words which I have spelt with R were written words which were given me. Adair says, speaking generally of Indian languages, they have not the Z, much less any such harsh sound as Tz; I have Haintclitz and che-hy-watz which appeared to me to have that sound. They are very fond of tch, st, ck, ks, tk, and the termination chay, ko, waw, ké or té or e preceded by any consonant, also a. The Indian, like the Latin, &c., has no articles; nouns have no cases nor declensions; the plural is expressed by magnifying terms as nethlé-day; days-nethle-mast-chay (many days,)

Spaniard-Spanalkay; Spainairds-Spanalkay-sulké-mastchay, or sole-ta-ulké. Sheh is what Adair calls the sounding criterion of the Muskogee Indians, wah-e-sheh—very, which I spell mastchay or mas-tschay; they have no comparative or superlative degree; they express a preference by opposite extremes; as you are virtuous, I am viscious, or by prefixing he adverbs little and much; and a double repetition of the same adjective, or ha added, makes a superlative." The Cherokees use the termination U, as osee—good; oseeyu—very good, most good. Nouns of quality and abstract terms seem not to be used, as for a liar, they say, iste-lockse, a person that lies. In Simmons' Vocabulary, Love is expressed in one word, Isteameheilst, the iste should be separate; ameheilst (from Spanish?); so mad: Istehachohawkit— that person is mad; strength—Isteichenowhee, &c.; they say also Iste-luste, black person; Iste-chati, red man instead of any single derivative word, like negro from niger. Makers of Vocabularies are apt to make a similar mistake by joining the pronoun my and your, as when they enquire what is father, they are given my father, your father. I have endeavored to correct these mistakes in my vocabulary, but I may have omitted a few. The Indians are particular in distinguishing old brother and young brother; they either prefix or add che for young as che-chose, young brother; hoktoche young girl—also for the young of animals, hey have no terms like colt, fawn, &c., but chelucco (itcho-cluckko) che. Echo che, young horse, young deer. According to the same poverty of language, for general, orator, &c., they say,

Tustenagge-cluckko, great warrior; Yatikka-cluccko, great speaker, &c.; words compounded are generally long, and many of their names of different things are periphrastical; the Cherokees, for instance call a Dove, Kuleteeskauneh, (a bird that cries for acorns,) for our short word a Spy, the Seminoles have to say Iste-hay-chulkay, one who goes out to see; pale, saput-hatké (half white) peace, shaking of hands in friendship. But, on the other hand, some are short of which the English would be periphrastical; such are the names of places as Palatka, flinging in the water; cheestatee, river of hunting fire lights, &c. In composition, they often drop the last syllable of a word as Fus-chati, instead of Fuswachati, red bird; wee-luste instead of waw-luste, black water; they also use religious emblems and typyfying vowels, and this radical language is simple and short, (see examples, Adair 69.) Adjectives follow the nouns and the accusative precedes the verb as in the dead languages. From the few phrases in my catalogue, (as these remarks are intended only to illustrate it, and my limits will not allow me to enter more at large into the subject,) it will be seen that the imperative mood has the pronoun added: Likas-chay, sit down, like the French asseyez-vous; Attes-chay, come in; Wykas-chay quit; but instead of Donnez-moi, or give me; A-mis-chay, give me (you); the pronoun precedes the verb and adverb, as how do you do, instead of as in English or in French, is *che*-he-loseli? A negative is expressed by a strong affirmative, as it is not good, hulwak-stchay, it is very bad. (see Adair, 73.)

{The Great Spirit, or, the Maker —Ophunkay.
{*God—Hesakitamisi, Simmons' notes on Florida.*

REMARK—They hold up their hand to heaven as the pronounce this word; they have no name for the Devil or Evil Spirit; when suffering under adversity, they do not ascribe it to the influence of a malignant demon; but regard their misfortune as the punishment of the Supreme Being, whom they adjure Tehan-chaste-methle-chay, which is as much as to say, You (my Maker,) over punish me.

A Spirit— Wyhômè (same name for Rum.)

A person—Iste, (Man in general. *Lieut Pettis*)

A man—Nuntakay, or Hanaunoway (Honanowaw, *Simmons*, Hon-on-war, *Pettis*.)

A woman—Hok-tak-kay, or Hokte, (Hockta *Simmons*, Oke-te *Pettis*.)

Old woman—Hokte-huktutnez.

Young woman—Hokte-mè.

An American or Virginian—Fotchè-nolkè, (Wisanalki, *Simmons*.)

Englishman—Metachak-ulkè

Spaniard—Spanalkay (Spanalki, *Simmons*.)

(For plural add, hoè-yâne mast-chay, or sulkè-mast-chay, or Soleta-ulkè, many or a great many, or an army of Americans, &c)

An Indian—Iste-chati, (a red man.)

REMARK: They call persons who are not of pure blood either of their own or any other race, Maletulkè.

A white man—Iste-hatkè

A negro—Iste-luste, (Stelasti, *Simmons*.)

A tribe—ulkè

The Seminole tribe—Seminolee ulkè

Cowetas—Coweta-ulkè.

Uchees—Uch-ulkè.

REMARK: They call the Upper Creeks, Ta-loph-ulkè, people who have a home or town.

Father—Chacteka; do. *Simmons*, (etauteh, my father, chatokta your father; *Cherokee*

Mother—Chatske, do. *Simmons*, (aatse, *Cherokee*.)

Brother—Chô-se.

{Brother, as used in Council—Chapawa, or my old brother or {best friend.

Young brother—che-chôse.

Sister— E-wun-waw.

Son —(Chakpootsi, *Simmons*.)

Daughter.—(Chackshosti, *Simmons*.)

Boy—che-paw-nee.

A little girl, (Hocktoche, *Simmons*.)

Husband—ehee (Acahay, *Cherokee*) (chahi, *Simmons*,) expression of love, Ahi?

Wife—che-hy-watz (chahiwa, *Simmons*.) cha your, Awa (*Cherokee*,) (from Eve *Adair*,) Ewa?

———

A king or head chief —Mico or Micco; a leader—Omathlie.

Orator or Great Speaker—Yatikka-cluckko.

Warrior— Tustenagge; do. (*Adair*), (Tustanuggie, *Simmons*.)

General, or war captain—Tustenagge-cluccko.

Magician, (in our sense), iste-hulwa (bad person)

A brave—iste-hanaunowaw-mauaoo-st-chay.

REMARK: This expresses he is a *very* brave man; the *mastchay* is dwelt on long to make a strong superlative.

Spy or scout—iste-hay-chulkay, (one who has gone out to see.)

Trader—Isneesay.

Council— Timpana-cluccko.

Council house—Mico-etchay (the king stands strong.)

Town house where the dances are celebrated—Epala-cluccko.

Great square where religious ceremonies are celebrated—
    chucco-cluccko (or the big yard)
Medicine bag—Halist-châway, (Halistwa, root or physic,
    and châway, bag,) (Hilliswaw, physic, *Simmons.*)
Pipe of peace and Pipe—Echipukwa,
    (eche-puckawa, pipes, *Simmons.*)
Green corn dance—Pùsketa.
    REMARK: The Bosk or feast of first fruits which is celebrat-
ed with much fasting and purgation and concluded with dances
and rejoicins; it is their principal religious ceremony. Adair
thinks it alludes to the Passover; it takes place when the corn
ripens; with the Seminoles in the early part of July.
Flute, (made of cane about 2½ feet in length, with double set
    of holes, and a mouth piece,)--Fifpa.
Drum, (made of dressed deerskin stretched over a large gourd,)
    Cosatulki, *Simmons.*
Rattle or Chichicoe, (made of a gourd with
    pebbles inside,)—Sulka.
Ball play—Pokitcha.
Ball—Poko.
Racket or hurl, like a battledour, the hollow part with which the
    ball is caught and town, made of crossed sinews of the
    deer—Tokônay.
War—Soletâwa.
War-cry, or gathering word—Yo-ho-ehee. Of Victory—
    Caha-queene.
Peace, or the shaking of hands in riendship—
    Esse-ka-phutcha-la.
Cassina drink, or black drink, used on religious occasions,
    at Councils, &c.—Wee-luste, or black water

Tobacco pouch—Itcha-suchay, (Hitche, Tobacco, *Simmons*)

REMARK: This is a very important article among Indian accoutrements, and they are never seen without it; their care is tasked to adopt some fine and suitable skin to make it of, and the wife of the warrior, or the maiden who bestows her smiles upon the young hunter, exert all their ingenuity in decorating it with beads and other fancy work; it is made of the skin of the wild cat, fox, wolf and other animals, with the tails hanging to them, and sometimes of the skins of birds with the feathers on, that of the Whooping Crane is much valued; these pouches are armorial bearings, and when they come into Council, each clan or family throw its down separately, and when the ceremony of smoking commences, uses its own tobacco. As soon as a youth is of an age to go upon the hunt, he carries his tobacco pouch, which, besides tobacco, is furnished with flint and steel, a piece of punk, and a knife.

Hatchet or Tomahawk-- Put-chuswâ.

Cannon—Itcha-cluccko, big gun.

Rifle—Etcha-sut-a-hay, [sutcha; pouch?] [Its sahihi, *Simmons*.]

Knife— Slaphka, [do. with w, do.]

House—Hotay } Choco, a house or home, *Pettis*

Camp— Choco} [Soko. *Simmons*.]

Fort or enclosure—To-pe-kee.

Town—Talopha, [Talaopho, *Simmons*.]

Pen—Tohope-ke?' [same as enclosure.]

Canoe—Pithlo, [Boat, Pithlo, Vessel, Pithlohocto, *Simmons*.]

Bed—Potarka, [*Pettis*,] [Topa, *Simmons*.]

Blanket— [Archeta, *Pettis*] [Ashelahatki, *Simmons.*]

RELATING TO THE BODY.

Scalp, Num-haar.
Head—[ecar, *Pettis.*]
Eyes, Luthphwa [eye, chatalthewa, *Simmons.*]
Tongue, Taluswa, [Chatolaswaw; *Your* Tongue, *Simmons.*]
    REMARK: In Simmons' Catalogue, the cha is prefixed and
joined; it should be separated as cha-talthewa, *your* eye, cha-
chockwaw, *your* mouth, &c.
Mouth, Chuckwa, [Chockwaw, *Simmons.*]
    {Hair,
    {Whiskers, Issè
Mustachio, Chack issè, or beard on the mouth
    [Beard on the mouth, chatchockhissi, *Simmons*, *your* beard, &c.]
Hand, Chinkee, [chanki, *Simmons.*]
Blood, Chattè, [chati, *Simmons.*]
Heart, [Effagà, *Barton*]

———

RELATING TO DRESS.

Scalp-lock, Issè.
Hat, Kuppa-tuka.
Plume, [Black,] Tafa-luste, [Tafa, feathers, *Simmons.*]
Any thing tied around the throat, Notchka.
Gorget, or silver breast plate, Chaluccanawaw,
    [Chateknonowaw, money, *Simmons.*]
Handkerchief, Enoche-eaw.
Bracelets, or arm bands, [of silver] Chaluccanawaw.
Beads, [Con-nar-wa, *Pettis*] [Conowaw, *Simmons.*]
Mantle, Kappa-cluccko.

Cloak, Kapa, Caupa, Jacket, *Simmons.*
Hunting Shirt, Fuksaykè.
Leggins, Uphe-taykê,
Moccasin, Stillepika.
Leather-shoe, Stillepika-wauhe.
Dressed deer skin, Chôsee.
Frock, or garment of women, Hunna.
Jacket or wrapper of women, Huksaykè.
Leggins or garters worn below the knee, Takfulwa
Needles, [Thlar-bate-ar, *Pettis,*] (Eslapota, *Simmons.*)
Scissors, [Scote-ear, *Pettis*]
Spoon, Hockka.

————

Sun, Hassè.
Moon, Hassè, (Hatliesi, *Simmons,*) Nethle-hassè, night sun?
Stars, Hutte-chumba, (Cochosompa, *Simmons.*)
    (Hotchot-chumpa, *Barton.*)
Day, Neth-lay.
Daylight, hayutt-schay, (morning, Hatatki, *Simmons.*)
This day, Mutche-Nethlay.
Night, Yomot-skay, (Nithlee, *Pettis,*) (Nilthi,
    Simmons, Dark, Ymochecks, do.)
Fire, Toteka, (Totekar, *Pettis.*)
Ground—E-cunnaw.
Dirt—Fucke.
Hill—E-cun-holwa, (or tall ground, ulwè, tall.)
Trail—Nini; Road, Nini, (*Pettis.*)
Water—We-wa, (We-waw, *Simmons.*)
River—We-thluccko, (or cluccko, big water.)
Creek—hutchee.
Branch—Hatch-uchee, (small or head of a creek)
Spring—Wekîwa, (Wekewa or Weliki, *Simmons*)

Lake—Wetîkay, (Wepalokesi or Itteniah, do.
Cypress swamp—uchenna-kulkè or cluccko, (big cypress.)
Savanna or prairie—We-hatkè (white water.)
Wind— Hutallay.
Wind storm-Hutallay-cluccko-mast-chay, (very great wind.)
Breeze or gentle gale—Hutallay-stômasin (little wind.)
Thunder—Tenêt-kay (Tonitkee, *Simmons.*)
   (*The Cherokees have a much finer word for Thunder,*
   E-en-taqua-roske,)
Wood cut for burning—Etotus.
Hammock—Ett-say-cha.
Ice—Hittotè.
Snow—Hittotè hatkè (white ice)

———————

NAMES OF TREES & PLANTS.

Tree, itto, *Simmons.*
   { Orange tree,
                        Alaha
   { Orange,
Sweet orange, Alaha-chayna, (yallaha, *Simmons*)
Sour orange, Alaha-Tomocks,(yallaha-chena) *do*
Magnolia, Oke-tockse, (sour water sweetened,) (Loblolly Bay,
   Itto-Mico, the chieftain of trees, *Simmons,*) (Magnolia,
   Tolo-cluccko, Big Bay; Red Bay, Eto-mico, *Bartram.*)
Live Oak, Alatcha-chumpa [sweet acorn]
   [acorn, sockcha. *Simmons*]
Palmetto tree, Tala-la-kulkè or cluckko [big cabbage.]
Palmetto cabbage, [Palmetto, seopho; cabbage,
   Talalocko] *Simmons.*
Saw-palmetto, Tala.
Cyprus, ucchenhahô [Atcheanahoe, *Simmons.*].
Pine, Chuli   do

Gum, Helocoppe *Simmons.*
Ceder, Atchena do
Maple, Haino do
Sugar cane, Halist-chumpa [sweet root,]
    {Water melon, Châstalay, [melon, chastali.]
    {Musk Fomischa, [Connalalaco *Simmons.*]
    {Arrow root, Conti-katkè
    {China-briar, do
    {Root like a tannier which they eat with leaf like wampee—
    grows in wet ground, Hehla
    {Indian potatoe, Ah-hah. [Ah-hah or Indian Potatoe is the
    Apios tuberosa, not Arum.]
    {Indian turnip, [Arum?]
Corn, Atchee [Archee *Petis*] (Atschee *Creek.*)
Bread, Tuckalargie   *do* Aspeen (*Seminole,*)
    Simmons. [Tockliki, *Simmons.*]
Grass; Pahke.   [Rope Tocka. *Simmons.*
    {Grass of which they make rope, Sowena.
    {Bear Grass; or silk Grass. [Yucca,]
Cider or Beer, Wee-toksce (sour water,)

NAMES OF ANIMALS AND BIRDS.

Horse, Echo-cluccko, (big deer) do *Bartram.*
    cholocko, *Pettis,* caballo, (spanish) chelucco, *Simmons.*
Deer, Echo, (do *Simmons.*)
Buck, Echo, hanaunowa   (male deer.)
Doe, Echo-hotké,   female do
Fawn, Echo istuchay,   (young do,) (echoche, *Simmons.*
Cow, Wauca (spanish vacca) do *Simmons.*)
Wolf, Yah-hah, (Eyaha *Simmons*) yah-hah is an exclamation of
    grief, wailing, *howling.*
Tiger, Catsha, [Caatsa do)
Dog, Efa, do
Groundmole, Tôkole.

Bird, Fuswa.

Eagle, yah-chelâne, (of golden color) Lamhi *Simmons.*

 Parroquet, yah-lâne, (yellow) (Pochelâne do)

 {Sandhill Crane, Soleta, (Wortola-lacha,

 {or whooping do *Simmons.*)

Heron, Wauco-cluccko, (big throat) red curlew or heron,

 Alolo-chate, *Simmons.*

Pelican, sochahaka,   do

Buzzard, soole, (do *Adair.*)

Owl, Huppa, (Opa *Simmons*) ooppa *Chickasaw,* (Adair.)

Bat, sukbulbar, (Micasaukie.)

Duck Futcho, (Fotcho *Simmons.*,]

English Duck, Futcho-cluccko,

Summer duck, Futcho-Chôtekus (small do)

Wild turkey, Penwa (do *Simmons.*)

Red bird, Fuschati, (do do.)

Mocking bird, (Fuswahaya do)

 {Dove

 {Ground dove, Patche-chôbe [Pochewawaw do

 Patche, pigeon; Easooba, bewildered *Adair*

REPTILES, INSECTS.

Snake—Chitta

Rattlesnake—Chitta-micco, (chieftain of the snakes)

Mockasin, or water snake—Wee hatkè, (white water, from

 the color of the belly, and living in water.)

Alligator—Hulputta, [hajo] they generally add 'hajo' or 'crazy.'

Bull Frog—Saputka.

Turtle—Lûcha.

Gopher, or great Land Tortoise—Kowikay [the

meaning of which is 'mourning' from the black color of this Tortoise.]

Mosquitoe—Okeeha.

Fire Fly—Hofka hatke.

Jigger—Hofka-hatke [white flea]

PHRASES.

Good morning—[They do not so express a salutation; but say 'Alaka-ischay' 'I am come,' to which the answer is 'ho' yes, and the person saluted or visited adds 'Lagaschay'—'sit down' (Hat-hat-que-hinks-cha) (used only very early in morning *Pettis*)

How do you do?—chehelosele (addressed to the sick) *Simmons*.

Salutation after a long absence—Ailkatesa *do*

{Good evening—(They say Aeepa-ischay—)

{Good bye   I am going, to which the other replies

               'Ho'—yes—you are going.

"A man goes forth on his business or avocations; he calls in at another town, if he wants victuals, rest, or social conversation, he confidently approaches the door of the first house he chooses, saying: "I am come;" the good man or woman replies "you are; it's well." Immediately victuals and drink are ready; he eats and drinks a little, then smokes tobacco, and converses either of private matters, public talks, or the news of the town. He rises and says, "I go;" the other answers "you do." He then proceeds again, and steps in at the next habitation he likes, or repairs to the public square, where there are people always conversing by day, or dancing all night, or to some more private assembly, as he likes; he needs no one to introduce him, anymore than the black bird or thrush, when they repair to the fruitful grove, to regale on their

luxuries, and entertain the fond female with evening songs."
    Bartram.
{It is well or good—Mathint-a-mas-tshay
{Very good   (Hinkla-mastchay, *Pettis*, good—Hinklas, *do.*)
It is not good—Hulwak-stchay
Yes--Ho (Incar, or, Car *Pettis*) (Enca *Simmons*)
No—Cooree.
Sit down—Lagaschay, (Laguschâ *Pettis,*)(Likas-che, *Simmons.*)
I do not know—Stentôse.
I don't understand— Kit-lox-cha.
Give me—A-mis-cha.
Come here—Attes-cha, (come in, Acheeschee, *Simmons.*)
Go away—I-e-pus-cha.
It is all gone—Souks-cha, [all gone, Atesche, *Simmons.*)
Be still, quit—Wykas-chay.
    REMARK : The little boys, when they are plagued say this,
when they get more vexed they say, 'Wykabus-chay', and 'Holy-
waugus,' 'bad,' [or Hulwak.]
When is it?—Stamartee?
You are good or pretty—Che-hink-las.
It is a lie—Iste-loksè-ta-mastchay, [that person lies very much.]
He is a liar—Iste loksè.
When a man is angry ,he says, Iste-hulwa-stchay
    [that's a bad man; getting more angry they add,
    Leech-as-chay, [I will kill you.]
When suddenly astonished at anything they exclaim,
    I-e-ela, [with a long drawl.]
Come and play ball—Pokitcha-lis-chay.
It is a bright morning, (they say, 'the sun rises good.')

Sunday—Nithla-chà-ko.
Tomorrow—Pokse, (Apockse; *Simmons*.)
Day after tomorrow—Pokse-â-sa mâ.
The day after day after tomorrow—Pokse-a-sa-ma-a-sa-ma-sa-tly.

ADJECTIVES, &C.

Good—Haintstche.
Bad—Hulwak.
Pretty—Haintclitz.
Hard—Hunela-mastshay, (very hard.)
Tall—Ulwè.
Short—Kachuckanosis-tschay, (very short.)
Little or small—Chotkwa, Chotekus.
Dark—Yomotchay, (Ymochecks, *Simmons*)
Light or pale—Saput-hatke, [half white.]
Dry—Efar.
Young—Manittè or che.

PRONOUNS.

I—Aneh, [*Barton.*] Anowah, *Adair.*
   {Thou, Cha? [Chemeet, *Barton.*]
   {You, do
He—Iste ? (oeesaw, he or she, *Barton,*)
My or mine—Eny.
Your—Cha.

COLOURS.

Red—Chati.
Blue—Sopa.
Black—Luste.
White—Hatkè,
Green—Ockola.
Yellow—Lane.

NAMES OF CHIEFS

Miconope [*sic*], his name means a King upon a king, or twice a governor; his original name was 'Sint-Chakkè,' or 'frequenter of the Pond,' [see page 21 for a more particular account of him, [Opae---a war leader, *Adair*.]

Oseola, or Hassè-ola, [Rising Sun.]

Jumper or Hoithle-mattee.

Charlie Omathlie,

    {Iolase Omathlie, (a friendly chief, [his brother,
    also friendly] killed by Oseola.)

    or Emartla, [Leader or one who goes before]

Catsha-Tustenagge-hajo, [Mad Tiger warrior,]
    a chief of the Micasaukies.

Fucke-luste-hajo—(Black dirt.) friendly; he has been shipped
    to Arkansas wih 400 of his tribe.

Hulputta-hajo—(Crazy Alligator.)

    {Eyah-hajo,

    {Yah-ha-hajo, (Mad Wolf)

    {Tusta-lak-kka-hajo—(Tusta-la-ka—the howls of a wolf.)

This was a chieftain of considerable note and consequence; he ranked third; he was one of the delegation sent out to examine the territory to which the Seminoles were to emigrate; but he took a violent part with them in opposing the removal, and he was active in endeavouring to stir up the negroes—he was a great hunter. He was slain by Gen. Shelton, of Newberry, S.C., who being in company with Col. Butler's battalion of horse, at a skirmish which took place near the Okle-wahaw, spied out this chief and pursued him alone; coming upon him at full gallop, Gen. Shelton shot him with his double barreled gun. Eyah Hajo fell upon his knees, mortally wounded, but quickly recovering himself, shot Gen. Shelton in the thigh with his rifle;

the Gen. then drew one of his pistols, but before he fired, some one coming up advanced within a few paces of the Indian chief and killed him—he was buried on the way by the surgeon, and on the return of the army, taken up and his head preserved—caution, firmness, and destructiveness, were largely developed.

Koè-hajo—(Mad Partridge; koe, the cry of a Partridge.)

Yah-oluche—(the great cloud.)

Semethlè.

Mithlackè.

Ho-pa-to-pha—a young chief (reported lately to have killed Powell.)

Uchee Billy, or Billy Hicks—a chief of consequence, who headed the Uchees at Spring Garden; he used to reside at or near Berresford, on the St. John's; he had from 25 to 30 warriors. He was killed at the crossing of the St. John's, by an individual of Col Brisbane's regiment when Ashby's and Fripp's companies were attacked.

Tiger Tail—A partisan chief with only 5 or 6 warriors who used to live formerly about Tallahassee, and was in the habit of hunting for the whites; he was expelled [by] the nation for some cause or other, his friendliness to the whites perhaps, as he was friendly during the winter campaign; someone having inconsiderately threatened him, he lately resulted to join his hostile countrymen, and he and his warriors carried off several scalps as passports to their safe admission into the nation.

Philip—See page 19.

Apel.

WOMEN.

Futttatike, Miconope's wife.

Suktayike.

Sette-ta-kulka.

Waukistchay.

Talhecheeko.

———

NAMES & DERIVATION OF NAMES OF RIVERS, TOWNS, &C.

St. Johns River—Hilaka [ylaco (Spanish?) Hist. of Florida.]

Head of the St. Johns— Hayuppa, or large marsh

    Withlacoochee—River creek.

Okihumkey—Bad water.

The Withlacoochee takes it rise from a very remarkable spring called Oakihumky, which is said to resemble an artificial fountain, being surrounded by a lime stone wall of regular form, which continues lengthways along the stream, in parallel branches." *Simmons.*

Wewa-ki-a-hacke—Crystal water.

Okle-wahaw—Muddy water.

Silver Spring on Lake George—Wekiwa St spring

Palatka signifies "flinging in the water" as it was formerly a great

    crossing place where cattle were driven across.

Pilaklikaha—Scattered hammocks.

    Tohopeke-like*—A place where cowpens are stationary,

    not transient.

Wacahouta—Cow pasture.

Chichuchaty—The red houses—so called because the Indians

    who lived there, had their houses painted with red clay.

———

*The islands in the Lake on which this Town is situated, exhibit evidences of ancient breast works—and there is a tradition among the Indians that the Spaniards who visited Florida fortified themselves there. Probably De Soto stopped there as it was in the direction of his route. Yellow Beard formerly lived there with 150 warriors—it is since known as Philip's Town.

Hitchipucksasy—Tobacco patch.

St. Sebastian's river—Tiketa, or the crossing place.

Haw creeks or Savannas on road from St. Augustine to Volusia.

Chala-pâpa or trout-creek as there is a creek there where trout is plentiful

Choochee—Canoe creek?

END OF VOCABULARY.

Part the Second:

SKETCHES

DURING A CAMPAIGN

SKETCHES DURING A CAMPAIGN
CHAPTER I.

Militia Draft—Different opinions of—The military appearance of the Carolina Regiment—St. Augustine compared to Santiago in Cuba, with a difference—Draught of Mounted Men—Disposition of the several forces for the Campaign.

In pursuance of the requisition made by the General Government, upon the State of South Carolina, for a Draught of six hundred militia for three months service, against the Seminole Indians, Gov. [George] M'Duffie[70] immediately ordered a Draught to be made, from the Brigades of Gens. Bull, Trotti and Hamilton, comprising the militia of Abbeville, Edgefield, and of the middle and lower Districts, from whence the transportation could be soonest made to Florida in vessels. The requisite number of troops might have been furnished from the district and city of Charleston alone, but it was thought best not to take so large a force from one small portion of the State, which might be jeopardized, in case of sudden invasion, or other alarm from any quarter, should the militia be weakened or disorganized; especially as it was already partially so, three of the finest companies from the city having left it for St. Augustine; and as the government, with its small and scattered army, would be obliged to despatch companies from the nearest posts, in order to assemble a sufficient force to act speedily against the Indians and check their ravages, the forts in the harbor might be (and Fort Moultrie afterwards was) left to the state to garrison. Moreover, it was more just and fitting that all should take a chance in the dangers and honors of an Indian campaign, than that a few should be selected out to bear them; and it was thought best that the back and low country should unite in furnishing warriors for the service. In the orders issued by the commanding officers, there were no superfluous appeals made to the chivalry of Carolinians, but a confidence expressed that they would evince the same alacrity on the present occasion, which had always distinguished them, in obedience to the laws of their country; and that they would promptly come forward, to meet and share the perils of their suffering brethren of Florida. Lists were opened for volunteers, who were to be received in lieu of a draught, and before the time appointed for draughting, almost the whole of the number demanded was supplied by Volunteers. In the districts generally, there was great enthusiasm and much concern that each might save itself from the compulsion of a draught; with a few exceptions, fine volunteer companies of from 60 to 120 men, were instantly raised in each district. In the city, one company, the Irish Volunteers, a very ancient corps, volunteered their services. Some regiments were draughted from in the city and parishes adjacent; from the 16th in the city, the draught went into operation as the regiment had furnished volunteers at the previous call, and from the nature of the Beat companies, composed for the most part of men in business, whose avocations demanded personal attention, and of transient residents, who were not much interested in the honor of the State, the military enthusiasm, and *esprit de corps* of volunteer uniform companies was not to be expected. In the country beats of the 18th and 19th regiments but few volunteered. Many men looked upon an Indian campaign as a very disagreeable sort of thing, and valued their scalps a great deal more than they did the barren and uncertain laurels of Indian warfare. They regarded the matter of a draught, and all the specious talk about the glorious necessity of volunteering, to save their own credit, and that of the State, as sheer nonsense; and having soberly and cooly made up their minds that they would not go, such as were draughted availed themselves of the privilege allowed by law, of finding able bodied substitutes to go for them; this was not regarded as in any way derogatory to their honor or courage; a value was set upon the risk to be inclined, and the losses their business would be likely to sustain in their absence; and, according to the extent of these, men were willing to pay; some gave much higher prices than they needed to have given. Five and six hundred dollars were offered by some, when the substitutes, in many instances, would have readily gone for a fifth or sixth of the amount. Besides this draught, there was one made in Abbeville also.

By the middle of the month, the Carolina Regiment, to the command of which Col. Abbot H. Brisbane was appointed, was in camp at St. Augustine, in an open field to the south of the town; soon after, Capt. Elmore arrived, with a fine company of one hundred and twenty riflemen, from Columbia and. Richland, which was intended to act as an independent corps. With the exception of these latter, who wore the

usual dress of riflemen, viz. drab frock shirts trimmed
with green fringe; and the Irishmen whose dress was of a
similar stuff, but darker hue and who were clad in close bodied short coats, lined with their favorite green, abroad
stripe of which ran along the outer seam of their trowsers,
the companies were scarcely distinguished by any difference
in their attire; all wore plain dresses and such as were best
adapted to the woods and swamps; Capt. Jones' company,
the Edgefield Blues, wore an [a] uniform dress of plain
dark blue cloth coatees, ornamented with a few brass buttons
on the skirts and sleeves, and trowsers that corresponded; the
rest were clothed in woodmen's suits, in native homespun,
or in their usual home garb; almost all wore mocknuters, or
foraging caps of the fur of the muskrat, rabbit, or fox, with
tassels, and pink and white cockades affixed to them. Many
of the men carried pocket and rencountre pistols, and all a
large woodman's spring knife or a dirk, in their belts or
pockets. There was more variety displayed in the costume of
the officers; some retained the silver winged, dock-tailed, stiff
militia uniform coat; others rivaled the more handsome liv-
ery of United States officers, and shone conspicuous in gold-
en epaulettes and superfine blue broad cloth; while others
merely added the necessary accoutrements of the officer,
such as sword, belt, and sash, to their plain but soldier like
suits of fustian; all had fatigue dresses calculated to withstand
the wear and tear of marching and camping, for convenience
and protection from the weather, and to supply the place of
epauletted dress uniforms in encounters with the Indians,
which were both unfit to charge through hammocks

with, and presented too conspicuous and enticing a mark for the rifle of the enemy. In these there was a singular variety. The water proof Caoutchouc of dingy hue and buckram starchness, contrasted with the soft green and motley colored blanket coats; some wore the simple military round jacket, and some the easy backwoodsman's hunting shirt, while others were content with less military looking citizen long tail blues, that had seen just service enough to recommend them for a campaign.

They commonly had on trowsers of strong cloth or fustean to which some added leggins to protect against the mud & saw palmettoes which they would have to march through. As Indian warfare is irregular & partisan, and a nice observance of military appearance and decorum in the dress and equipments of an officer is not requisite as in the formal warfare of civilized enemies, but the great object is the extermination of the savage foe, and in many cases officers as well as men are compelled to defend themselves behind trees, if a successful charge cannot be made, some of the officers carried muskets, rifles, or doubled barreled guns, a practice of which the officers of the regular army had previously set the example. By some it was discountenanced as derogatory [derogating] from the military character, and as tending to a neglect of the duties of command which an officer should not for a moment be diverted from, and General Scott, after the campaign was concluded, expressed his dissatisfaction of it, and said that henceforth all officers must appear in battle in their proper uniform and equipments, and in those only. Notwithstanding a General might not think it proper openly to sanction any departure from strict military usage, such a transgression might be winked at, and most persons would be of the opinion that, for wood and swamp fighting, gilt epaulettes and fine cloth would not agree as well with hammocks and mud, as plain woodsmen dress, and that in these bush battles with Indians whose keen eyes are always on the search to pick off the chieftains of their foemen, so that they may produce confusion and loss of confidence in their ranks, the policy of war would demand that the officer should not render his person unnecessarily conspicuous, provided he does not sacrifice any of the gallantry becoming officer, or act in a manner to diminish the confidence of his men. There would seem be no objection to an officer arming himself with a musket, or any other species of gun, which might not equally apply to his arming himself with a pistol and sword. It is seldom that an Indian fight is at close quarters, so as to call into requisition the latter weapons; at least, our Seminoles were never anxious to come within pistol shot; whereas, the musket was useful, and while their chiefs were making the best use of their rifles, ours might as well be employed in the same way; and an officer would lead on his men with more spirit, when he had the means of participating in the fight, than if he had to stand idly, a mere looker on, and mark for the enemy.

The good old times of Indian border war never saw a finer set of men collected together, better suited to follow up the fierce and wily son of the forest through his devious paths, and rout from his secret ambuscades; more ready to plunge head and neck into the wild fight, or patient to endure the hardships and toils of the wilderness and the privations of a long campaign; with few expections, they were elite of the substantial fine healthy looking class of farmers and laborers; they were officered chiefly by young and middle aged gentlemen, some of the list families in the state; many whose birth and fortune fitted them for high stations in society, preferred the wild adventure of the forest to the luxury of the drawing room; and in their zeal to do their duty, volunteered as privates, submitting to innumerable hardships, and disagreeable necessities and privations, to which they were not accustomed.

The assemblage on the mild shore of Florida of these gallant and select troops, reminded of the turning out of the Spanish Hidalgos, under De Soto, for the conquest of this territory. Many a Carolinian indulged in a similar lavish personal expense, though the Spaniards may have excelled in magnificence; but the latter expected to be renumerated in fair principalities, in wide and fertile lands, and mines of silver and gold. The former left their homes at the single instigation of patriotism, and looked forward to the approbation of their countrymen as the only guerdon for their toils and dangers.

St Augustine was like another Santiago in Cuba, on the occasion—stopping place of civilization previous to an entry into the savage wilderness, but the parallel went no farther. The accomplished translator of the Inca says, that the inhabitants of Cuba flocked to the town, to receive their adventurous countrymen, and welcomed them with all manner of festivities;

every night balls and masquerades were given and every day witnessed a tournament or bull fight; but at St. Augustine, there were no such festivities and junketings, to do us honor. Spanish magnificence had long since faded here, and it was only a little town of American and Minorcan thrift. The worthy cits thought more of the importance of filling their pockets, while the season for turning a penny lasted, and the town was crowded with the liberal-hearted money-spending volunteers, than of filling subscription lists for a dinner or ball. There were complaints that articles were over-charged, and no very good feelings existed towards the Minorcans. But though there were no public rejoicings at the arrival of succor, and at the prospect of Florida being once more restored to quiet, and rid of her troublesome enemy, instances of private hospitality were not wanting and much real regard and interest were expressed for those who had voluntarily left the bosom of their homes, to risk their lives in dreadful savage warfare for strangers.

On the 2d February, additional orders were received by the Governor, for the State to furnish 750 mounted men also, and in the course of a short time the Districts of Anderson, Laurens, Abbeville, and some others of the upper Districts supplied the requisite number, most of whom were volunteers. These horses were ordered by Gen. Scott, to rendezvous at Purysburg. Thus, the Carolina quota of militia consisted of two Regiments; one of foot commanded by Col. A. H. Brisbane, and the other of cavalry, commanded by Col. Goodwyn, and the Brigade was commanded by Gen.Wm. Bull of Abbeville. Gen. Abraham Eustis, of the U. States Army, was to conduct the Carolina troops as the left wing of the Army; Colonel Lindsay,[71] the centre division, consisting of the Alabamians and some Louisiana Volunteers; and Gen. Scott, the commander in chief, was to accompany the right wing, with the Georgians. The Regulars were distributed, a portion in each division.

————

CHAPTER II.

Depature from Charleston for St. Augustine; Sunset at sea and fading away of the shore; Feelings and Reflections awakened; Slight sketches aboard ship.

On the 10th of February, I left the harbor of Charleston for St. Augustine, having volunteered as a Lieutenant in a company that had been made up in pursuance of a draft from the 16th, 18th, and 19th Regiments. It was rather a motley command, the chief part of the men being substitutes, some from the town, and some from the country; the materials, though heterogeneous, were upon the whole good, and the company might have been considered as partaking of the mixed character of volunteers and hired recruits; they were mostly adventurers who were willing to fight Indians, seekers after novelty, and men who were ready to do the duty which the State had been summoned to perform, for an adequate consideration. It did not argue aught against their patriotism, that in serving their country at the same time put a little money in their pockets, for who do not? and if the worth of an article is to be judged by its price, they were better than ordinary enlisted soldiers, for they got much handsomer pay.

Our schooner soon got a gentle breeze after the steamboat which had towed her out of the harbor left her, and evening saw us far upon the sea-billow, and out of sight of land. We gazed long and silently upon the fading outline of our native shore, for we were leaving it, and parents, and friends, perhaps never to return. If one has resolved to break those dear ties, and sees himself about to sacrifice every thing he loves in order to rush into field of wild adventure, it is at this time that he re-pents, accuses himself, and thinks how much better it would have been to stay at home. As I sat on the poop of the vessel which was appropriated to the officers, and looked back upon the last speck of land, all other thoughts for the moment gave way to the one saddening feeling. The sun mingled his last dying efforts, and his purple shadow with the blue steak of the horizon, and as that dwindled slowly away, night and ocean began to assert their solemn and divided empire over all things. There was a melan-choly cadence in the shrill whine of the sea-loon which chimed in at intervals with the ripple of the wake behind us, and rose clear and sadly upon the evening breeze long after we ceased to catch a glimpse of her dusky speck riding upon the restless wave. The desultory laugh, and noisy conversation of the men who had been long enough together to get tolerably sociable among themselves, grated harshly on my ears, and reminded me that I was surrounded by perfect strangers, with whose character I was totally unacquainted, and with whom I had no sympathies but the one common to us all which had brought us together, and although with my brother officers I was upon terms of sufficient sociability, still there was a sense of loneliness, and a want of accustomed intercourse with intimates.

My thoughts assumed a sickly hue; and I began to weigh the motives which had placed me in my present situation; as long as I could reconcile them to a solid sense of duty, and persuade myself that I had the "Mens consciarecti,"[72] I felt all the spirit of the enterprise; but I own, I was disturbed by doubts and misgivings, I began to fear that a false principle had actuated me, and the exciting causes which had induced me to the step I had taken, evanished from before my imagination like the fading rose hues that I gazed upon, and left a dark uncertain blank, which filled my soul with disappointment and dismay. I felt like the adventurer merchant in the Arabian Tales, who, in the midst of his exalted enthusiasm, kicked and overset his basket of crockery, and found himself reduced to nothing; it seemed to me as though, in Scripture phrase, I had strained at a gnat and swallowed a camel. Whilst others were arrogating to themselves credit for volunteering upon the "Indian Campaign," I pictured to myself, that, in the opinions of those whom I should most value, I had lost, instead of gaining praise, and what was the paltry gratification of mere popular, general applause; the idle pull of the streets which meritriciously kisses and passes compared with the approbation of relatives and friends; that sweet and abiding incense which is put up in the temple of the heart and breathes for us alone? Methought I heard these say, "it was wrong in an only son to leave his mother in this cruel way. What folly where there was no necessity, to go to fight Indians, to endure hardships and every thing that is disagreeable, when no honour is to be acquired by it!"

It is true I had anticipated such sentiments as these before I made up my mind to volunteer, but I expected them only as the natural expressions of persons whose regard for my immediate welfare would induce them to dissuade me from my purpose; having settled the matter of conflicting duties and inclinations calmly in my owe mind, I did not communicate the result to any one until after I had enrolled my name, and it was too late to retreat, for fear lest those imposing arguments, urged by such pleaders, might divert me from what I had concluded was right and proper; and here I must take the occasion to remark, whilst I acknowledge my error, that, in adopting any step in life, it is a false maxim that we always know best ourselves what we ought to do—no one is too old, or has arrived at sufficient maturity of judgment, not to profit by the advice of others, and to slight that altogether is to be wanting in that becoming reverence to others, and decent respect to their opinions concerning us, which we should carry along with us through life—for what says Tully *"Nam negligere quid de se quisque sentiat, non solum arrogantis est, sed omnino dissoloti."*

When duty to one's country or honor clashes with the love and gratitude we owe our parent, if we act up to the strictness of the moral code,

we, in every case, should consult the wishes of a parent in preference to our own inclinations, and though they oppose what
we deem right and necessary to be performed, and this, in
despite of the world's opinions; for though the desire of glory is
the strongest passion of youth, "*prima igitur est adolescenti commendatio ad gloriam, siqua ex bellicis rebus comparari potest;*" and love of country and of mankind be the best and noblest of feelings; yet, says
the same philosopher; "*prima igitur commendatio profiscicitur a*
MODESTIA, *tum* PIETATE IN PARENTES, *tum* IN SUOS
BENVOLENTIA"*

Another reflection which gave me pain, was, that I was apprehensive that I had mixed up with my motives no small share
of that unworthy *vis animi*, termed by the Greek philosophers,
Ogun—by which I mean love of excitement, of adventure and
novelty, and such like selfish inducements, which sustain and
give zest to action while they last and are felt, but, like the spar-
kling effervescence of a glass of champagne, when they depart
and no longer animate the surface, leave the soul, like the vapid
glass, dull heavy and mawkish. As we jolt the glass or put a
crumb in the wine, to stir up its life, so I endeavoured to rouse
the same spirits which I was just condemning, and whose momentary absence was the cause of my melancholy, and according
to the vulgar recipe of using the hair of the dog for the bite, I
summoned up the anticipations of the new scenes, which were
awaiting me—the wild hazards and novel adventures I was
about to encounter among the Indians, and the many little
pleasurable associations 1 had formed in my mind with my excursion to Florida

---

*Cicero de officiis.

and came to the conclusion that it is easier to speculate about, than to act always in strict conformity with the most perfect principles of conduct, and that those which had guided me were sufficiently so, and I became reassured in conscience that unfilial unkindness was in reality remote from my heart. Our conversations in the course of the evening, while we were on deck, was chiefly on the interesting topics of the campaign, and I speedily recovered from my qualms and the vapours of home sickness, which had given rise to them, and awoke from my berth the next morning, having during the night accomplished more exploits, and seen more Indians than any one did afterwards throughout the whole course of the campaign, without thinking once of home.

Our men became merry as they got more intimate, and so long as the bounds of correct behaviour, from private to superior, were not infringed upon, we did not refuse to join in the laugh and jest with them. In the contact of dissimilar elements, which had met together this society there was developed much character and originality worthy of observation, which offered an amusing study to beguile the tedium of the voyage and promised to afford no small interest when united on the theatre of stirring events. As a vessel at sea, however, can scarcely be considered such a theatre, it generally stirring the stomachs more than the faculties of men into action, and as no incident of sufficient importance occurred, upon which an interesting description of character and contrasting modes of action might be engrafted, I must content myself and the reader must likewise, with a few simple sketches, such as they are, which I may perhaps occasionally renew, as I find opportunity when I get more "in medias res."

We had on board an Irishman, that belonged to another company, but by some mistake, had got among us. He was sorely afflicted with the epidemic common among sailors and soldiers, yelept "the horrors." As he suffered much from heat in the hold, and there was danger of his getting overboard if left to himself on deck, we had him tied in a large Tub, as the most convenient place out of harm's way and set a sentinel to watch over him; he was a tailor by trade, and as he sat with his duck legs crossed under him in the tub he indulged in all the nervous extravaganzas of the peculiar mania under which he was laboring; at one time he would be sowing in idea, and make the wryest faces, at not being able to thread his needle. At another, he imagined that the ravelly rope which secured his arms and hung about him, was a piece of fine silk that had been given him to work up, and he alternately cursed, and piteously besought those that were near him, that they would not play tricks on him and cause him to be losing his time. His appearance was so ludicrous and cynical, that a witty mechanic of the name of Bettison observed 'he was a second Diogenes in his tub.'

This remark puzzled an illiterate swamp sucker from the cypress, and he wanted to know where the first was—this led to an amusing, conflict of language in which our wit and poet Bettison riddled the ears of his antagonist, Turbeville, with grandloquent expressions, and the latter paid back his coined words; in occasional heavy lumps of original bullion.

"Pray, Mr. Turbeville," quoth B——, "if I may be permitted to enquire, where did you receive the light of erudition?"

"I don't know what sort of light that is," answered Turbeville.

"I mean, did you never look through the classic authors." "Glassy orders? 1 don't reckon I know what kind of orders them be—oh you mean specks like them the Lieutenant has on—why can't you speak English? I dont understand your Africa."

"Why, don't you live in Africa?"

"You may call it Africa, I call it America."

"The gentleman is disposed to be laconic—will the gentleman relate what peculiar ramification or topography of the country, has the superlative honor of giving birth to a genius so remarkable?"

Poor Turbeville began now to be the common butt of all, and several joined in to aim a shaft of ridicule at him. He was a poor little dried up; being, looking like any thing else than a soldier. As he stood up, his meagre little body bent forwards under his lath legs, and he gave you the idea of a benumbed sand piper, or a half starved Chewicker about to run. His complexion was sickly and sallow, as if he had lived on the drainings of a swamp, and the languid expression of his countenance betokened that his whole career of life had not hitherto extended farther sauntering about the pine barren purlieus of a log house after poultry and hogs, shooting birds and catching fish and terrapins—yet, notwithstanding the profession of a soldier was the last he seemed fitted for, he was one of a class of woodsmen who are accustomed from earliest boyhood, to handle the rifle or any thing in the shape of a gun, and to shoot like Indians half the time for their subsistence, and there could be found few better qualified in all probability to match an Indian in hush manoeuvring, and hammock-craft.

"Say, where *did* you come from, where were you raised Turbeville?" enquired a dozen, teazing and flouting him—"Why," answered the swamp sucker, with dry composure, "I was raised just at the head of nowhere—where rivers freeze, snakes never die, and turkies gobble—just above where Homminy Swamp runs into Mushley river—in the middle, there's a big pond and the scum grows so thick upon it that you can drive a team over it." This bold attempt at a coarse, but ready species of wit, whose ingenuity consists in the invention of odd originalities, and in walking slip-shod over the understanding of one's opponent, seldom fails to stump the banterer, and poor Turbeville was left alone in quiet for a time, while his annoyers looked about for another subject on whom to vent their idle gibes—"Where's Matthew Eagle? hallo Eagle;" and the new victim was shouted for through gangway and hatchway, and summoned to receive his share of torment and ridicule—they soon spied him out, ludicrously enough engaged. Our Captain, not wishing to lose all the precious time aboard-ship, which might be so advantageously employed in drilling his raw recruits, had taken 'Matthew Eagle' in hand, commencing with him as the most difficult job. Matthew was, in sooth, a beautiful boy; he was a Wassamasaw of the first water; with smooth, turgid, yellow cheeks; a quiet, dumpy nose, thick lips, reaching almost to his ears, which gaped always with a vacant but placid and good humored smile, and displayed a set of large projecting teeth; coarse black hair, like an Indian's, which fell smoothly over his forehead, and half hid his clear, simple, hazle eyes; he was of middle height, and his stomach swelled out like a genuine clay eater's; to his uncouth figure he added a pair of knocked knees and huge splay feet. As on coming to town for the first time in his life, the shops looked inviting and he had ready money in his pocket Matthew had rigged himself out in a full new suit, every portion of which was too large for him; his dove coloured coat was long and loose in the back could be, the skirts reaching below his knees, and the cape jutting away far above the nape of his neck, its proper boundary, into the occipital regions, so that he seemed literally over head and ears in love with it; it stuck out in front, and could have wrapped twice his girth—underneath he wore a waistcoat of the same color, which covered all the lower extremities of his belly, and his pantaloons, which were likewise of the same hue were so much too long for him that he kept them rolled up in double reefs over his ankles. With such natural and adventitious deformities the Captain seemed to despair of making any thing like a soldier of him; he was what would have been termed in the regular service, one of Uncle Sam's hard bargains, it was in vain to try to make him turn his toes out, and keep his heels together; to keep the straight easy position of the shoulders and arms, and hold up his head military-wise. In addition to his ignorance of these things, poor 'Eagle' had to strive against a difficulty not usually attendant upon drilling; the roll of the vessel to which raw countryman as he was, he felt a squeamish antipathy, constantly disturbed his equilibrium.

When he would about face, his arms fluttered in every direction in the air; his legs straggled from under him, his chin rested upon his breast, and his eyes remained anxiously fixed upon his tottering feet, instead of at the proper distance before them. At last the captain in an humor half wrathy and jocular, tied a handkerchief round his arms and bound them to his hips, and put a prop under his chin. In this constrained and pitiable attitude, "Matthew Eagle" was descried by the party in search of him, marching and toddling along the deck in most promising style, until a luckless lurch of the vessel threw him off his centre, and not being able to use his arms to balance himself, he was most unfortunately cut short in his career, and precipitated against the gunwale upon his beam end; in this sad encounter, his cap, which like the rest of his clothes did not fit him, flew overboard, and henceforth he had to go without any covering on his head, in consequence of which they called him 'Bald Eagle.'

As he was one of those sort of characters who do not shine in lively dialogue, and are most conspicuous for their dumbness and extreme simplicity, I will spare the reader any further notice of 'Eagle' at present, except to recall his memory once more in one little tribute of praise. He was a quiet and unoffending lad, simple on the surface, but possessing at bottom a sufficient share of natural shrewdness; perfectly good natured, and always willing to oblige I never knew him to refuse his comrades a favor but upon one occasion; and that was, when he had filled his havresac with raw potatoes, which he had obtained in a foray into some of the deserted plantations; they were the first he had met with upon the campaign, and Eagle's affection for these sweet old friends, was of too foil, engrossing, and greedly a nature to be divided with keen delight, he made all possible haste to introduce them *sans cere-monie*—that is, perfectly crude and uncooked, into the more comfortable and spacious apartments of his stomach, ere others might anticipate him; utterly indifferent to the entreaties of those around him, who had not got any of the spoil, and regardless of their abuses and curses of him for being so stingy.

Poor Eagle! He has winged his way from this sad earth, to the pure and happy realms of air, where spirits dwell. Nature did not intend that, he should live a soldier's life, and fate decreed that he should not die a soldier's death. Before the campaign was half over, he took the measles, and we had to leave him on the way with a sick company; the company became convalescent, and marched; but he had not sufficiently recovered; without a murmur, he braved the hardships of a three days dreadful march through swamps and bogs; took a pleurisy, and died. Poor lad! it grieves my heart to think of his sad end—away from home—with no mother's tear to shed pity and consolation on his desolate soul—no friend's kindly care to soothe and cheer his miserable, lonesome pallet—unknown—unwept—unwillowed—without even the simple inscription of a simple name, staked over his shallow grave,

ALAS! POOR MATTHEW EAGLE ! !

CHAPTER III.

Arrival; Harbor, Town, and Fort of St. Augustine at sunset; Private ac-
commodations abroad [aboard]*; Adventures of a night on Guard; En-*
campment in the country; Amusements and Exercises.

As the winds at this season of the year are generally unfavorable, we were nearly a week at sea. As it was not our own, but Uncle Sam's time that was thus squandered away, we did not much care; but when we got in sight of land, and were compelled to beat about almost a whole day, without gaining an inch headway, then every one began to be impatient; all were anxious to exchange the tedious schooner, and monotonous sea, for the novelties of St. Augustine, and dry land once again. At length towards the afternoon, the wind shifted a little, and we made sensible progress, and in two or three hours beheld the pilot in his little skiff, dancing among the breakers of the bar, and waving his white pocket handkerchief. In the course of an half hour we had taken him in, passed the shallow bar called the north and south breakers, and the white sandy cliffs of Island and main; turned the Point, and beheld before us the stupendous, gloomy quaint old Spanish Castle of St. Marks; capping the head of the small town, like an enormous, dark, shadowy Sombrero, swallowing up the head of some little insignificant looking Spaniard. The sun was just shedding his mellow parting ray upon the antique pile pencilling wall and watchtower in the blue water, and amber welkin; and the white houses, the smooth plains and and glacis, and the distant trees, and in our rear the shining sand hills and partial verdure of Anastasia Island and the North beach looked like a miniature landscape done on ivory, or scenery viewed through an inverted opera-glass. This peculiar softness, delicacy of tint, and perfection of outline in objects, occasioned by the mild and gentle air of Florida has since frequently struck me in the interior; where the atmosphere is rarer, and the country opens into stretching glades and far savannas.

As it was late, and we knew of no Barrack or place of encampment, having been provided for us whither to repair, we resolved to remain on board of the schooner for the night, and she was brought to anchor in the Stream. The Captain of our company went ashore to see the Colonel, who we found had arrived the day before in the steam boat which had left Charleston the day after we did, and I was left in command, with instructions to keep the men below deck as much as possible, in order that we should not appear remiss in discipline, and that they might not crowd the gangways, and impede the sailors in their operations of getting every thing to rights aboard, and also to prevent shouting halloing, and all those noisy congratulations, in which militia soldiers upon an enterprize like ours, are so apt to indulge, with the other companies, two or three of whom wee in vessels anchored near in the harbor. This was a hard task to perform, as the poor fellows, crowded beneath the hatch in the shallow hold, were anxious to get air, as well as to look around them at the novelties of the place.

It was ludicrous to see the various countenances, and expressions of gladness, wonder, anxiety, and wry despair, as some who were taller and more experienced in taking advanges in a crowd, perched on their neighbors shoulders, got their bodies half out so that they could see all that was going on, others got a chin or a nose upon deck, and were striving and struggling to get a glimpse of different objects, while others, more unfortunate, were compelled to remain transfixed in the huddle, debarred from fresh air, and from the sight of any thing; then such a Babel of voices as there was; some singing, and laughing,and talking; others cursing for their mashed toes, and others bellowing to get out— but all in good humor. The serjeants were ordered to relieve them as much as possible and a certain number, at a time, were permitted to come on deck.

Our regiment, as before remarked, was encamped in a field, at the south side of the town, and a fortnight almost had elapsed, before we took up the line of march towards the interior. During this period, our time was employed in drilling which we much needed; in evening dress parades; and going through the routine of guard mounting. On the evening of our arrival, we heard the late intelligence of the burning of Gen. Hernandez' place, about 28 miles from town; and of Bulow's, 12 miles farther. The reflection of the fires was distinctly seen at St. Augustine; and from the direction, and the extent of the blaze, it was pretty well ascertained that those two valuable plantations with their large Sugar Mills, were destroyed by the Indians. The volunteers from Charleston stationed in the town, were in momentary expectation of a brush, as the Indians were known to be nearer now than they had been at all. They had had an alarm two nights previous; some of the Hamburgh volunteers[73] who were stationed at an out post, having fired several times at a supposed body of Indians, that they imagined they saw stealing towards them, and the companies had been immediately drawn out to meet the anticipated attack. It was a foggy night, and they had been deceived. It was reported also on good authority, that a mockasin track was seen at the spot where one of the volunteers had fired, at what he thought was an Indian, but this was afterwards accounted for, by some one having walked there in slippers.

Shortly after, the Florida militia was disbanded by General Eustis, there being no further necessity for their continuance in arms since the arrival of other troops, and the term of service of the young men who had volunteered for the defence of St. Augustine having expired, the out posts fell to our charge.

I happened to be the first appointed to act at captain of the guard detailed for this duty.—There were several picquets connected with the main one or guard house which was not many yards from the river Sebastian; this river flows to the west back of the town, and makes a Peninsula of the land on which it is situate. The Indian name for it is "Tiketa" or the crossing place, as it is fordable in one part. The guard house was opposite to this ford, and a sentinel was posted immediately at the Tiketa, where the enemy would be certain to cross if they came. After the sentinels were stationed, and the proper instructions given, which were to fire if Indians were seen, or to call the lance-corporal of the Guard if the sentinel wished to have any strange voices, or appearances investigated, I retired to keep my vigils for the night, to the guard house.

It was not long before Mr. Sentinel bellowed out at the top of his lungs "Corporal of the Guard—Corporal of the Guard." Away went the Corporal with his file of men, and I half way after him, for I felt all the responsibility of my important situation as commander of the guard, and was upon the qui vive that the alarm should be given in time if there was occasion, and that, on the other hand a false one might be prevented. The corporal on a run met me, and reported in a whispering voice that the sentinel had heard strange noises; a confused talking over the river in an odd language, and he was certain there were Indians, as he had formerly been among them and knew the accent—he had also heard croaks, and curious imitations of different sounds—I immediately went to the river—the night was clear and not more than ordinarily dark, but it was impossible to see with any degree of correctness, more than a few yards. I looked anxiously and listened attentively some time, but could neither see nor hear anything of a suspicious character.

Scarcely had I returned to the Guard house when the sentinel called again more obstreperously than before. I concluded that now he must have actually seen or heard the enemy crossing, and expected every moment to hear him fire. I repaired again to the river with my double barrel in my hand and accompanied by the corporal and several men, resolved to ascertain the cause of the alarm whether true or false. We preserved as much silence as possible, and after conferring with the sentinel who declared upon his oath that he distinctly heard, and thought he saw a long string of canoes coming down the river from the opposite side, we crept and extended ourselves along the marsh to watch and be ready to fire a platoon in case there were Indians, in order that the Camp, which was more than half a mile distant, might be certain of hearing the alarm. As I stood near the sentinel listening, sure enough there was such a splashing! it seemed as the river was covered with canoes. I even fancied at times that could see them putting off from the other side: but the next moment all was gloom and obscurity and uncertainty. The splashing at one time was soft like that made by paddles dipping in the water—-at another in increased into a noise as though a troop of horse were wading through the river; and what made me more certain, there was a snorting such as horses are accustom to make in the water. It seemed to be nearer. The sentinel, by whom I was standing, whispered to me and cocked his musket, but I ordered him not to fire unless he was sure that he saw Indians. I began now myself to get alarmed, for the splashing was now close under the marsh and I could plainly see several dark object stealing slowly and cautiously along towards us, out of the river. They seemed already to have discovered us, or to be upon the look out, for they stopped once or twice, and I could see something wave like the hand of a chief, and something pointed like a rifle. The sentinel raised his piece and aimed. I was on the point of following his example, but I recollected that we were not yet in a country where none but Indians might be expected to approach our lines, and thought it possible that some of the inhabitants on the other side of the river, a few of whom still remained on their farms, might have crossed over, though I could not account for their coming this way, instead of over the bridge which was above. The sentinel's finger was upon the trigger. I ordered him in a low tone by no means to fire before he hailed once distinctly. He did so. The challenge was unanswered, and the Indians, (for had they been whites or blacks, they would have spoken,) halted abruptly. It was a critical moment, a moment of life and death: for our situation was now discovered, and I expected incontinently to hear nothing less than the crack of a rifle, or the whiz of a tomahawk, but instead I heard a low moan like that of a cow, but whether a bona fide cow or not? to shoot or not to shoot? we still were puzzled—so notorious is the art of this treacherous foe in imitating the cries of beasts, birds and reptiles of every kind, that we did not know but what this was a deception intended to lull our watchfulness, in order that we might be surprised without our being able to give the alarm, so that they might steal a march upon the camp. On the other hand, if these were real cows and we should shoot them, we might perhaps deprive some poor Minorcan of his means of getting a livelihood by selling milk, and incur blame for creating a false alarm, besides being laughed at for our pains. I was resolved not to be mistaken, and crouching and concealing our position as much as possible, we waited with suspended breath, and our eyes fixed on the objects as they again advanced.

At length, all doubt was at at end. I beheld the ample arms and blazed face of a demure meek visaged milch cow, switching her tail quietly along, and followed by four or five other gossips.

I now thought how ridiculous it was to take every noise and appearance for Indians; it was as bad as imagining, and being alarmed at ghosts, and the strange delusions of the night were just as likely to arise from simple and laughable causes in the one case as in the other.

It was now apparent that the string of canoes and the splashing of oars that we saw and heard in the middle of the river, and towards the opposite shore, were nothing more than a shoal of porpoises, who were taking a midnight ramble and frolic up the stream, rolling their huge lazy bodies along the shallows of the margin, and puffing and snorting after the manner of horses on their way, they disturbed the slumbers of a crane who was taking her nap in the marsh, and who changed her roost with a croak; and after day began to break, I discovered a small house, the Baracca of a fisherman on the other side of the river, whose female tyrant had risen and begun to bustle and scold in rapid and villainous Minorcan, which, it appeared, the sentinel be construed into Seminole.

The concurrence of all these plausible circumstances, it will be acknowledged, was enough to alarm our fancies at the time, though since whenever I think of this, my first essay upon guard, and of the indifference which I felt on subsequent occasions, when there was much more real cause for apprehension, I cannot help smiling at the unnecessary trouble and excitement into which I put myself.

We changed our camp from the city suburbs to a plantation of Mr. Hanson, about two miles in the country. The movement was hailed with much satisfaction, and their was a smile of rejoicing upon the coutenances of the low-country swamp-landers and backwoodsmen, as the bland evening air, charged with the fresh odours of the piny forests and oak and myrtle thickets, conspired, together with the exercise of marching, to set the blood into motion, and give the spirits elasticity, and when they find themselves in their element in the woods. The scene began now to exhibit a more animating and active character. The troops in high spirits stepped over the ground in quick time; the mounted officers pranced forwards and backwards, giving or extending orders in a brisk, loud, tone of voice, and the flankers who were put out more for the sake of instructing, than because safety required this caution, skipped along waist high through scrubby bushes, and rustling saw-palmettoes, over knotty bogs and bay gall branches. Then came the bustle of pitching tents, felling trees, and unlading of waggons; the rattling of camp kettles, and the crackling of fires.

After supper, the remainder of the evening till tattoo was usually spent by our hardy yeomen in such favorite exercises as wrestling, leap frog, &c. The nights at this season being pleasantly cool (though the days were sometimes as hot as in May) invited to these violent pastimes, and the camp would ring with the boistrous shouts and cheerings of the crowded groups who took an interest in the manly amusement. 'Hurra Bill—Hurrah Wash—Hurra for Bill—Hurra for Wash!'

'Bill, don't let him throw you.'

'Stand up to the rack, Wash.'

'Hurra Wash,'

'Bill's down.'

'Bill, you fool, why did you let go your grip?'

'I allowed Wash could fling him."

'Boys, who'll wrastle?' exclaims Wash, now triumphantly jumping up, and challenging with arms extended, and reeking with the healthy moisture. 'I'll throw e'er a one on you. hug or trip, any how—bust my runnet, if I can't fling any man in the deestrict I come from!'

A champion is not hard to be found, who, with that sectional and clannish jealousy, Southern pride cherishes, thinks that the honor of his 'deestrict,' is called in question by this challenge, and consigned to his hands to vindicate, and that though he may not be the best man in it, it can beat any other in the State; and the game continues, with the same noisy mirth, except that it is now 'Hurra Barnwell—Hurra Edgefeld,' instead of 'Hurra Bill, Hurra Wash.' A rough and tumble fight might be thought the proper test on such occasions, but it was rarely that the order of the camp was disturbed by such practices.

As the heavy infantry exercise is not so well adapted to Indian warfare as the rifle, we every day drilled in the rapid, animating, and useful manoeuvres of the latter, beautiful exercise from morning till midday, and in the afternoon again, until sunset, we were practising double quick extensions through pine barrens; forwarding and rallying skirmishers over bogs and brakes; advancing and retiring by right, left and centre; firing by file, one man to draw the Indian from behind the tree, and the other to shoot him; &c. &c. and what with muskets, rifles, and pistols, there was scarce a sound piece of bark left upon the mutilated pine trees for nearly a mile around.

CHAPTER IV.

The Campaign commenced—A glance at the country—Plants on the way—Encampment and midnight alarm—Military incident and mistake—a Denouément.

On the 23d February, Captain [Thomas] Hibler's company of Edgefield volunteers, and a detachment of my company, under my command, were ordered on the march to Gen. Hernandez' plantation, the last place which had been destroyed, distant 28 miles. The Col., the Captain, and other officers were to proceed by the way of Matanza river, and we expected to meet at Hernandez about the same time. A portion of the Regiment had preceded us three days before, and a portion remained behind in case their services might be required at any other point.

Here, at the outset, I began to experience some of the inconveniences and deprivations attendant upon campaigning, and to be disappointed in some of the pleasurable anticipations which I had entertained of beholding and being gratified with observing the fresh varieties of scenery, the vegetable productions &c. of a country new to me. In pursuance of that strict principle of camps; that none but the commanding officer is to know when any contemplated movement is to take place, and that the soldier is to be always ready to march at a moment's warning, we no sooner received, for the first time, the command, than we had to put it into execution. My baggage, including every article except the clothing I had on, was huddled into a cart to go down to the river and be conveyed in boats, and among such necessaries as my sheep-skin and blanket, a small pocket herbarium that I had brought with me, expecting to relieve the tedium of the march by amusing myself on the way, when my duty did not prevent me, in collecting a few treasures from the chosen region of Flora, was left behind.

Instead too, of finding opportunties, as I had imagined I should, to stroll now and then from the road side to pick a flower, shoot a rare bird, or notice any thing uncommon, I had to attend to the duties of my command as advance guard, and my business was to look for Indians and not for flowers. I did not however lose much, and from the few and common specimens I met with on the road, I began to think that Florida was by no means that Paradise of ever blooming; flowers that I thought it was,* and with a few exceptions, there was little novelty to arrest and fix the attention. The country we passed over was chiefly open pine barren, the soil covered with dry yellow grass, low shrubs, and bristled

---

*It is a common mistake to think to that Florida derives its name from this circumstance—but it does not—it derives it from the Spanish term for Palm Sunday the Sunday before Easter which that Nation calls *"Pasqua Florida"* or Flowery Easter from the palm branches and flowers which the churches are decorated on that day, as the country was discovered on or about that time.

or *"logged over"* as they would say in Florida, with the everlasting saw-palmetto, (*Chamaerops serrulata*). The thick, tough, woody stems of this plant creep horizontally, spreading interlaced, in every direction over the ground before it bends upwards and forms its plaited fronds. These palmettoes in some places grow so dense and tall as to be impervious to the rays of the sun, and afford fine hiding places to rattlesnakes, and all other kinds of vermin including Indians; the interruption and annoyance they cause to the traveller on horseback or on foot is very great; at every moment he is liable to stumble over their prostrate, log like stems, which are concealed from view by their close fan-shaped leaves, and the unyielding stiff opposition these present to his progresses farther increased by the formidable serratures of their stipes, which cut the clothing and wound the skin.

In some places there were extensive patches of another kind of palmetto; a very dwarf species of fan palmetto, growing to the height of only a few inches from the ground. This is no doubt the same which Bartram mentions having met with in the plains of Cuscowilla, and calls *Corypha pumila stipit serratis.* (Sabal pumila*, Elliott*) a stinted variety only of the common fan palmetto perhaps. It presented a squalid and uninteresting appearance.

The beautiful and singular evergreen heathlike shrub *Ceratiola Ericoides*, Horn Bush or Sandhill Rosemary, grew in coppices over the more gravelly and sandy spots of the barren.

The shining, linear, regular leaves and the roughened brittle branches of this bush present very much the appearance of those of the Fir—

these that I saw, grew from two to five feet high (four to eight—
Elliott.) Its numerous and verticillate upright glaucous branches, and fine, revolute leaves, forming bushy leaves like the
Box, make it very conspicuous. It has no corolla, in which it
differs from the Heath, and the flowering organs are very small,
axillary, and sessile. Pursh places this plant Diandria class; Elliott and Nuttall in the Dioecia Diandria—Mr. Elliott assigns
the months of August and September as its blooming period
but doubtfully—whereas I found it in bloom in February and
March. I may possibly have mistaken some other plant for
this, but with the exception of the flowering time (on which
Nuttall is silent) it corresponded exactly with the descriptions of Botanists. Perhaps it continues in bloom through the
fall and winter in Florida. It is not mentioned by either of
these authorties as growing in Florida, but Pursh mentions it
at St Mary's.

Picked up near Hanson's, in a ditch, a plant which I have
not been able to identity—my notes of it were imperfect; but I
am pretty certain that it was of the class—Hexandria mo-
nogynia—stem about a foot high, and succulent with a few
lobed root leaves on petioles, and a few scattered on the stem—
Calyx five cleft, unequal; Corolla four cleft, unequal, white.
Flowers in a short terminal raceme.

When we stopped to dine on our salt pork and biscuit, of
which, with the aid of a bottle of wine, the only thing I had the
good luck to have along with me, I made a hearty repast, we
heard the firing of cannons in the direction of Picolata, and
were firmly under the impression

that the Indians had attacked that place. If so, we thought it probable that they would be driven our way, and should they cross our trail, we might expect a visit from them during the night.

Passed several dried up ponds with tall broom-like dried grass, and a squalid cypress or two, or pine growing in them. We had marched fifteen miles, and that we thought a very respectable distance for the first day, and were on the lookout for a good watering place where we might encamp, but nothing was to be seen like water, but these waste ponds which deceived us from a distance, proving always dry or nearly so, when we got up to them. At length after marching a mile or two farther, the evening being advanced, we had to halt at a scanty dirty looking pool, and pitched our tents, which occupied but a small space of ground, as we did not amount to quite a hundred men, and from four to eight men were stowed in one tent. To guard against surprise, our sentinels were stationed behind trees about 150 yards from the camp, and 60 or 70 yards apart. It was a wet and uncomfortable night, and at the time that it was rawest, about 1 o'clock, it came to my turn to act as officer of the camp. Between this and sunrise, we had been told was the dangerous time for an attack, as it is also the period during which the sentinel is less apt to be watchful.

I esteemed it my duty therefore, to make the rounds, every time there was a relief, and commenced the tour wet up to the knees with the reeking grass, the cold rain pattering in my face and the night so dark that it was only by the challenge of the sentinel that I could find where abouts he was. I had just got back, and was enjoying the comfortable glow of a small fire and pitying the poor sentry who had to remain for two hours in the miserable weather, when a flash of a gun at the pond where one was stationed made a sudden illumination; and the next moment, two of the sentinels came running in out of breath with their guns cocked. There had been alarm, and I was sure that the Indians were at hand, when I discovered that our man Simpson was the author of it: a tall strapping, lively, dare-devil, whole-hog, Kentucky-like fellow from St. George's. Simpson related that he had heard a splashing in the pond, and seen something about the height of a man, walking through it up to him, and he aimed to fire at it, but the powder flashed in the pan; he retreated a little way to another tree, primed, and saw the object stealing off, and this time his piece snapped; the sentinels adjacent to him were alarmed and concluded that the enemy had slipped between them into the camp; it being so dark they could not see anything move, except it was very near.

'Indians—Indians—up men, up,' cried those who were already awake, and those whose susceptible ears received the quick impression of danger.

The flickering embers, over which I had just been solacing myself, were in an instant and trampled into smoky coals and ashes, without a thought of the comfort they had afforded and might still afford; and in the dark, men in their first confusion tumbled against tents, and over camp-kettles and logs. Some called for lights, that they might inspect their priming, and others forbade it, as it would expose the ranks to the ene-my's fire, and were for putting out every spark, without consider-ing the trouble they would be at in rekindling the fire from wet materials.

We were formed quickly enough to meet an attack, but not so quick as, that had Indians been as nigh as the sentinels supposed, and rushed among us, we could have escaped being nearly all shot or tomahawked; for we did not know where their position might be, while they might easily distinguish ours; and besides that, we were raw hands, and this would have been our first essay in a midnight Indian encounter; the attacking party on such occasions, has always a great advantage.

It being my duty to investigate the cause of the alarm, and to report to the commander of the camp, I proceeded with Simpson to his station, and looked and listened for some time, but there were no indications of Indians; sometimes the ear would be startled with the sudden shrill hoot of an owl which the deep swamps would re-echo and multiply afar, and which our imaginations would be ready to convert into suspicious noises; or a frog after the long silence of deep meditation, would put up a most earnest and sonorous prayer to the rain with an unexpected salutation to our nerves, that, for the instant, they could not help being agitated. The least rustle in the woods: the flit of a bird from its roost: or a drop of rain upon a dry leaf was con-strued for the moment, into a sneaking savage: and then would follow the doubts and delusions of the "visible darkness." But there was no positive evidence of an enemy, and after cautioning Simpson not to shoot unless he was certain that he was not deceived, and above all, to be careful if he saw any thing more, not to snap at it a second time, I left him behind his tree to go and visit the other sentinels. Half of them only had come in; the other remaining two were still at their posts, being afraid to move lest they should be mistaken for Indians, and fired at from the Camp, and thinking the best chance was to stand where they were behind a tree. It was also their duty not to desert their posts, unless the enemy were really at hand. In this situation they remained crouching, in imitation of the Indians, who lay down, both for concealment, and that they may see objects plainer by looking up at them from a darker into a lighter medium.

I confess, it being the first time that our men found themselves stationed in the midst of woods and in the dark alone, with Indians, as believed, all about them, ready to rush in upon them, I was not a little apprehensive of being shot by them, as they would not think of hailing anyone who approached, as that would be altogether unorthodox in woods, inhabited only by Indians and wild beasts; and as they were some distance from the camp, and it was such a dark night, they might suspect an Indian inside, as well as outside of the lines; I therefore bent my steps as near the camp as possible, so as to avoid approaching the posts near the outside, and involuntarily, without considering whether it became an officer and was *comme il faut*[4] or not. I gave a hem, as a token by which I might be recognized, when, having advanced nearer than I had imagined to the sentinel, his quick, shrill, up-country accent, greeted me suddenly with the startling challenge "who-goes-tharr," and in the dark I could just see the motion, and as he rose and immediately clapped his musket to his shoulder. In a stentor voice I instantly shouted "rounds." The raw militia-man showed by his slight hesitation that he did not fully comprehend the reply, and half doubted whether we were friends, which term we were compelled quickly to substitute for the other, or a cartridge of ball and buck might yet have been discharged at us. Satisfied now that we were really not Indians, but that he was in the presence of the officer of the day, the curator of the camp, and the stern exacter of strict duty and discipline, recovering from the agitation which that moment of intense anxiety naturally produced, and desirous of atoning for the mistake he had nearly been guilty of, the volunteer put on all his military importance, as one resolved to show that he knew his duty, and fogetting all his previous caution, bawled out, "advance friend then, and give the countersign." At the same time his bayonet came down so fiercely in contact with my belt, that I was forced to retreat a step or two for fear of being run through the stomach.

The countersign was given.

'Stand—stand—I say,' again shouted the sentry in a fiercer tone.

Here was a ridiculous position for an 'Officer of the day' to be placed in; to be brought to bay by his own sentinel, and refused his own countersign. There was evidently some mistake and the sentinel resolved to take advantage of it and keep me standing in the rain as long as he had a mind to. It was in vain that expostulated with him, and endeavored to make him sensible, that, as there was some mistake in giving him the countersign, it was enough that he knew me by my voice &c. as the officer of the Camp.

It would not do—he could not be persuaded that I was not seeking to test his observance of his duty, and to trick him into the commission of an error.

I was not disposed to remain any longer in this disagreeable situation, and was anxious to report a false alarm, and get out of the rain, or by a comfortable fire once again, so I bade him call the Sergeant of the Guard, by whom the mistake was soon explained. 'Skirmish' had been the countersign ordered by me, but that was not a word in the up-country vocabulary, and the provoking and scrupulous sentinel would have it 'scrimmage,' which was the way the sergeant repeated it to him.

Having questioned him concerning the adventure of his watch, and finding no additional cause of alarm, and the other sentinel not having seen or heard any thing, the report was made, and after remaining under arms a little while longer, the camp dispersed to their tents, the bustle and confusion was superseded by snoring and quiet, and the silence of the dead slumbering hour that divides the night and day, resumed its reign, interrupted only by the heavy breathings of the fatigued sleepers, the occasional desultory conversations of some few half dosers who lay around the embers of the guard fire, and the tramp, rattling arms and low orders of the relief, going their monotonous rounds, and pausing ever and anon to exchange stern courtesies with the loud quick-challenging sentinel.

As soon as it was light enough to see, the grounds about the pond where examined for traces of the Indian or Indians, who, many yet were confident, had been prowling about us as spies, though the camp in general, now that the morning light had chased away the doubts and suspicious of the night, was disposed to discredit whether Simpson had seen anything at all. In a moment this tranquility disappeared, and looks of alarm and excitement, were interchanged. Those who had not yet got up and who were awakened by the bustle and the voices around them, were to be seen looking with inquiring countenances, out of their tents, and coming out with their muskets and their blankets over their shoulders. The cause of all this stir was a report that several bare tracks had been seen at the pond, the conclusion was immediately drawn that they were the tracks of negro spies, and it was no longer doubted that Indians were at hand, and that they would attack us at this, their favorite time for an attack. All were anxious to know whether the footsteps *were* naked—with toes, or without toes—mockasin tracks or not mockasin tracks—whether they were straight like an Indian's, or turned out; recent or not recent; which direction they had taken. Every one was for going to examine for himself, and exhibit his skill in this sort of wood-craft. In the mean time one of the men who had first been to the spot, coming up and being halloed to, what tracks he thought they were, satisfied our curiosity on the subject, by answering; "he reckoned they were Bear tracks or Wolf tracks, one." And so it turned out—the whole alarm had been caused by a thirsty bear who had come to the pond to drink, and seeing our tents, which were a novel thing to him, had, I suppose, risen on his hind legs to take a survey of the encampment, and being frightened by Simpson's flash, galloped slowly away.

———

CHAPTER V.

A deserted settlement—Indian Mound—A recreation—Palmetto grove—a night at Hernandez—March to Bulow's—Sketch of the Country—Parakeets—A Wigwam—Gophers and Salamanders.

At 8 o'clock we had struck tents, and prepared for our march, having only 12 miles to go to reach Gen. Hernandez'. We passed Palasiere river, and Moultrie's bridge over the Creek, so called after Gov. Moultrie of Carolina, who owned, near St. Augustine, a splendid stone mansion, and a country seat called Bella Vista.[75] Both were narrow but deep and dark looking streams shaded by a thick growth of oak, cypress, gum, maple, calycanthus, and other trees and shrubs, most of which were clothed in the young verdure of a Florida spring.

The face of the country began to assume a more hilly or rolling appearance, and we ascended the brow of a pleasant piny ridge, and discovered at the edge of a gentle dale, two settlements enclosed by fences made of whole trees cut into long huge logs, and piled up into a barrier inpenetrable to every thing but Indians.

The settlements appeared to have been but recently located and recently deserted; not a, soul was to be seen, nor a sign of any living thing, and I was struck with the unnatural stillness and cheerlessness of the scene. Instead of the ear being greeted with the social grunt of the aristocratic hog, the noisy scream of the pretty pet peacock, or the shrill clarion of the farmyard chanticleer, summoning the laughing dame's of the poultrie house to his strutting side, such genial sounds as always welcome us on passing by the humblest and most fever-stricken pine barren log house in Carolina, here the very genius of silence and of desolation seemed to reign; the curse of the Indian panic had passed over the domestic quiet of these simple abodes; the plough-share had been turned into a weapon of war; the sorry team had been taken from their ignominious drudgery to be made fierce chargers of; the master of the domain had left his rustic occupations to become a volunteer, and the cattle driver was employed in hunting Indian trails instead of following cowtracks. The grass was springing up in the fields. The corn crib shewed its skeleton frame stark and empty and the barn door gaped, and creaked upon its hinges in harsh dissonance with the death-like silence which reigned over the deserted settlement.

We had not met with a single human being on our way, and the sight of this abandoned habitation, the first we had come to after passing over a dreary country, caused us to despair of seeing any white person but ourselves in Florida, and we began to expect that we should encounter none but similar scenes of desolation and nothing but a barren wilderness the whole way that we should go along; which we did indeed afterwards verify.

A negro guide conducted us the way, and after having informed us, that we had but two more miles to go, which we were congratulating ourselves upon, as the day was excessively warm; we found ourselves, when the two miles were more than accomplished, brought to a halt, and in a dilemma. The guide expressed himself uncertain, whether we were in the right way, and stated it as probable that we were five or six miles out of the way. He left us, to return, and look for the right road, and took up a path, where there was a fork by a branch, with some ugly looking hammocks hemming it. Though the fellow was well recommended, and his countenance was not against him, we could not help feeling some doubt of his honesty, and suspicion that he might be leading us into an ambuscade; but he was permitted to go and look for the way, (as we could do nothing better) without any thing being said, except a muttered threat or two from the more suspicioucious of the party, and curses from nearly all for deceiving us about the distance. We soon beheld him, however, cantering back, and he informed us that we were in [on] the right road to one of Gen. Hernadez' plantations, but whether it was the right one or no [not], we could not ascertain. From the wagon tracks which were recent, and which were supposed to be those of the companies that had gone on before, we thought we must be going right, and after a mile or two farther, we came in sight of a habitation through the trees, and turning a bend, beheld one of the places alluded to. We passed on the side of the road a large tumulus, or Indian mound, of an oblong, roof-like shape. It seemed to be very ancient, as pines of considerable size were growing on the top of it. I wished to examine it more minutely, but there was no opportunity of stopping. I concluded that it was most probably a burial ground of the Yemassees, who, after many hard battles, were finally exterminated, a hundred years ago, by the Seminoles.

These mounds are generally to be met with on the banks of rivers, but this was more than half a mile from the river, which might, at that time, have been nearer. The old maps of Florida show many differences of this kind as peninsulas and islands, which the waters have since left large dry tracts.

There was nothing in the appearance of this mound, of that grandeaur and sublimity of conception which strike the beholder in those which are found in mountainous countries, In Pickens district in South Carolina, I once saw one of these ancient sepulchres, perched in lorn, and solitary rude magnificence, upon the summit of lofty mountain; it was constructed of huge, imperishable rocks which must have witnessed the lapse of half a dozen centuries; hundreds of hands must have been engaged in the pious labor of piling up this stupendous edifice of the Dead. Four large, smooth slabs, formed the coffin in which the dust of some renowned Cherokee chieftain slept. The sepulchre was marked around with rocks which had sunk deep beneath the surface of the soil, enclosing a spacious oblong area; in this perhaps were buried the vanquished of some great battle.

There was a two-fold moral in the grand and beautiful site which had been selected for this aboriginal monument; it was in accordance with the simple custom of the primitive nations who always sought the "high places" for burial grounds, that the dead might be nearer to heaven, and remote from the intursion of unhappy mortals; it was prophetic in design, for it seems as though they obeyed an instinct, or followed the precepts of some ancient tradition to commit their dead to spots where, in future times, when the curse of the ill-fated race was to fall upon them, and the besom of civilization was to seep them from the earth they might be most secure from the profane tread of the white man, and lie undisturbed by the ruthless invasion of the plough share.

When we had got opposite to the settlement we had a glimpse of, we found that it was the wrong place—two of the gentlemen who were mounted rode on to see if they could get a view of the encampment at a higher point on the river; and in the mean time we halted at a deserted overseer's house. Here, besides the shade of a cool piazza, and a few trees that grew by, we met with two other luxuries; a shed of pumpkin's, and a field of sugar cane. 'Eagle' was, I believe, the discoverer of the former, for I beheld him, among the first toating two huge ones under each arm with a most complacent grin of delight upon his countenance. He could not have been better pleased had he made a foray into some Indian wigwam, and gallantly borne off two round-cheeked squaws instead.

As our rations had given out entirely, these, at a season of plenty and luxury, despised vegetable, were an acquisition not to be thought lightly of. It was getting late in the day, and as we were uncertain how far we might be from the camp, we thought it best, rather than undergo any more marching, and having a halt perhaps at worst quarters, to put up here where there was a house, and a supper of boiled pumpkins, with juice of the sugar cane for beverage of lieu of coffee, if nothing else. We did not despair, however, of finding some stray beeves or hogs in the neighborhood. It was not long before a fine young steer was spied out walking through the marsh near the river, and a detachment was sent after it; but in the meantime our two reconnoiterers returned, and brought information that the camp was in sight not far off. So, after a refreshing rest in the cool shade which was as welcome in February in this tropical climate, as it is in most other parts of the union in May or June, and a rural regale of sweet sugar cane, we resumed our march towards the river. As we had got pretty much over our apprehensions of encountering Indians immediately, and had not met with any tracks on our way, there was some relaxation from the severe order of the march, and our appearance, though not actually disorderly, was that of a party returning from a foray, or militia-men from a muster. It was vain keep the men from loading themselves with pumpkins and sticks of sugar cane. The rear was straggling ever so far; sticks of sugar cane were shooting out in every direction from havresacs, pockets and belts, and some were carried in triumph on the tops of bayonets. Every now and then a pumpkin would be tossed into the waggon, and the road was strewed with them as they joined out again. Soon, however, our files began to get regular; for we were approaching a dense hammock which extended from some distance on both sides of the road. It was a beautiful grove of tall and shady palmettoes, (*Chamaerops Palmetto*,) the first we had seen, though I had expected to have met them the first objects on our arrival in Florida. In Carolina on the islands and coasts I had seen them only isolated or in clumps, but here was a magnificent forest of them. Some of the individuals with tall, smooth, glaucous stems; others with stiff imbricated leaves, or ladder-like processes growing on them tempting the natives of the woods to climb them, and gather their generous vegetable fruit; all straight stately columns of a beautiful regular growth, and crowned with their long triangular-striped, bright plumed, or fan-like leaves rustling harmonious music over our heads, and enticing us to linger beneath their oriental shade.

When we arrived at our destination, we found the tree companies encamped in a field; they had met with no Indians, and had seen no signs of any except the ruins of the place—but they had several alarms.

The sugar mill, which had cost $40,000, was burnt, and the barn had been broken open, and a great quantity of corn was lying out exposed to the weather. They had been living gloriously on homminy, vegetables, and beef.

I put up this night in tolerable quarters, (having no tent with me;) a comfortable negro house which had escaped the flames; it was made entirely out of palmetto leaves, thatched from top to bottom, and had only one small low aperture to crawl in by; it looked very much like an oven, but I found when I got into it that it did not feel like one—there was no door to close, and in the course of the night the camp robbers pulled down half of the hovel over my head to make bedding from their tents, and the old night air, which, in this unequal climate at this season, follows the torrid day, poured in upon me. My captain woke me about midnight; he had just arrived, and was glad to share my quarters, bad as they were. The two other Lieutenants had a more uncomfortable time of it; they passed the night in the open flats on the Matanza, after a tedious time of it, the night previous having enjoyed the rain, and the next day the heat upon a shoal. The Matanza takes its name from the key or island which is so called; the Spanish word means 'slaughter', which was given to it in consequence of 300 Frenchmen who took refuge there once after being wrecked on the Reef, having been massacred by the Coloosa Indians, the original inhabitants of Florida.

We took up the line of march early the next morning the Bulow's plantation, twelve miles farther, our Colonel conducting us. The division of the regiment consisted of the Irish Volunteers, our detachment, Capt. Hibler, Jones, and Quattlebum's companies. Capt. Parker's was left behind sick with the measles, and the residue of our company did not arrive in time to join us, so that we had to march again without baggage, hardly a tent and camp kettle.

Our road lay through a sandy pine and fan palmetto barren, intersected occassionally by branches and narrow swamps. The pines were very stunted, growing not more than fifteen feet high and forming scattered groves, intermingled with a few scrubs, (*Quercus Catesboei*) and having an underwood of low oak bushes, (*Quercus maritima* or *myrtifolia*) Cassina, and a few other scraggy shrubs.

In these pines we alarmed a flock of Parakeets, which were clustered on the tops; they flew around us, setting up a most outrageous screaming and chattering, and after making two or three rapid, graceful circuits, enlivening the woods with a beautiful maze of varied colors, green, gold and orange, settled again upon the bare branches of a scrub close by. Here they watched us as we passed, seeming very tame, and as though they wished to be familiar, and make some sort of an acquaintance with us, inviting our notice by their ludicrous grimaces, and awkward antics, rubbing their grave hooked noses together, plucking at each other, like a group of lazy childish old Turks in their painted robes, pulling at one another's beards; and stupidly hanging on by their bills and toes to the branches, and crawling around them, like painted circus clowns around a tight rope. As they thus slowly revolved, sunning themselves and presented in succession the different parts of their rich plumage, they reminded me of the fairy tale descriptions of enchanted birds in the desert, and out-of-the-way demesnes of some sorceress.

The flight of these birds is singularly beautiful: rapid as that of the wild pigeon, or swifter perhaps. They cleave the air with graceful meanderings, dazzling the eye with a path of fleeting, gorgeous hues. They generally take a direct course when their flight is high, but always with these gentle inclinations; when they are lower, or among the trees, they make more circles or swoops. They are usually seen in rather dense, though not large, flocks, but I have noticed single ones occassionally wending their sinuous way from forest to forest. When on the wing, they keep up a constant shrieking jabber, and by this peculiar clamor, their approach or presence is instantly known.

Like all of the parrot species, they are a silken, luxurious, lazy, conceited, doltish, vain-wordy race, and literally the *"fruges con-sumere nati"*[76] of the society of birds; for they are born epicures, and they gormandize all kinds of fruit and grain and what they do not devour, they take a pleasure in wasting. They are desperately idle, and when they have nothing to engross their appetites, they don't know, for the life of them, what to do with their bills and toes, and they are much addicted to the Americanism of cocking up legs and whitling, for they will exercise their bills upon a piece of stick, if they can get hold of nothing else. They differ from others of the parrot tribe in being great dunces, and are incapable of articulating a single word.

In Florida, their food consists principally of the seed of the cyprus balls, which tree they are fond of frequenting; of the luscious fruit of the pawpaw, palmetto-royal, and in fact, of every kind of fruit.

They are very good eating, but a singular fact is related of them by Catesby: that their brains and intestines are a deadly poison to cats. The experiment was tried by Wilson, and after Puss had supped heartily on this delicious fare, she was found the next morning as well as usual; but the Parakeet, he supposed, might not have eaten of the cockle-burr, which they are remarkably fond of, and which is supposed to give thes partys their poisonous quality.

The Carolina Parrot, as the Parakeet is called, is also a native of North and South Carolina, and has been found as far north as Maryland, but it has entirely disappeared now, I believe, in these districts—it is common in the West.

The Seminoles call it "Yah-lâne,", or the "yellow bird."

It is singular that Bartram, whose poetically descriptive genius, and admiration of every thing beautiful in nature, was apt to exhaust itself on every occasion; whose pages are sometimes almost tedious with repetitions of the 'Transcendant Palm,' 'Elysium groves,' the 'Seraphic crane,' 'beautiful golden fish gliding,' &c. should have merely given a slight notice in a scientific way of the paroqueet, and does not once mention after his poetical wont, the splendid appearance of these birds, enlivening with their brilliant plummage the dark and solemn cypress groves, and the dull monotonous pine barrens, and imparting gaiety and attraction to the most uninviting forest homes of nature, who is always surprising us with beauties, and wonders where we least expect them.

I was anxious to shoot some of these birds, and having a load of small shot in my pocket, whould have stopped to take a crack at them, but a rumor of "Indian tracks" diverted my attention. Some one rode up and reported that a trail where they had been driving cattle was seen across the road. We were instantly formed into platoons, expecting an attack, or flankers thrown out, and every one was peering through the far pine boles for the colored skirt, or dark plum of an Indian to appear. While we were upon the look out we beheld before us a large white object, which, at a distance, bore the appearance of a large Marquee. It turned out to be a high sand hill, and in two or three other spots the earth looked as if it had been washed or blown up into similar ridges.

The trail proved to be an old one. However our expectation was still kept alive by the sight of a solitary wigwam seated among the sand hills a little way off. A detachment was in a moment off in double quick time to surround it and take its inmates prisoners, but we were again disappointed. It was deserted.

Met in the pine barrens, and amoung these sand hills, with the dens of the Gopher or great Land Tortoise, and the hillocks of the Salamanders.

The Gopher* is a large species of land tortoise, to which the appellation *Testudo Clausa*[77] is given; on account of the remarkable faculty it possesses of closing all parts of its shell entirely and protecting and fortifying itself at pleasure within its impregnable castle. This it effects by means of the peculiar construction of the nether shell, the compartments or divisions of which are not knit closely together by sutures like the upper shell, but are connected by a horny cartilage, by means of which the animal is enabled to move as on hinges, this shell, which

---

*Testudo Polyphaemus, (*Bartram.*)

is likewise continued in such a way round the margin, that when it withdraws its head and legs, the under shell closes up to the superior one effectually. The anterior part of the belly shell extends forwards 2 or 3 inches in the form of a shovel; when full grown the shell of the Gopher measures about 15 inches in length and 12 in width, and is of an ash or dark clay color; it is very convex and high, and this shape, together with the hardness or the shell, enables it to support an astonishing weight—it will walk easily under a man, and can support 5 or 600 pounds weight. It has loose skin hanging about its throat; the legs are strong talons; the hind feet are more compressed and stumpy, and have more nails. The head is well proportioned to its size; its eyes large and keen, it peers forth from its walled domain with the hard and severe aspect of a visored knight cased in armor. When it sallies forth from its cave it is with great caution, and it remians a considerable time at the entrance reconnoitering around, and if it sees anything suspicious, retires immediately to its fortress. With its long talons it digs itself a spacious den in the sand hills, which slants into the ground, and is about 10 feet deep. These have a singular appearance, and from the mounds of earth dug out of them would be supposed to be the retreats of some large wild beast by those who did not know what they were. They many times were an annoyance to our horsemen, and in riding along slowly, or full tilt upon a charge, one would find himself rolled on a sudden into the sand, and his horse floundering up to his breast in a "cursed gopher hole."

For an animal which nature has provided with such an extraordinary, and almost perfect defence against harm from all others, it is, instead of a bold adventurer, an arrant coward, living in retirement almost constantly out of harm's way under ground, and only leaving its den, when it is forced to go in search of food or water, and that mostly in the night. It is said to live on vegetables chiefly.

They are esteemed very delicious eating, almost equal to green turtle, and their eggs, which are larger than musket balls, are much sought after. The Gopher is first met going southerly, after passing the Savannah river, and is very common in Florida. It derives its name from the word *Gouffre* (French) from the *Pit* it makes in the ground. The Indians call it Kowikay, (*in mourning*).

Those hillocks, or little mounds and burrows which appear so frequently in the barren tracts of Florida are caused by a little animal known there by the name of 'Salamandar.' Of these hillocks and of the animal itself, my researches enable me to give only the following limited account and I have not met with the creature myself.

Their burrows are exceedingly numerous in various places, and give an appearance to the plains similar to that produced by ploughing up the ground—over their burrows hillocks of loose earth are raised resembling in some respects those thrown up by the shrew mole and something like large ant hills—the mounds are of various dimensions from the diameter of a few inches only to that of several yards—the quantity of earth thrown up consequently varies from a pint to 2 or 3 bushels; the earth is loose and naturalists describe it as having the appearance of being emptied out of a flower pot—no hole is to be discovered under the mass of loose soil, but if it be carefully removed, it is seen that the earth has been broken in a circle of an inch and a half in diameter, within which space the ground is loose, but still without any distinct opening.

The animal belongs to a genus called the Pouched Rat; they are distinguished by their voluminous cheek pouches which are perfectly exterior to the mouth, from which they are separated by the common integument; they are profoundly concave, opening downwards, and towards the mouth—the legs are short, the fore feet large, and armed with very long claws—the hind feet small, and although it walks awkwardly, yet it burrows with the greatest rapidity, so that the difficulty of getting specimens from which this animal might be better known to naturalists, may be, in a great degree attributed to the facility with which it passes through the soil, removing imperceptibly at the slightest sound which gives notice of the vicinity of danger. The head and body are large, giving to it a clumsy appearance. There are peculiarities of the teeth which also distinguish it, they resemble those of the squirrel.

The animal in question vulgarly called Salamander, Pouched Rat, Sand Rat, Gopher (*Pseudostoma Bursarium*;)* Say; Long's expedition to

---

*From Pseudo, false, and Stoma, mouth; false mouth; or cheek pouches.

the Rocky Mountains. *Canada Rat* Shaw, Gen. Zoology; *Mus Bursarius* Lin. Trans. v. p. 227; *Mus Saccatus* Mitchell, New York Med. Rep. 1821, Lewis & Clark; *Cricetus Bursareous* Desm. Mannuel, 312,) is found in Florida, Georgia, &c., and the plains adjacent to the Missouri. Shaw's description and plate of the Canada rat is very different from Godman's species. That of the former has a large heavy head, the pouches are inflated and hang inverted like large bladders from the jaws, the colour of the back is cinereous, and the animal looks like a mole. In the engraving of Godman, the Pseudostoma bursarium has no perceptible pouch, the head is quite small comparatively, and of a different shape, and the color is reddish brown, lead colored at base, on the under parts paler.

The following notice was sent me by a friend, Dr.——, a gentleman of Charleston, who was upon the campaign in Florida; "On the Pease creek trail—caught a live Salamander. It appeared to me to be a species of Rat. The eyes small, projecting, and very black—ears round—color of the animal reddish brown on the back, inclining to a greyish yellow on the belly. The feet were furnished with long claws—tail naked like the rat—teeth like squirrel. No pouches in the jaw that I could discover—(Mr. Bachman says that he has seen one with pouches,)—from which I infer that there are probably two species. I let it go on the ground for the purpose of watching its movements. It was very nimble, and active, penetrating the ground with astonishing rapidity, in throwing the earth out of the hole which he made, he formed a triangular pouch with the under part of his jaw and his fore legs, throwing the earth forwards."

Coxe, in his description of "Carolana" called Florida, and "Meschashebe," mentions "a rat with a bag under its throat, wherein it conveys its young when forced to fly."

In an account of the *Mus bursareous* in the Trans. of Lin. Soc., the cheek pouches are said to serve for temporary reception of the animal's food. Shaw's specimen of the Canada Rat had the pouches filled with dirt, which it was supposed the Indians who brought it had done to fill them out. It is most likely that the pouches subserve the purpose of bags to carry the earth temporarily in, by which the animal is enabled to work with such rapidity. Our guide Ben. Wiggins informed us that seen them carrying the earth and emptying it from their pouches.

Bartram's only notice of this animal is that of "a large ground rat, more than twice the size of the common Norway rat, which in the night time throws out the earth, forming little mounds or hillocks."

Barton, in his Medical and Phy. Jour. says that a species of mus allied to the M. Bursareus of Shaw is common in Georgia and Florida. That he examined a living specimen, and was convinced that it was no other than the Tucau of Hernandez, and the Tuza or Tosan of Clavigero.

This animal is so entirely subterranean that many persons have lived for many years surrounded by its little edifices without knowing the singular being by whose labours they are constructed. They are extremely hard to catch

—the only method by which to procure them is to dig over their hole and let the sun shine in upon it, and to wait secreted and in perfect silence—he will be disturbed by the heat and light and come forth when you may shoot him, or if he leaves the hole any distance, run and put your foot over the hole.

The growth on these sand hills consists almost entirely of saw palmetto, prickly pear and wiregrass. Nothing worth mentioning occurred on our route further, and we got in sight of Bulow's early in the afternoon.

————

CHAPTER VI.

A wilderness of Dead Oaks—Palmetto grove—Fort—The detachment left to garison it—employments and notices at Bulow's—Large Steam Sugar Mill—Sugar Lands—High and low Hammock—Timber trees of Florida—A fact or two concerning Sugar.

The first object that struck us as we approached the plantation was an immense forest of dead *Live Oak*, if any thing more gloomy looking than a Santee cypress swamp. It must once have been a beautiful grove, and had I been an aristocrat, instead of a plain republican, I might have indulged the reflection; how criminal it was to destroy so many fine trees, whose venerable antiquity gave them a paramount right to the soil, in order to make way for your upstart rummy sugar-cane. It was one of the many sad instances of the levelling, grovelling order of things in this country, which sweeps all before it, melting down our golden time-worshipped idols into base coin, sacrificing ever the *beautiful* to the useful; which causes us to prefer the sight of a dunghill to that of a mountain, and to have, instead of a beautiful lawn in front of our doors, a forest of corn and an underwood of pease growing up to the very steps.

This dead wilderness had something frightful about it; the huge, scraggy branches stretched out, and interlocked in the harshest, and most graceless attitudes, forming every imaginable variety of rude, dire, and ghastly shapes. Some tall and crooked topped cedars of the size of cypresses leant their slant and uncouth shapes to add to the fantastic horror of the scene, and by way of foil to render the picture more strikingly grim and ugly, two or three graceful palmettoes, on whom the ringing blight had not fallen, inclined their plumy heads among these monarchs of the waste, looking like scarce, and modest belles beset by a ball-room-full of stiff and awkward overgrown beaus.

Out of the midst of the gloomy wilderness arose the blackened walls of a large stone buiding. This was the Sugar Mill which had been recently burnt. No more suitable scenery could have been devised by the imagination for the horrors of an Indian midnight attack. It recalled the many tales I had read of the early forest settlements, and the atrocities of ruthless savage invasion. I beheld the lurid torch-lights dancing and flashing among the grisly, cadaverous, wilderness branches, and heard the shrill echoing demon yells piercing their awful solitude and waking the distant mournful howls of the wolves. Then I pictured to myself the mother pressing her baby to her bosom, and flying distractedly through the pathless woods; the planter looking back upon his burning dwellings, and vowing vengeance against the marauders, and by the flashing flames, I saw the exulting visages of the red men rioting through the horrid maze of the war dance.

I was diverted from this dismal prospect, and the train of imaginings it gave rise to, to one pleasanter. We were passing a long hammock a little way off to our right, which consisted of an almost entire growth of palmetto trees forming a beautiful dark grove, or rather forest. This deep swamp which skirted the horizon had rather a threatening appearance, and it seemed impossible that it should not contain Indians, but nevertheless, we passed it without seeing a sign, except a lean dog which perceiving us, streaked over the field towards it; by the direction, however, which he took from the negro houses, we concluded that he belonged to the plantation.

We halted by the ruins of the dwelling house, from which an alleyway, made of substantial squared cedar posts 10 feet high, led into a Palmetto fort, having four angles or bastions. The palmetto logs were laid horizontally, and morticed in one another, to a height above that of a man and loop holes were cut between them. On one side of the fort there was a terrace, or log platform for a sentinel to walk on, and a fine well was in its centre. On the outside, some little way off, there was a high tree with steps, like those of a ladder, reaching to its top, which commanded an extensive view of the country around for a mile or more, and had been used as a look out.

This fort had been built by the proprietor,

who, having a large force of negroes, intended at one time to defend the plantation, but afterwards concluded that it was safest to remove them.

It was reported at St. Augustine that a large body of Indians, some said 500, had fortified themselves in this fort, and were in possession of a swivel. It is not to be wondered at that they did not do so, for they knew better than to pen themselves up in that way for slaughter. They would then have given us a chance at them. They are every way safer in their natural fortifications in the woods, for there they can always employ thier skill in retreating, which constitutes glory and science of their warfare. As we were, however, at that time unacquainted with their manner of making war, we thought it not improbable that we might find them upon the premises, instead of which, we took quiet possession of the Fort, and of a four pounder, which had been spiked.

It was here that Maj. Putnam and the St. Augustine Guards had been stationed, who were engaged in the Battle of Dunn Lawton.[78]

As soon as the men had grounded their arms, they flocked to the well to enjoy the luxury of good water once more, and to fill their canteens. While they were in the midst of this, and congratulating themselves upon the fine accommodations there were for camping, on a sudden the most dire consternation and dismay became visible in their contenances. Some one had reported that the Indians had poisoned the well and as this was known to be in keeping with their other savage customs, many did not doubt the fact, but others who had not quenched their thirst were willing to run the risk, and laughed at the fears of the rest, who were quieted in their apprehensions after they did not experience any strange symptoms.

Our detachment was quartered in the Fort, which we were to be left to garrison, and the other companies tented on the outside. They left us next morning to proceed ten miles farther to Carrickfergus, the plantation of Duncan M'Rae,[79] where they were to remain until provisions were forwareded on, and more particular directions obtained from head quarters. A temporary depot was to be established at the Fort, and we were charged with the duty of gathering in the corn, great quantities of which remained on the place.

Our situation here, though comfortable, was not altogether relished by us, as we were unwilling to be left behind, and to lose the chance of the first brush with the enemy; but nevertheless, the duty of garrisoning the Fort was assigned to us as an important one and our post was honorable, considering the danger that so small a body as we were, numbering only 28, was exposed to, in case of an attack by a large number of Indians, such as were represented [to be] in the immediate neighborhood.

We spent part of the first day in gathering in the corn, and such articles as were of use to us. The Indians had not burnt the negro houses, and every thing in them seemed to have been left untouched, since the hasty flight of the inmates. There was more corn in them than we could take away, and a good deal of useful negro furniture. There were a great number of these houses, and Mr. Bulow had upwards of two hundred negroes—they surrounded the Fort in a semicircle, and were distant about 150 yards from it. As they afforded the Indians a fine screen to crawl up behind unseen, and a favorable position to make a attack from, we, at one time thought of burning them down, but did not, as we did not wish to create more destruction than the plantation had already suffered.

We amused ourselves the rest of the day in sauntering about the place, and seeing what was to be seen. We came to where a large chest of books, papers, and other articles had been buried, and been dug up by the Indians. As these were of no value to them, they had left them scattered about; but they proved afterwards a great acquisition to us, and served to pass many a wary hour while we were in camp.

The dwelling house, out houses, and a small well [mill] adjacent were all destroyed. The former was a neat moderate sized mansion, built of the shell rock of the country. The situation had not much to recommend it, looking out on one side upon a creek that was close by, and an extensive cotton field and marsh beyond; and on the others, upon the dreary dead oak field, and the thickets, and cabbage swamps that bounded the horizon.

We next visited the ruins of the magnificent steam sugar mill, which was over a quarter of a mile from the house, and to which a wide road led through the wilderness. This fine building was constructed of the same shell stone that the house was, and was about one hundred and fifty feet in length. A good deal of the steam apparatus was uninjured; there was also some lead about the building, most of which the Indians had carried off, as this was an article they never left behind, if they could conveniently carry it off.

This mill cost $60,000, and before the Indian disturbances, the plantation would have sold for $100,000. The sugar lands were extensive and fine, being what is called "high hammocks." —The high and low hammock lands, which consist of a growth of live-oak, hickory, magnolia, red bay, and palmetto or cabbage trees, with an alluvium of mixed vegetable mould and loam, based upon clay and rotten limestone, are the most valuable lands in Florida, for sugar, cotton and corn. These are to be found in greatest perfection and abundance on the rivers south of St. Augustine., and east of St. Johns, on Mosquito, Tomoka, Halifax &c. and the inlets.—About Matanza, the soil is more like that of our Sea Islands, apparently very barren, but producing cotton of the finest staple. Other extensive portions of the country in this district are uninviting to the agriculturist.

The above mentioned lands are rendered additionally valuable, from the quantity of fine timber on them which may be exported, principally live-oak, cedar, and Florida mahogany, or red bay. The first is the most valuable, and large supplies are furneshed for ship timber.—The second grows to a great size on the Florida coast; I measured some hewn pieces here, that were full 2 1-2 feet square. Florida cedar is in great demand—it constituted a considerable source of profit on this plantation. Most of the large trees on the coast, farther north, have been used, and it is obliged to be obtained from Florida, for the construction of the upper timbers of vessels, in which it is much used with live-oak, its lightness compensating for the weight of the latter material. The Red Bay, (*Laurus Caroliniensis*) also grows very large in Florida, where it is called "bastard mahogany." It is to be distinguished from the smaller variety, which grows in what are called the Bay Galls. This is a fine tree, growing to the height of 60 or 70 feet in the rich hammocks, occasionally in dried up ponds, and in great perfection on the shorer on the lakes. Forbes mentions one, which stood as a prominent beacon on the western border of Lake Mayaco. The wood is fine grained, and is susceptible of nearly the same polish as mahogany, though not so dark, being of a beautiful rose color. If the trees were as large and plentiful as the Acajou or St. Domingo mahogany, and could be furnished as cheap, they would be in more demand.

Besides these trees, I may mention as a source of increasing profit, the Palmetto, the utility of which, for marine purposes— for the construction of wharves, breakwaters and the forts, owing to its peculiar quality of incorruptibility in salt water, and its toughness and capacity to resist violence, and the effects of cannon balls, is well known. These trees are becoming scarce on the coast of Carolina, and bring a good price in the Charleston market. They grow to a considerable height in Florida, but I never witnessed one of the altitude that Forbes mentions, 100 feet— fifty and sixty feet is their greatest height. They are valuable for many purposes of domestic economy; the leaves make mats, baskets, hats, &c. and are much used in thatching; the embryo leaves supply the table with a delicious cabbage; the wood, when dry, is excellent fuel. Orange groves are also sometimes interspersed with the above mentioned growth.

This plantation made from 4 to 500 hogsheads of sugar. So much has been written upon the cultivation of this staple of the South, that what I might say on the subject would be only repetition and might swell into a treatise unsuited to the plan of this work—my intentions is only to mention a fact or two in relation to the growth and product of this plant in Florida. The sugar cane is planted in Florida in February, but the season for it is regulated by the dryness or wetness of the weather. The seed should be put in the ground when rain may be expected as like most other plants its germination is forwarded by water. About a foot of the top part of the cane is cut off to make slips for planting. The slips or cuttings are put in the ground at different distances apart according to its fertility; in poor land 3, and in rich 5 feet apart—it appears out of the ground early in the spring. The sugar cane grows well and seeds in Florida which it does not do in Georgia and Louisiana. It is said to possess one great advantage over the cane of Jamaica; that it may lay 2 or 3 months on the ground after being cut without injury, whereas in Jamaica it cannot lay longer than 10 or 12 days. They are obliged there to use great despatch and employ extra hands to get it in, which is avoided in Florida. The quality of the sugar depends on the dryness or wetness of the season when it is maturing and on the rapidity of the process of boiling. If the cane is too much saturated with water, it takes longer to boil, and the sugar is dark colored. If it remains too long before it undergoes the process, it ferments and is injured—but the whole of November and December may be profitably employed. The expense of a sugar establishment is great, and on plantations which make from 3 to 500 hogsheads, Steam Millscosting 40 to $60,000 are indispensable, to enable the sugar to be made speedily, but on smaller plantations, mills working by horse power may be erected at a cost of 10 or $15,000, which answer well enough.

The African and Otaheite cane grows best.

The product of an acre of cane planted in the very best land, and with the best cultivation, will yield 2 hogsheads of sugar; but the average product and what is considered a very good crop, is from 1,000 to 1,200 pounds or about a hoghead.

At 13 cts. a lb. a hhd. will be worth $130

It yields also a barrel and a fifth of

     Syrup, say worth,   __20__

The value of the product of an acre

     therefore is, $150

A hand will tend better than 4 acres without provision.

From three to four acres, if provision and fodder is also made, so that the profit of a hand is from 4 to $500, calculating moderately for the best sugar.

The following extract of the profits of three plantations in Alachua in 1832, is taken from a Savannah paper.

1st Plantation, 47 hands.

160 hhds. of sugar,	$11,200
14,000 gals. molasses,	2,800
4,006 bushels corn,	2,500
Fodder, rice, beans, peas &c,	1,000
Total	$17,500

2d Plantation, 20 hands.

90 casks sugar,	$5,400
7000 gals, molasses,	1,000
Fodder, beans, &c.,	1,008
Total	$7,400

3d Plantation, 12 hands.

50 casks sugar,	$2,500
7,000 gals, molasses,	1,500
2,000 bushels corn,	1,200
Fodder and extras,	500
Total	$5,700

The first produced $372 to the hand—second, 270—and third, 475—price of sugar 7 cents.

———

CHAPTER VII.

Print of a Foot-step in the Mud—The Alarm Gun—A 'Daisy Clipper'—The Contagion—Jack O' Lantern—Out-posts wounded, and Tents fired upon—More Tracks—A bull in a Boat—Irishmen—The first sight of Indians.

In the afternoon, the Capt. Dr. A——, who was left with us to attend the garrison, and myself, set out, to make a tour of observation about the outskirts of the premises, and see if any Indian tracks were to be found. We had not proceeded more than 300 yards, on a road which led through the marsh, to a cotton field, when we discovered the print of a mockasin sunk in the mud, by the thicket of a bay and myrtle, which appeared to have been made recently.

We endeavoured to trace its direction, but the ground getting hard, we lost it, or only imagined that here and there the grass was pressed down like Robinson Crusoe's, was enough (not exactly to excite our alarms, for we had come out expecting and wishing to see Indians, and moreover thought ourselves a match for at least a hundred of them, but) to satisfy us that they were in the neighbourhood, and we thought it probable that this might be a spy of the preceding night, who, at the sight of our camp fires, might have been despatched to watch our movements, and if so, he would have given intelligence of the departure of our main body, and nothing was more likely than that they would come down upon us with the expectation of cutting off our small number, and taking an easy boot of scalps.

We did not prosecute our reconnoissances any farther, but returned to the fort. At sunset our sentinel saw some objects emerge out of the field. It was too far to distinguish at first what kind of animals they were, but they were not Indians. They proved to be a small drove of pigs that were domestically coming home to supper, having *carte blanche* of all the corn on the plantation. Two gunners went out after them, and returned with two; so that this evening and the next day, we fared sumptuously on fresh in lieu of salt pork.

It was now time to post our picquets. One was placed on the bridge that led over the creek to the road on which we had seen the mockasin track; the others in front, on the other side of the negro houses, concealed as well as they could be, by stumps or trees, so that the Indians might not approach unseen behind the houses.

The first hour passed quietly.

The twilight was superseded by a faint cloudy moonshine. The sentinel on the platform began to take slower turns, and stopped every minute to throw his doubtful eyes as far as they could penetrate amid the shadowy recesses of the gaunt spectre-looking oaks, on the darkened margin of the circumjacent palmetto swamp, and skirting forests, and over the wide plain of marsh.

A gun went off.

There is smething very exciting to a beginner, in this sudden alarm, and single signal of an approaching enemy, arousing the echoes of the still night, and bidding everyone be at his post. It is, (with the exception that in this case there is a spice of danger) much like hearing a rousing report in the woods of your next neighbour's double barrel gun, on a stand at a deer hunt; and feeling your blood dancing in a thousand queer movements about your heart, as the next moment, you imagine the woods crashing with the leaps of an enormous basket-horned buck. In like manner, at the discharge of the sentinel's piece, one expects immediately to hear it followed by the piercing onset yell, and the cracking of rifles, and imagines in every bush or stump, that he sees the wily foe, stealing up to the onslaught.

If the Indians had been as rapid in running in, and storming our fort, as the picquets were, we should inevitable have been all massacred in the twinkling of an eye. The horrid apprehension of being shot down and scalped, before they could get inside the fort, put wings to their feet. They cut the air and dirt, and vaulted over ditch and curtain, with the ease that circus riders would have turned a somerset on the spring board. One man (I fear to mention the circumstance, lest I may not be believed) had webbed toes; he lost his shoes at the start; the next morning, his track was plainly to be seen where he had 'streaked' it over a turnip patch; and every unfortunate turnip top that had come in contact with his toes, was sliced off as neatly as if a pair of scissors had been applied to them. He was of the breed of racers, yelept "Daisy Clippers."

The picquet who fired was the one stationed at the bridge. He related that he saw two men, like Indians, come out of the marsh, and as they were walking up to him on the causeway, he fired. This was all that he positively knew—he could give no account what became of them afterwards; whether he had hit them or not.

After this, we concluded that it was risking the lives of the men too much, to put them outside of the Fort, without its being of any benefit, and only productive of false alarms; so sentinels were set in each bastion, and one at the gate of the passage way, and the four ponder which we had found, was prepared, loaded with musket balls and slugs, and placed on the terrace, so as to range the entrance of the passage.

Before this wa completed, the sentinel at the gate had fired; he was certain that he had seen several Indians prowling about the tents, (which were still standing on the outside, having been left); he was rebuked by the sergeant for firing at nothing; but the Sergeant himself had not been there two minutes, before *he* pulled trigger. The contagion now spread. Everyone's imagination suggested that we were surrounded by Indians, whose object it was to keep as quiet and concealed as possible, until they got near enough, when they would rush in, and make a mouthful of us.

As all the men were under arms, and on the look out, several would declare that they saw objects approaching. Bang!—bang!! —they would fire two or three at a time; still, the Indians, like phantoms, the next moment glided away into air, unseen. If it could have been ascertained, that the soldiers were acted on by their fears, or prompted by the love of burning powder, to blaze away as they did, it was the part of the officer to put a stop to it; but officers as well as men, were puzzled what to think of the matter, for, to corroborate the appearances which those that saw them, swore to, and the presence of Indians, a large fire was now seen not very far off, which we thought might proceed from the main body of the Indians, and about the same time a light, nearly the height of a man, from the ground, was observed, taking a uniform direction along the negro houses, like a lantern or torch in the hand of some one walking.

While we were gazing at it, it suddenly changed its direction, and made rapidly for the Fort, and in an instant it had whisked over our heads and vanished. It was one of those singular vapours called *Jack O' Lanterns.*

This admirable deception caused us to laugh at our previous imaginings and delusions, and as every thing remained quiet, and the men got tired of straining their eyes at shadows of stumps and bushes, we retired to our rest, leaving a strong guard in case of a real alarm.

In the morning the first thing we did was to look for tracks and dead bodies. Instead of the two men at whom Picquet No. 1 had taken such deliberate aim we saw a cedar stump with a ball through it, which proved, that however the ocular nerves of the sentry had been affected, he had taken cool aim.

A more serious havoc had been committed upon the tents. Some of them were torn in several places with the shots; but here were no such things as tracks to be found, and we began to think that Florida Indians were like Florida cows, that it took six of them to make a shadow.

Spent the greater part of the next day in shooting; as I had a double barrel, and had provided myself with shot—game in abundance, partridges, snipes, and birds that were game to us, being good eating, among which I may mention a flock of tame pigeons which afforded me two or three days excellent sport. With such catering as this—the fish which we caught in the creek, and the remains of the pigs with a garnish of vegetables, which a small garden afforded, we had a dinner, the memory of which caused us many a gastro-dolent sigh on future occasions when we were restricted to our oleaginous diet of fritters and salt pork.

Saw many mocasin [*sic*] tracks on a trail through the marsh, some seemed fresh, and they led to the causeway in the direction where our sentry had fired into the post. Changed our opinion again about the alarms of the night, and concluded that Indians must actually have been about us, but could not account for the absence of tracks elsewhere, and why some of them had not been shot, or why they did not shoot at the sentinel or the Fort.

In the evening beheld a dust in the road which we had marched—got under arms, but supposed it must be some of our troops. It proved to be the remainder of our company under Lieut. Pinckney with provisions and our baggage. As may be supposed, we were all very glad to see one another again safe, after almost a week's separation, and the risk our small parties incurred of being attacked by a superior force of Indians. We learnt the desertion of two of our company, who had walked away from Hernandez' by themselves.

At midnight or one o'clock the next morning, a party of the Irish Volunteers arrived in the boats from Camp M'Crea. They narrowly escaped being shot at by our sentinel, as the orders were generally not to hail, none but Indians, it being presumed, would visit us: but each sentinel was cautioned to use discretion in case any of our troops should happen to come, and to hail in those directions where they might be expected.

It was a suspicious time to hear oars on the water, and the sentinel forgetting this caution, the next moment would have fired, had not one of the Irishmen quickley shouted:

"Friends ay to be sure we are. Blast your liver, if you *kill us*, by my shoul, wont we be for *reporting* ye to the Colonel?"

"My sake," exclaimed the countryman, recovering his breath as they drew nearer, "I reckon I was worser scared than you! Kill you? Don't I know nothing can kill an Irishman but Lightning?"

It was raining torrents, and these fine hardy fellows had been out all the night in the open boats exposed to the miserable weather, and their small party, which did not amount to ten, liable to be discovered by the noise of their oars and way-laid by the Indians from the numerous hammocks which bordered the narrow creek. The distance they had come was 16 miles from them we learnt what adventures had befallen the troops since they left us. As they were passing on a causeway between Dummit's and M'Crea's plantations they heard the report of three guns, and six or eight Indians were soon after seen at a distance, who had observed the troops. An encounter was now certainly expected. It was no longer all "talk and no cider;" but here were the red devils at last, in legitimate red skins, body and bones, alive, and looking at them as unconcerned as so many wild brazen-browed stags, gazing down archly from a crag on the hunters below, conscious in their superiority of limb to bound away over fell and flood, the instant danger approached nearer.

Some wild young fellows were for having a scamper on the instant after these grave warriors, and two or three dashed off helter-skelter 'on their own hook,' as the saying is, as eager as

Indians themselves for a scalp; but the Colonel commanded them back, and they obeyed, but reluctantly. He, as it was proper he should, was for taking things more cooly. These Indians might be a decoy, and an ambuscade might be near, and it was necessary that a certain disposition should be made, so as to surround, and prevent the escape of these Indians. Two companies were sent in advance to meet them, while the other two formed the main body in the centre.

In the meantime, the skulking rascals diappeared. Hammocks and scrubs were scoured, and men posted every where to intercept them, but all to no purpose. They passed through all this circumvention, as easily as water would pass through a sieve; and when our troops thought that they had cut off their escape in front, a glimpse of them, and they had given them the slip altogether.

In the search, they had got to McCrea's, where a corn house was yet on fire. The place was recoinnoitred, and then they retired back to Dummitt's, where they intended encamping. On the way they came across a fine fat Bullock, which the Indians whom they had been in pursuit of, had shot, and partly skinned, and just had time to take out the tongue, when they were surprised—our troops took possession of the bullock. The next morning they went on to McCrea, and a part of them proceeded to scour the adjacent country. They met with several recent trails, and came upon the embers of a camp fire, which must have been the fire that we saw from Bulow's.

CHAPTER VIII.

Escort command marches to Camp McCrea—Notices on the way—Cactus—Shell rock—Grove of oaks—Halt at the encampment and return—Parakeets—Wild cats—Excursion at Bulow's—the Palmetto grove and the Palmetto tree—Leave Bulow's—Bivouac—Cockspur Burrs—and Musquitoes—Day and night in Cantonment.

The next morning, (Feb. 28th) took under my comand 20 picked men, and started from Bulow Fort, to escort the provision wagons to Camp McCrea.[80]

Our guides were one of the volunteers who had lately left the Camp, and a negro boy belonging to Col. Dummitt, employed as a servant by Lieut. Pinckney, who knew all the country thoroughly.

Our small party set out soon after sunrise in fine spirits, and in the full persuasion that we would win the first Indian laurels, as Indians were now known positively to be in the intervening neighborhood, and our number could not frighten any ordinary number of them.

Our road was tedious and sandy for the first part and led through low thickets, occasionally swamps and ponds, the most favorable country that could be for an ambuscade. We next passed some deserted houses, and then came to a long, dark, death-concealing hammock which stretched fully a mile upon our left and which the road touched the whole way. Here every disposition was made to meet a sudden attack, but we passed it in safety —Saw in the sandy fields Cactus opuntia, Prickly Pear, or Indian fig growing in great perfection, beautifully erect, much taller, and with more numerous articulations than near Charleston, and on Sullivan's Island. These were three or four feet high—Bartram mentions some eight feet high, and strong enough to bear the weight of a man. Mr. Elliott says that it is probable that there are three distinct species on our coasts covered by this name. This should certainly be distinguished from the common dwarf Indian fig; its height being so considerably greater, and it is destitute of the fascicles of setaceous, barbed prickles, which render the common prickly pear so noxious to the touch. The spines on it are very long and sharp.

About here, there appeared above the surface of the ground, much of that singular freestone, or concretion of shells, which forms the foundation of the land that runs parallel with the coast and near to it, of which, when I come to speak of Anastasia Island, I will say more.

A beautiful grove of Live Oaks now appeared in sight; though not to be compared with many on Ashley river, and in other parts of Carolina, yet the even canopy that their wide limbs spread, the enticing shades of their mossy curtains, and the sweet woodland breath that pervaded the soft russet carpet of leaves beneath, had charms which welcomed us to a halt, and to take a momentary enjoyment of them.

This was the plantation of the Marquis de Fougières, formerly French Consul at Charleston. Here we again witnessed the effects of savage fury in the blackened relics of buildings, not one of which had been left standing.

We passed, besides, the plantations of Darley and Dummitt at Tomoka, which were likewise in ruins. Our volunteer guide had informed us that a scouting party had been detached that morning by colonel to beat the bushes for Indians, and having heard several reports of muskets on our way, we had no doubt that they had started some. After we had nearly arrived at the camp we encountered the detachment under command of Maj. Walker, and proceeded, in company, to Camp M'Crea. They had met with no Indians, and the firing we had heard were the discharges of bad loads.

Passed on the way a mule, which had been shot by the Indians.

We found the Col. busily occupied with the Capt. of Pioneers in the construction of a Fort. The provisions were very welcome, for they had been on a short allowance.

The encampment was in a spacious field close upon the Tomoka river, and the balmy sea breezes swept across it, laden with the resinous fragrance of the surrounding pines, and the saline breath of the marshy savannas. Reclining under the sapphire canopy of the soft, warm sky, I enjoyed that delightful state of tranquil, and at the same time buoyant, spirits, which health and exercise, and banishment of care produce, and undoing the contents of my havresac, I made a repast more exquisite than all the boasted *bons mets* of Delmonico could have furnished, accompanied with a rural *rinfresco* of cool, luscious sugar cane; whose juicy luxury far transcended your city medicated creams, and tasteless sherberts.

In the afternoon we set out upon our return, not feeling in the slightest degree fatigued, though much of the road was heavy sand, and a good part of it boggy. Not having any waggons to detain us now, we started at a rapid pace to march the ten miles in two hours, or a little more.

Swift sweeping, like spirit-birds from their wizard tenements in the green pine-tops, on wings of gold and emerald, glance their devious way through the azure ether the gay Parakeets. They do not endeavour to get out of our way, but rather seem anxious to show off their gaudy plumage, and the air is pained with their eternal chattering. I had no small shot, and if I had, would not have fired for fear of giving alarm to the camp needlessly. I omitted to mention having previously shot one of these birds, and I had found out by experience that shooting at them was no way to silence their clamouring. On the contrary, when they saw one of their company fall, and bleeding on the ground, they fell to abusing me in the most violent language, and instead of putting them to flight, it drew them more about me, and they flew back two or three times to the same tree, evincing great concern at the fate of their slain companion.

Soon after these lively Elegantes of the forest had disappeared, we heard a crashing of the bushes in a hammock close by, and two brindled wild cats came leaping out, one after the other, in beautiful style across the road a few feet from us. It was with difficulty we restrained ourselves from shooting at them, but we thought it was best to reserve our fire for the Indians, in case some of them might be lurking in the hammock, who had started the wild cats out; but we returned, as we went, without having the glimpse of a plume or war shirt—we got to the Fort just as the sun was setting, having marched 20 miles, and spent better than 4 hours at Camp M'Crea.

The following was a most charming Spring morning, and Dr. A— accompanied me in an excursion of pleasure into the adjacent forests and fields—we went well armed with guns and pistols, and believed that we could engage 20 Indians, and keep them at bay until assistance could arrive at the Fort. It was well for us, that our vanity and courage were not put to the test—we first struck a coruse [course] into the dark, and deep palmetto hammock. Here we enjoyed the "Tanscendent [*sic*] Palm" and beheld this beautiful tree in all its perfection. The eye revelled on the Corinthian richness of the graceful plumy capitals which crowned these stately colonnades in this, the most magnificient of Nature's forest palaces, and the sense was enchanted with the tropic luxury, which breathed in its temperate airs, murmured in the gentle rustle of its fanning leaves, and lived in its grateful contiguity of shade.

THE PALMETTO TREE.
I.
Tree of the South! our country's pride and boast,
Sacred to the war—the bulwark of our coast,
How peaceful yet thy shade—thy mien how calm!
Serene, delightful and majestic Palm.
II.
In sultry noontide hour, the Indian maid,
Here erst beneath they rustling bower delayed,
Charmed was the air—enchanted was the spot,
Her's were the dreams that waking blighteth not.
III.
Her hopes were present pastimes—her young sighs
Were presnt ecstacies—not miseries

Her thoughts were nature's pleasant precepts, not
The lessons false which harrow many a maiden's lot.
IV.
And Love and Innocence, and Joy entwined,
Led the soft hours, and left dull care behind;
And as he gazed upon this maiden's face,
The hunter thought not of the morrow's chase.
V.
Such theme, sweet shade (mine own it fain would be)
Doth best beseem for pleasant reverie,
Shall I not dream of such, and while the hour
Of wished for bliss 'neath the Palmetto bow'r?
VI.
Alas! vain thought beware—Fly, Fly! These shades
No nymph doth haunt; but cruel war invades.
Not here Love's arrows from soft eyes; but see,
The Rifle points from from the Palmetto Tree.

Picked up a few early and common flowers. Saw no Indian tracks, or Indians, and emerged again into daylight.

Resolved upon an expedition up the creek, and paddled in a canoe for a mile or two. So still was everything around; not a sound but the ripple of our little bark as it glided through the breeze-kissed sluggish water, the rustling of some solitary palmetto, and the distant roar of the ocean; so primitive and wild did the landscape seem, that I could not realise that I was living in this age of wide-spread civilization, Rail Roads, and mushroom settlements; but imagined myself carried back half a century or more, wandering like a second Bartram through new and untrod regions, inhabited only by Indians, wolves and alligators; and the country was, indeed pretty much the same at the present time; what settlements there were bring distant, and not a white man living any where in the country.

On our way, we discovered an Indian canoe tied by a rope of marsh close under a hammock, and took it as a prize.

Met with no farther adventure, and returned.

Next day, (2d March,) nothing of consequence occurred. Passed the day in the usual way, shooting, fishing, and making excursions. Began to find time hang heavy, and wondering why we did not go after the Indians.

Had no alarms now. The men who gave false alarms were put on double and treble duty unless they could show tracks of the enemy where they fired.

3d, 4th, and 5th, passed in the same monotonous way.

On the 6th the, Col. arrived at our Fort, from St. Augustine, whither he had ridden to ascertain the cause of the delay of the rest of the regiment, and to get orders to move on. He brought the news of Gen. Gaines having been repulsed at the Withlacoochee by the Indians, the particulars of which were much exaggerated at that time—of the Indians having fired upon the steamboat as she was returning from Volusia down the river St. John's; and of the Lieut. Col's, having been ordered on with the remainder of the regiment to Palatka, where some Indians were said to be in force.

We received orders to move on to Camp M'Crea the next day with the elite of our men, and without tents and baggage, as a forced march was to be made to Spring Garden, in which neighbourhood the Indians were known to be assembled in considerable force. This order gave us much satisfaction, as they were getting tired of being stationary so long, having remained now near a fortnight in garrison, though we could not expect more comfortable quarters. 15 men were left, very much against their will, in the fort, under a sergeant, who were not considered competent to the march, and the charge of the depot was left to them.

Started after dinner, and got to the camp after sunset. As we were without tents we bivouacked in the open field before fires. The first part of the night was mild and pleasant enough, but there was no getting any rest on account of Cockspur-burrs and Musquitoes. The Cock-spur-burr (*Cenchrus Tribuloides*) is very common in the sandy fields on the coast of Florida, and is extremely annoying to the feet and hands, its hooked spurs adhering in the flesh, and producing much irritation. Every time I turned, my sides and back were covered with these prickly abominations, and I could not touch my great coat to pull it over me, but what these affectionate pests of the earth stuck by dozens to my fingers.

The other pests of the air are so intolerable, that this part of Florida takes its name from them. They are much larger and more poisonous than our city musquitoes, and are a foridable breed, like our *gallinippers* of the swamps. They were peculiarly obnoxious to our up-countrymen, who swore that they saw some as large as Turkies, carrying brick bats under their wings to sharpen their bills upon, and that they were in two gangs, one of whom raised the covering, while the other rushed in to the attack. At Key West, I have heard, they are so bad that whole droves of cattle will be seen at night lying to windward on the beach, much in the same way that horses are seen to turn their tails to a storm of rain; and the deer are also obliged to leave the swamps and seek the breezes of the sea shore. These must have been the "*winged serpents*," of which Nicholas Challusius paints Florida full.

In the mid'st of our sufferings, it began to rain and towards morning poured. All our fires were extinguished, and clothing and every thing soaked. After a while, we found a shelter in a dilapitated negro house, about half a mile from the camp, but this was like getting out of the frying pan into the fire. We were crowded to suffocation, and as a fire had to be made in the house to cook by, the smoke was abominable. The palmetto thatch however soon took fire and made a vent, which let in as much rain as it let out smoke, so that we were annoyed the whole day by these two elements, as much as we had been the whole night by the cockspur burrs and musquitoes.

At night, I lay on a single plank, as narrow and sharp as Mahomet's bridge to Paradise, but, notwithstanding slept soundly, and getting up by sunrise, walked out into the fields to pick sugar cane. Today, we sent by the boats for our tents, as we found we were not to march for some days yet, and when they arrived, we moved from our cantonment to the camp. A great number of the men were down with the measles, and the only accommodation there was for a hospital was a fowl house. The dwelling house, sugar house, and every building on the place except those two mentioned, were destroyed.

CHAPTER IX.

A morning's visit from the Red folk—The Indian war whoop—turn out after the enemy—Dead men scalped—Old Ben's information, and warning—A burial—Expedition down the creek—Alligators, Pelicans &c., at Fort Bulow.

"Pow—Pow-pow-pow—Pow-pow—Whoop—Wholu—Pow-pow—Wbo-lu-lu-lu-lu—Pow-pow—Whoo-whoop."

What the devil's the matter with the men, (thought I, as I turned over on my sheep skin, awakened by the cracking of rifles, and these shrill cheers shooting against orders in this way, and whooping after pigs, so early in the morning. The next moment I heard several voices exclaim "Indians—the Indians are shooting down our men." "Injins for true," shouted my boy—"for God's sake, master get up—dem is Injins—great God how dem da shoot and hollow." I was now wide awake, and the woods continued to ring with the desultory, quick, startling spang of the rifle, and the piercing, thrilling war whoop, which intermingled with the murderous sounds. It was animating and exciting in the highest degree, to hear them. For the first time in my life, my ears were saluted with that terrible savage yell, of which I had conceived an impression of such indefinite horror, and which is said to strike a panic into the stoutest heart, and though there was nothing so formidable in the sound itself so far as strength of lungs could render it so, one good Kentucky *scream* being worth a dozen of them, yet there was certainly a peculiar, inimitable intensity of savageness and cruelty, and fierce triumph, in these native wild notes of the forest, which was far from disappointing my expectations, and I could readily imagine the panic, that in an unprotected situation, would strike into the heart of an individual, at hearing the sudden war whoop.

It is not the heroic battle shout of a generous enemy, but something less human, pertaining more to the cruel instinct of the bloodthirsty wild beast; like the howl of the carniverous hyena, or the suppressed ferocious scream of a feline animal.

The yells followed the discharge of the rifle, and the triumph of taking a scalp—like their firing, they are desultory, repeated at different intervals, and the compass of the whoop is similar to that of the cheer on a fox chase.

The Serjeants had called the roll, but few of the officers had got up when the alarm commenced. The Col's voice was soon heard shouting to fall in, and giving the necessary orders cooly and deliberately, and our companies fell into line with the order and alacrity of veteran troops.

The Indians were seen when they made the attack, some to rush from behind the walls of the burnt sugar house which stood at about 250 yards from the Camp, where they had concealed themselves, others were shooting through the windows at our men, about 30 of whom had gone unarmed into the brush to get wood, and some to gather sugar cane as usual.

Hennesy, an Irishman, was one of the first who was seen, endeavoring to make his escape at the top of his speed. The Indians tried to cut him off in the road, which ran by the sugar house, to the Camp, but he passed by them through a shower of bullets, some of which cut his clothes, and got safe to the Camp. Some others were fired at and narrowly escaped.

As soon as the Indians saw that we were preparing to attack them, they made off—running in extended single file across the cane field into the woods. They were painted in their war colors, black and red; some had blankets on them which flaunting in the breeze, and their long scalp-locks streaming in the air, gave them a singularly wild and warlike appearance, and one of them, who appeared to be the chief, rode on horseback. In less than five minutes after the alarm, we were on the march; the Lexington riflemen being thrown out in the van. The Irish Volunteers were left to protect the fort and the sick.

We made a circuit passing by the mill, and on our way came upon tracks of blood, which led us to one of the men belonging to our company, who was shot and scalped and lying on his face. We picked him up, and then halted a while to give a general whoop by way of challenge to the enemy, to show themselves and give us fight.

The woods rung with our shouts and screams, and from the earnestness and vigour with which the countrymen raised the shrill wood whoop, they no doubt thought, as the Kentuckians did, who exclaimed, when they went to fight the savages fror the first time, and heard their yells, "Oh wake snakes my red hearties—if you are for screaming that a sort we can *outscream* you any time."

The challenge had no effect except to create

from them in return, a kind of chuckle, which several thought they heard at a distance in the woods, as they were retreating.

After skirting one or two hammocks in which we thought they were, but not being able to find them, we returned, and on our way back came across two other men dead; one a veteran Irishman, whom they had not time to scalp, and another man of our company, who was scalped.

In these instances, as in others that I afterwards saw, the hair was not all taken off, but only a portion around the crown; as much as they can grasp in the hand, and peel off.

> "From the skull they had stripped the flesh,
> As ye peel the fig when the fruit is fresh."

It was a horrid sight! my feelings shrunk within me. It was enough to cause one to shudder with horror to think of the dreadful sensations of these murdered men, when they thought themselves suddenly shot down in cold blood, and in the power of the barbarous scalping knife, without the slight satisfaction of being able to defend themselves for one moment and to die warmed with the spirit of resistance.

Winster, the first one we picked up, was seen by some one who was near him to fall on his knees at the first fire—he ran wounded a short distance; was again shot in the head and other parts of his body, and fell dead.

A negro who belonged to the Camp was walking in company with him, and they had approached to within 20 or 30 yards of the ruins of the sugar house, when the nengro whispered to him not to go any farther, that there were Indians concealed behind the sugar house, but Winster disregarding the caution, went on; the negro knew the way in which to deal with Indians, and was careful not to betray to them that he had discovered them—he turned slowly and indifferently on his heel, and did not run but walked back, whispering as he passed others on his way, that Indians were there to fly. The Indians did not shoot at him.

From the number of balls in the bodies, as many as seven or eight being taken out of one of them, the assassins must have fired at them on the ground after they were dead.

After we returned to camp, we gave another whoop, in order to show the Indians, who might think that we were dismayed and terror stricken by this bold and successful sally of their's, that we were not in the least dispirited, and only wanted them to give us a chance.

Orders were given to breakfast as quickly as possible, to be ready for an excursion through the Swamps, to pursue the trail.

Every one now assembled about Ben Wiggins, the guide, to hear his opinion of the number of Indians who had made the attack—what part they were, and whether it was probable they would come back again or not. Ben was a mulatto, who was rather advanced in life, had high cheek bones, like an Indian, and was generallly thought to be a half-breed, but he asserted positively that he had no Indian blood in him. He used to drive cattle among the Indians, and was well acquaited with them, and the country. He was at the battle of Dunn Lawton, and had got severely wounded during the retreat in the boats, and still had one of his arms in a sling.

He said there might have been about 40, or

50 of them. That they were Philip's party, who had ravaged that part of the country. He did not think they were more, though Philip had upwards of 150 warriors.

He did not think that they would make another atttack, unless it might be the next morning early, as they would spend the rest of the day and night, in rejoicings over the scalps they had got.

He said they would halt after going a short distance, to stretch the scalps on a pole—they would then paint them red inside, and fix them on sticks also painted red, and carry them to their chief. Old Ben had repeatedly warned the men that "if they went running about in that way without guns, they would one day or another, some of them get *sculped*."

I could not help congratulating myself on my narrow escape, having been at the precise place an hour the morning previous, gathering sugar cane.

It threatening to rain very violently, the expedition was countermanded, and we proceeded to the solemn duty of burying out men. The funeral escort consisted of a corporal's guard of eight men, and the officers followed in reversed rank—no arms were carried, and there was no solemn dead march; but in silence we proceeded to the burial ground. I thought of the beautiful lines on the burial of Sir John Moore, which have been attributed to Byron.

> "Not a drum was heard, nor a funeral note,
> As his corpse from [to] the rampart we hurried," &c.

It was an awful occassion, and inkling of the hard-heartedness of war who is no respecter of the dead. The imposing scene of a burial at sea has been often described—where the sad relic of mortality is launched on a plank into the deep and gurgling ocean, which closes frightfully over its victim—but in this, I thought that there was as much to awaken intense, and unpleasant reflection: the hasty consignment just as they were in their bloody garments, and caps, drawn over they gory heads, without coffin, or consecration by prayer, to the shallow trench of three fellow-beings, who not two hours since, had been enjoying like us, the breath of life.

The following morning, I had to take command of eight men in the boats, to go and bring what provisions [provision] was at Fort Bulow, and our men who had been left there.

The Tomoka river, which is pretty wide here, continued for two miles, the right side being nearly the whole way a sandy bluff—its embouchure united with that of the Halifax, which is here a wide and beautiful ocean stream. Soon after, we came in sight of the ocean, and after passing a large bay, entered Bulow creek.

It was a fine warm morning, and the Alligators were more numerous than I had ever seen them any where in Carolina, and some very large—the shore was alive with their unwieldy shapes, launching into the water out of the mud every instant.

Met with many different kinds of water birds, among which most numerous and conspicuous, was the Stolid Wood Pelican, taking his siesta on the gentle wave, and looking, with his long, ponderous, curved bill resting on his neck, like a grave Turk smoking his Chibouque.

These stupid, heavy birds, are about the size of a goose. They let you get very near them, and are easily shot. They are called *Pelicans* from the pouch which they have, which however is small, and *Wood Pelicans*, because they frequent the forests sometimes, and are to be seen perched on the tops of tall Cypresses, resting their bill in the manner described on their necks. They are common with us in Carolina.

"The social prattling coot, enrobed in blue, and the squeeling water hen, with wings half expanded, tripped after each other over the watery mirror."

I am uncertain whether the bird I saw was the common coot, or the Florida Gallinule, as described by Charles Bonaparte. It appeared to me as it flew across the creek a little distance off, to be much darker and of a more glossy hue than the coot. Wilson's print of the purple Gallinule, the Sultana hen or Porphyrion of the Ancients, differs from Bonaparte's. The former is of a shining purple, with red legs—the latter a sooty black, with lighter or cinereous under parts, and yellow green legs. The bird I saw was much of this latter description. It seemed of a beautiful satin black, appeared of solitary and shy disposition, and skimmed the glossy surface with a moderate and graceful flight from marsh to marsh. The gallinule is said not to frequent brackish marshes. This was a little brackish.

Startled from her silent recess in the rushy coves, the tawney Indian Pullet. With short and interrupted flight, now resting, now rising again on low, and straight bent pinion, she fled before our bow.

The soft, delicately mottled plumage of this bird is handsome, when viewed near. They are common in our rice fields, are of a solitary nature and are great hiders. Their flesh is esteemed good eating.

In one of the deep cabbage swamps, we beheld two fine, fat steers browsing, and were strongly tempted to shoot them, but it would have been disobeying orders, and the report of our guns might have drawn Indians upon us, whom, in our present situation, we were not particularly anxious to encounter.

After a row of about five hours, we arrived at the Fort. We found our Sergeant and his men bolted and barred, and looking broken and haggard, from the constant fatigues of watching. They expected every day and night to be made a sacrifice of, and nearly the whole garrison was on duty every night. A very hearty welcome, it may be supposed, was given us—and Hartley soon placed before me a huge Corn bread, of the size of an English Cheese, just fresh from the oven, the brown crust half splitting invitingly, and leaving the crumbling, mellow, white inside, and perfuming the air with the delicious odour of the bakery. Next to this, he placed on the table (for this was another luxury we enjoyed at Bulow's, which we did not elsewhere) a large platter of beef-steaks!—part of a present which a teamster from Hernandez' had lately brought; enough to have dined four men, to which generous fare my appetite it did ample honor, and with the addition of a glass or two of cold water, (those who have ever drank out of a tin cup, know what the luxury of a tumbler is) I made a repast which left me in an excellent humor.

The Sergeant, mean time, who was a tall

thin, sharp-featured, good-natured Santee-man, obliging, bustling, and withal extremely loquacious, entertained me with a narrative of the hardships, and constant anxieties the garrison had suffered, and the despondency they had labored under, thinking that we had gone on, and left them to stay here, they did not know how long, and he gave an account of how he had disposed every thing in the best possible way for the safety of the garrison.

"Lord! Lieutenant," said he, "you don't know the trouble I have been in. I hav'nt slept a wink hardly, since you left us here. I know'd, Sir, every thing depended on me, and it was my duty to do the best I could, and make every thing as comfortable, and secure as I could. Now, Lieutenant, I ask you, war'nt I right to keep the men up as much as possible, when I know'd Indians were a covorting about us all the time? I know the men think hard of me for it, and abuse me, and look on me as wanting to hold a high hand over them, and all that, because their towers of duty has to come round so often, and I tell you what, Lieutenant, I had a pretty tight job to make one or two on 'em obey orders. The Doctor must have told you of the scuffle I had with that fellow Walters?"

'Yes, he drew his knife on you?'

'That's what he did—and would have put it into me, if I hadn't a been a little too sharp for him; but it takes a cute man to get the better of me.'

'Why did you not have him put in the guard house, if he would not obey orders?'

'Oh, I had that done pretty soon—we hai'nt quarrelled since then. The Captain left me here, Lieutenant to do my duty, and I did not care for any man, while I know'd I was doing it.'

Hartley now took me, as night was drawing on, to show me his arrangements.

'You see, Lieutenant,' said he, pointing to a huge block or two of wood, 'I had those rolled in to make fire of, as they don't blaze—its nice, good, dry wood full of the heart, and one of them blocks will burn a whole day and night.and make fire enough to cook and warm the men, and wont throw a bit of light in the sentinel's eyes, nor show them. Then there's water in a pail, always ready by, to out it, in case there's any alarm. The first relief is going on now; you see Lieutenant, we are obliged to have five on a tower, and three reliefs; its very hard for us, and we have two down sick, and one getting the measles.'

'And Eagle, what's the matter with him, that he is making such wry faces; is he too sick.'

Matthew was plucking away at his nose, and working his countenance into all kinds of contortions, without making any answer. At length he smiled, and pulled a jigger out of his nose, which had lodged itself in one of the thick lobes of his nostrils, producing great pain.

———

CHAPTER X.

—"Zounds!
What, more strange sights and sounds?"

I had not lain down ten minutes, before Hartley appeared at my side. 'Lieutenant,' he whispered, 'one of the sentinels says he hears strange noises—he has heared them two times—I hear'n them once myself.'

'Well, Hartley,' I answered, 'I will get up and listen.' The sentinel was questioned, and said that he heard distant noises like whooping and loud noises, as of negroes going through the woods. I listened some time, but could hear nothing except the clatter of the sergeant's sword as he visited each sentinel, the whispering that passed between them, and the constant, loud coughing of the. men, which prevented every fancied sound from being distinctly realized, and I lay down again—but it was vain to think of sleeping.

'Lieutenant,' whispered Hartley again, at the shed door, 'there seems like there's a fire not far in the woods; you better come, and take a look at it.'

So up I got again, put on my great coat, for the night was damp and chilly, and looked over the curtain in the direction the sergeant pointed out.

'If that ain't, a fire, and pretty nigh too, my name ain't Hartley. Boys,' he whispered louder, 'don't all of you be looking this way—keep a good look-out t'other side—keep a good look out—they only put that fire to blind us.'

There was a light appearance upon the horizon, but whether it was a fire, or only the sand reflected from the road, through the opening in the dark woods, I could not be certain,

'Lord, sir, how can you see sand in a dark night like this,' said Hartley, 'trust me I have seen fire too often in the woods, not to know that that's one.'

As however the light whatever it was did not increase nor diminish, but remained the same for some time, and everything seemed quiet out of doors, I concluded that there was no use for me to remain in the disagreeable air, and advised Hartley to follow my example and take some rest, and to leave the care of the garrison to the corporal, who should wake us immediately if any thing occurred to excite farther [further] apprehension. He really seemed in want of rest, and so we lay down. The moment Hartley's head touched his knapsack, he fell into a profound slumber, and began to snore—I also was inclining to a doze, when my ears became sensible of a strange sound; I got wide awake and listened. I heard it immediately again. At first it sounded like a shrill horn wound long and clear close under the curtain of the fort. The next blast was louder and more sonorous—a dismal and horrid yell which was prolonged, and ended in a hideous moan.

I sprang up and seized my gun. The Indians, thought I, have surrounded us—they know our small force and the better to secure their prey they think to terrify us, and strike a panic into us with their yells, that they may rush in upon us at a greater advantage.

The Corporal ran in to wake us—he said these were the same sounds only much louder and nearer that had been heard before.

Hartley was as sound as a top—it went hard with me to wake the poor fellow, but it was necessary to have, instantly, every man of our slim force out, ready to meet the assault in time, and I roused him. It does not take more than one push, or a single utterance of the startling monosyllable "up," to make a good soldier, upon an Indian Campaign, however worn down he may be, jump up; and it is astonishing, how quick, in these cases, the faculties recover from their somnolency. The Serjeant heard but the fag end of the yell, and making no other than the exclamation. "That's them," he was on his legs in a second, grasped his musket in one hand, and his drawn sword in the other, and sallied out; his sharp countenance looking from beneath his fierce, hastily put on Mocknuter, as savage as Don Quixotte's. [Quixote].

No sooner had we stepped out of the threshold of the shed than a volley (for I can use no more appropriate term,) of the most horrific yells, screams, howls, whines, and moans jumbled up together in the most dreadful confusion and prolonged, and alternating with deafening and most dismal cadences like the distracting uproar and caterwauling of all the fiends and furies from the Infernal regions, greeted our ears.

The first object I beheld was the sentinel running in, half frightened out of his wits, from the gate where he had been stationed. The blood mounted into my veins—I cocked my gun—I knew that by the stern laws of war, his life should pay the forfeit of his cowardice, but I could not do what a more heated temper or severer discipline might have prompted, and through he really appeared overwhelmed with terror at being alone in an exposed situation and the enemy upon us as he thought, there was some allowance to be made for his panic, and his belief that the fort was already stormed by the savage host, and that he might as well be fighting in company, as perish alone.

I threatened, and ordered him back and put

another sentinel with him, as the post was an important one.

The yells appeared to be in the direction of the Dead Oak wilderness, about the sugar mill, and at times as close as the negro houses. They ceased, and then were renewed with the same violence. It was a moment of intense suspense, every man crouching and straining his eyes throught the loop-holes—every bayonet fixed and ready, expecting every moment to see let slip the dogs of war. But no enemy came.

'What think you, Hartley,' said I, 'are they wolves or Indians?'

'Not a bit of wolves," he whispered, 'no wolves would make so many different noises.'

'Nor do I think now, that any human beings could make such sounds as those.'

'Listen—listen.'

And again the awful conclamation arose—it had changed position and now filled the wild recesses of the black and frowning hammock south of us. It began with one deep richtoned lorn, and protracted howl, something like the baying of an ancient hound, but infinitely more hollow, more savage, and more wildly musical—other howls then joined in with it—gradually they arose to a frenzied pitch—now they united in an exstatic discord of snarling yells, feline screams, and whooping barks, in a manner similar, (only ten times more loud and sonorous,) to the furious baying and yelping of various dogs at the moon.

'It's all a contrivance,' whispered Hartley, when the noises ceased, 'to gully us—an Injin can imitate like the Old Boy; so they says that knows them.' I was inclined however to think otherwise; and that the noises proceeded from a pack of wolves, and may-be panthers, or wild cats, who had encountered each other in their nightly prowl.

The men began to get tired of watching; and one by one slunk off to the embers to warm themselves, chat, and interchange different opinions. Some had heard wolves howl before, and were satisfied that no Indians could holla like them, while others still doubted. Some continued to watch, and others quietly wrapped themselves up in their blankets, and began to snore before the fire.

The moon by this time had risen, and in her pale light the forest of tall oaks and cedars dimly appeared, with an aspect of increased desolation and wildness, but on the other side, her beams fell brighter, and with softness upon the winding marsh bound creek; and flickered pleasantly among the quivering tops of the stately Palms. The discordant orgies of the wolves no longer interrupted the sweet hush of the night, and in their stead was only to be heard the feeble skreigh of the night bird, flitting over our heads, and the faint chirrups of the crickets at our feet. I mounted the terrace, and looked abroad over the wild and solitary scene, indulging in one of those melancholy, yet not unpleasing moods one experiences, in finding one's self thrown by accident, or by one's own seeking, into a situation full of romance, of hazard and peril—in that sentimental absorption which a sense of loneliness and adventure away from home produces, which leads into the many dried up channels of thought, awakening the bliss and bale of other times, and scenes

recalling one's self to one's self, and contrasting the strange vicissi-
tudes of life.

I became discontented with the present, and already ere the
cup of excitement had been scarcely tasted, the charms of the
'Indian Campaign' began to lose their rest. With the tender floating of the moon-beams, with the gentle sighing of the tranquil,
love embowering Palm, and the soft flashing of the fire-flies
which had not yet 'paled their ineffectual fires.' and still illumined
the dark leafy coves, I associated nought but peace, the luxury
of a voluptuous and civilized clime, and the enchantments of
love—but alas! I was in the midst of war and wolves, of barrels of
salt pork and beans, and felt that I was exiled among men. A
weariness and despondence crept over me, and so did the chill of
the night, and recollecting that I had to get up before sunrise to
return to the camp, and that it was now past midnight; I retired
to bury my vagrant thoughts, which were getting troublesome in a
few hours of repose.

CHAPTER XI.

Return to the Camp—Orders to move on—Report of the defeat of the Indi-
ans by Gen. Gaines—Arrivals at Camp—Old Ben—An Indian
Tale.

By daylight, all was astir in and out the Fort—some cooking and
baking large corn breads to carry with them—others rolling
the barrels of provisions into the boats, while others kept
guard; for our mishap at M'Crea's had taught us the danger of
going any distance from our lines, without arms. As the boat
could not carry more than 8 men, the rest went by land, and I

returned in the boat: we all arrived at Camp without any adventure in the afternoon.

In the evening, a party who had set off the day before at, the same time that we did, for William's plantation, on the Halifax, where two companies of regulars were stationed, for despatches, returned and brought orders from head quarters, for our regiment to move on with all speed for Volusia, where the left wing was to be assembled, and from thence proceed through the Indian towns.

This news gave us much gratification, as we were tired of being inactive so long, and having been a month coming 50 miles, we were in reality disgusted with this delay, and with the extraordinary mismanagement which had subjected us to the inconvenience of a want of supplies and of the necessary transportation. We seldom had more than three or four days provisions at a time, and had constantly to be sending small detachments after them, which only, by the luckiest chance, escaped being cut off and massacred. Then we had no wagons but a few miserable patched up concerns, and though a great many horses had been sent out from Charleston, we had not enough to pull them. The militia abused Uncle Sam and his officers, for treating them, as they thought in this contemptible manner, and swore, that another time they would 'fight on their own hook,' but that as it was, they would 'stand up to the rack, fodder or no fodder,' and 'go ahead like wheel horses.'

At the same time, we received other news which was neither agreeable nor disagreeable; a courier had brought intelligence that Gaines had defeated the Indians with great loss, and that he and Clinch had them, and all their women and children penned up. The war, it was supposed, would then be closed—we regretted that we had taken all this trouble for nothing, and that while we had been kept idle all this while, others had slipt in, and got all the honor. But on the other hand, some were not sorry that the campaign had proved so short a one, and were consoled at the prospects of seeing home again so soon.

We were joined this evening also by the General of our Brigade, accompanied by a body guard, of 20 horsemen. The rest of the horse were to come on in a day or two, and the remainder of the Regiment, one company of which arrived that evening, were upon their way. The camp looked more animated after this addition to our force, and the excitement of the expected move.

The Col. and old Ben, his right hand man, got no peace from the numerous inquiries about what direction we were to take, what distance we had to go, what kind of road, and whether there was any probability of meeting Indians or not on the way. Such questions as these usually led to others about the Indians, their habits, customs, &c., and as old Ben had been living among them a great deal, he would, when he chose, relate many little anecdotes and tales concerning them, which simple as they were, made an hour pass pleasantly enough, around our camp fires. I found though that he was always most fluent when inspired with a dram, and having lately received an accession of St. Augustine muddy Cognac, to my Caoutchouc magnum. I plied him up to the communicative pitch, and as I have preserved in memory the substance of one or two of the tales he repeated on this occasion, I will relate, only adopting a dress and language of my own occasionally, to suit a civilized taste, without departing from which old Ben said he got from the lips of the 'Blind King' an aged, and loquacious sage, who departed life now many years.

————

NOTCHES
ON THE LIFE AND ADVENTURES OF
YAH-HAH-HAJO.
From the Sticks in the Lodge of the Blind King.

A long time ago, (said the Blind King) before my fathers came into the land we now inhabit, and conquered it. Many years before the people they conquered had come into it, all the tribes of animals upon the earth that walk, or fly, or crawl, lived just as we do—sometimes in peace, sometimes in war with each other; and held councils, and hunted, and lived in towns like us, and spoke as we do.

Now there lived at that time, a Prince of great renown——a great warrior, and a great hunter, whose name was Yah-hah-Hajo. His towns were built under the ground, and among the rocks. He was of a very ancient race, and in his lodge there were many marked skins to show the great deeds, and age of his fathers.

His tribe was the most fierce and warlike of all others, and they roved about every where, and destroyed the people of every other tribe they met with, so that they were very much feared by all, and all, from the Great Deer* without horns, down to the Tokôle** that hides in the earth, sought the alliance, and became tributary, and were subject to Yah-hah-Hajo.

Yet Yah-hah-Hajo was very poor; he was never content with staying any time in one place, and would be out day and night for many moons together from home, hunting, of which he was very fond; and he leapt the forests and the streams, until he was bare of flesh; and as he planted no corn, but depended on the chase for his subsistence, he was always very hungry.

It happened one day that he lay down tired and panting and half famished, after a long chase, by the sea shore. He had not long been napping under the cool shade of the Tala Trees*** before he was awakened by a strange barking which did not seem like the voices of his people or those of any of the neighbouring tribes. He looked and he saw trotting up to him several animals of a tribe which he had never before seen; their bodies were formed like his, but they had not the same red skin; they were besides flatter about the ears, and had not such high cheek bones; but what was most remarkable they were not lean and gaunt like him, but their bodies were covered with fat, and sleek with soft hair, like the feathers of the Wortola.****

Yah-hah-Hajo did not know what to make of these strange looking creatures. He took them for spirits, and as they came up to him he would have fled, but he was so weak from hunger and fear, that he fell backwards and could not move.

---

*The Horse, —so called by the Seminoles.
**Mole.
***Palmetto Tree.
****Whooping Crane.

The strange animals saw his fear, and to show him that they did not intend any harm, they all went away to a little distance, and one of them advanced up to him, and spoke, and said in a soft tone: "Yah-hah-Hajo do not be alarmed, do not think that we are enemies who have come into your country to make war upon you. We are of a peaceful race, and have come from a far country to make friends with you. I am the queen of a powerful people, and my name is Efa—that of my family is the Spaniel—we are the most mild of all the creatures that the Great Spirit has put upon the earth. We are a favoured race, and the happiest that can be—having always plenty to eat—hunting only for pleasure, and not caring to eat what we catch—having so many nice things else. We will take you along with us, and show you how we live."

While she spoke, Yah-hah-Hajo could not help admiring Efa's soft white skin, her chinque pin eyes, and her beautiful curled tail that swept the ground like a flake of snow —he compared it with that of cunning eyed Choola, a maiden of the Fox tribe, of whom he was once enamoured, and thought Efa's much the handsomest. But what pleased him most was her round plump figure, which he eyed so hard that Efa blushed, and hid her face in her paws—but she had much more cause to have run away, for had not Yah-hah-Hajo being restrained by the fear of her people, many of whom were sufficiently fierce looking, and seemed of different dispositions from her, he would have devoured poor little Efa on the spot

He thought it would be safer and wiser to accept her proffered hospitality, and satisy his craving hunger on some of those good things she spoke of—but he was half unwilling to trust himself in the power of strange people whom he did not know, and hesitated.

Efa perceiving his doubts, scratched off a silver collar that she wore on her neck, and put it on Yah-hah-hajo's neck, and barking, and making signs to her attendants, several of them came up with strings of beads in their mouths, and parcels of curious fine skins of Animals, which Yah-hah-hajo had never seen before, and laid them at his feet, and by these presents they succeeded in persuading Yah-hah-hajo to go with them to their town which they had built upon the sea shore.

Here he was surprised at all that they saw. The dogs, (for so these animals were called) lived in a very different manner from the wolves. They had large kennels above ground, and workmen to build them; whereas the wolves scratched out their own holes, or lived in the first cave they came across; the dogs eat out of platters, as we do, and lapped their victuals softly, whereas the wolves tore the flesh of every thing they eat, on the ground, and would swallow a whole rabbit at a morsel.

After Yah-hah-hajo had satisfied his hunger, and eaten up all the good things which Efa had set before him, of which many were new kinds of roots, that he had never seen in the woods, and much was game, of which the dogs are fond, though not as much so as the wolves; he got over his desire to devour Efa, and did not show his teeth, and look at her so hard, but he now admired her more, and glanced roguishly now and then at her large, soft dark eyes, as he smoked his pipe, with his raggy tail drawn under his legs, and one of his paws laid on Efa's, at the door of her lodge.

Nor was Efa displeased with the noble countenance, and magnanimous qualities of so great a chief as Yah-hah-Hajo, and she hinted, that she thought they might exchange sticks*, and live very happily together.

But Yah-hah-Hajo, who was very proud, and had a hankering to pay his court to the daughter of Catsha-Tustenagge, a powerful warrior, with whom he wished to be on good terms, which he thought a more suitable alliance for him, paid little attention to Efa's advances, and he was so ungrateful that he spent only half the year with her, (it must be recollected, said the blind king, that years with the brutes were the same as days with us), and one night, as soon as it was dark, all of a sudden he started up on his feet, and with the most dreadful howlings, that alarmed the whole town, and made the heart of Efa very sad; he dashed off wildly into the woods for home.

Efa was much grieved that he should treat her in this way, after all her kindness and hospitality to him, and concluded that some evil Maneto must have suddenly possessed him, to make him howl so, and run off in such a hurry, and she called her councillors together, to devise means to bring Yah-hah-hajo back.

Then the conjurers, after drinking much of a drink like our black drink, said, that they would send another spirit to drive the evil spirit out of Yah-hah-hajo; and they raised a spirit whom

---

*Marry.

they called Wyhôme, and sent her after Yah-hah-hajo.

Wyhôme overtook Yah-hah-hajo at midday, at the river Hil-aka*—sleeping on the shore of the Big Pond;** by the side of the silvor [silver] Wekiwa*** under the shade of the fruitful Alaha and Tala**** trees, and as she knew he would drink from the cool fountain, as soon as he awoke, Wyhôme mingled bitter waters with the waters of the Wekiwa.

Yah-hah-hajo awoke, and he was surprised to see the water which before was still, and only a little pool, now dancing about, bubbling up, and tumbling out of the rocks, and wide deep enough for two or three canoes to float in, and he saw a stream, besides, flowing from it, through a beautiful meadow which was not there before.

As the bright waters sparkled up before him, they kept singing out continually, *chumpa, chumpa, chumpa,***** so invitingly, that he thrust his whole head in, over his eyes and ears, and drank till he could drink no more.

When Yah-hah-hajo took his head out, he felt as if he was all on fire, and the first thing he thought of was to run and plunge into the deep middle of the Hilaka to cool his body.

As he stepped on the mud of the river bank, and jumped off, his foot lit, by accident, upon the tail of a cross, fierce old chieftain, who was snoring in the mud, whose name was Hulputta-Hajo.

---

*The St. John's.
**Lake George.
***Silver spring on the Western side of Lake George.
****Orange and Palmetto.
*****Chumpa, sweet.

As Hulputta-hajo and his Tribe lived the greater part of their time in the water—and Yah-hah-hajo lived altogether on dry land, they had not much to do with one another, though occasionally they met. It was upon one of these occasions that Yah-hah-hajo stole some fish, which Hulputta-hajo was drying in the sun, before the mouth of his lodge; and ever since, Hulputta-hajo had owed him a grudge.

His anger was dreadfully aroused at being disturbed from his nap, and when he found who it was had trod upon his tail, he became furious, thinking that Yah-yah-hajo did it out of contempt for him.

'Wah!' he grunted, as he slid his corpulent body from the mud into the river, at the same time spurting a torrent of water into Yah-hah-hajo's face—'Ho! it is well—I have you in the water, brother; I will chastise you for stealing my fish, and mashing my tail.'

So saying, he raised the war-whoop, so terribly loud that all the fishes in the river near by were stunned with the noise, and came floating down the stream like dead—at the same time he brandished his tomahawk with his tail.

Yah-hah-hajo was almost blinded by the floods of water that came pouring in torrents into his eyes, but he returned the war-whoop with fierce spirit, and shouted 'TUSTA-LA-KA-A' with such a dreadful howl, that the fishes were startled out of their trance, and fled from the top of the water to the bottom again.

At the same time, he rushed forwards to the battle with all his might and main, thinking he was encountering more than one enemy, but he vented all his fury upon a shadow; for the bitter waters were in his eyes, and he saw forked.

This mistake had nearly cost Yah-hah-Hajo his life, for the real Hulputt-Hajo made at him in the mean time, with his mouth wide open, to swallow him, which he would have done, had not Yah-hah-hajo, with the expert dexterity of a renowned and cunning Warrior, aimed a blow at his head, which struck Hulputta-Hajo under the lower jaw, and cut through the muscles, so that Hulputta-Hajo could not use his lower jaw at all, and was obliged to raise the upper one, and in making a Yah-hah-Hajo, he missed his stroke, which passed clean over Yah-hah-Hajo's head, while his jaw fell empty on the other side of him, with a crash, like the falling of trees, in a storm wind.

And (said the Blind King) he carried this wound to the grave, and it is thus with Hulputta-Hajo's children to this day. They cannot raise the bottom jaw.

Before Hulputta-Hajo, who was very corpulent and un-wieldy, could turn round again, Yah-hah-Hajo leaped upon his back, and fell to scalping him—but Hulputto-Hajo's head was so hard, he could make no impression upon it.

While he was trying his utmost, Hulputta-Hajo gave a whirl and a flirt, and spun round so rapidly, with his head and tail cocked up out of the water, the Yah-hah-Hajo, who had the bitter waters already whirling through his brain, be-came so giddy, that he fell into a trance, and Hulputta-Hajo, seizing him by the tail, pulled him down into his dark lodge, deep under the waters.

When Yah-hah-Hajo had recovered from his

trance, he found himself laid on his back, in a dark, dismal-looking, stinking place, full of skeletons, of bones of deer and other animals, cranes, and other birds, bull frogs, and all manner of fishes.

'Umph,' said he, 'Hulputta-Hajo is making his fire to roast me; I suppose he will be here immediately—Well, Yah-hah-Hajo will die like a warrior.'

While he was taking matters so cooly, his paw happened to rest upon some long, cold thing, that was near him, and seeing something like a coal of fire, he took it for a pipe, ready lit.

'Ah hah!' exclaimed Yah-hah-Hajo, 'I see Hulputta-Hajo has been kind enough to leave me a pipe—I will smoke.'

As he took hold of the pipe, a voice cried out 'Wah! Wykas-chay. (quit) Let go my nose.'

'Ugh!' exclaimed Yah-hah-Hajo 'who are you?'

'I am Esapanota,'* answered the voice, 'what do you take my snout for?'

'Good,' exclaimed Yah-hah-Hajo, 'I took it for a pipe. Well, I suppose you are Hulputta-Hajo's executioner, and have come to slice off a part of my body for his supper—if you will just cut these strings, so that I can turn over I will shew you a nice piece of the loin that you may have.'

'Do my eyes deceive me in the dark," exclaimed Esapanota, 'or do I not hear the voice of the great king and destroyer of nations, Yah-hah-Hajo?'

---

*The Gar—This part of the Blind King's of the Gar fish living on friendly terms with the Alligator, is supported by Bartram, who says that the Alligator does not prey on the Gar, either because he is too hard to digest, or out of respect to their similar avocations and they hunt in company for fish.

'You see—you hear—I am Yah-hah-Hajo.'

'You have mistaken my intentions,' said the Gar 'Yo-hee! by the name of the Great Spirit; but it grieves me to see so great a warrior confined in chains, and I would fain release you, O Yah-hah-Hajo, only I fear it might cause me my life, for I am almost the only company that Hulputta-Hajo sees, and if he suspected me, being so much stronger than I am, he would kill me. But—let me see—there is the Terrapin, I will put it upon him, he is always about some mischief or other, nipping at this and that, and Hulputta-Hajo will readily believe that he cut the strings; besides he has the knack of hiding his head from danger and always gets out of a scrape better than I can.' So saying, Esapanota, with his sharp teeth cut the thongs, and Yah-hah-Hajo found himself at liberty.

'Now be off quick,' said Esapanota, 'or Hulputta-Hajo will be back from fishing.'

'By my Scalp-lock,' said Yah-hah-Hajo, 'I wish that he would come, that I may be revenged on him; but first, let me get out of this dark ugly mud and water hole; can you show me the way, good Esapanota, out of this cursed place?'

'I can go with you as far as there is water enough,' said the Gar, and leading the way, he piloted Yah-hah-Hajo to an end of the hole, where he could see a glimmering of light and a dry passage leading upwards. Here, after embracing Esapanota, and thanking him, Yah-hah-Hajo scrambled up, and found himself once more on dry land.

The entrance to the hole was at the side of a cove, and the first thing he saw when he got out was Halputta-hajo dancing his war dance in the water, and rehearsing his exploits in the presence of his squaws.

'Ah-hah! Tusta-la-ka-ha-ah,' shouted Yah-hah-Hajo, overjoyed, and raising the war-whoop; 'what are you making such a fuss for, Hulputta-Hajo?—your squaws are laughing at you.'

Hulputta-Hajo was so enraged with passion, that his prisoner should have escaped, and should taunt him thus before his squaws, that he drew in so much water through his nostrils that all the streams which flowed into the Hilaka were dried up, and he swelled himself out to so terrible a size, and so much smoke came from his mouth and nostrils that there was a fog on the river for a week after, and losing all caution in his violent rage, he ran full speed on the shore after Yah-hah-Hajo; but Yah-hah-Hajo had now the advantage and his activity eluded with ease all Hulputta-Hajo's strokes—while, furious to avenge himself on his odious foe for dragging him into his nasty hole, he belaboured and lambasted Hulputta-Hajo most severely, making every stroke tell, until the scales flew from his back like leaves from the yellow trees in the wintry moons—and he was half dead.

As the noise of the dreadful combat reached the ears of several of Hulputta-Hajo's tribe, whose war whoops could now be heard setting the whole river in a roar, Yah-hah-Hajo thought it was time to take to his heels, having gained the victory, but he would not go, before he carried away some trophy with him, and as Hulputta-Hajo's scalp was too difficult to take, he contented himself with biting off his ears and a piece of his tail, and took his tomahawk.

As Yah-hah-Hajo was pretty tired after this adventure, he did not go far, but halted in a deep hammock, where he knew he would be safe from his enemies, and laying down, he soon fell fast asleep, and did not wake until after day night.[light]

After the fatigues of the preceding evening, he was very hungry, when he rose to renew his journey, and after going a little way, meeting with a Gopher's hole, he stopped to get some refreshment. The master of the lodge was sitting at his door.

'Kowîkay—I am come,' said Yah-hah-Hajo, saluting him; but the Gopher made no answer, and did not welcome him, and Yah-hah-Hajo saw that he was in mourning, and fortified in his shell, as if he expected some danger.

'How's this,' inquired Yah-hah-Hajo, 'are any of your relations dead, Kowîkay? and do you fear me, that you are shut up in this manner. I am your friend.'

How am I to know that,' said the Gopher—'Early this morning, the Eagle passed this way, and informed me that my cousin, the Terrapin, was killed by Hulputta-Hajo, or some of his tribe, who cut off his head, while he was sleeping, unsuspecting, on a log—either that fierce tribe wish to extend their hunting grounds, or are enraged at some injury. They are at war with all their neighbours. The Eagle was at the Hilaka, hunting peaceably as usual, and as he made a swoop after a fish, one of Hulputta-Hajo's warriors made a slash at him, and took off his scalp—he was perfectly bald-headed when he stopped here on his way, to collect some allies to go against them. This is the cause of my mourning, stranger, for my cousin, the Terrapin's death, and I have enclosed myself in this fortification as, for aught I know, you may be one of Hulputta-Hajo's allies, and on account of my kin to the Terrapin, I expect an attack every moment.'

'Convince yourself to the contrary,' said Yah-hah-Hajo, if you will take a look brother Kowîkay, I will show you what will prove that I am not the ally, but the powerful foe of Hulputta-Hajo.'

At this assurance, Kowîkay sidled a little back towards the mouth of his hole, and cautiously opening the door of his shell a little, he peeped with half of his black eye out, and seeing the end of Hulputta-hajo's tail, and his ears and tomahawk, which Yah-hah-Hajo flourished about his head, he was at once aware of the valiant and powerful friend whom he had the good luck to meet with, and almost jumped out of his shell for joy, that the death of his cousin had been avenged. He gave Yah-hah-Hajo such a hearty gripe by the paw, that he was fain compelled to howl out with the pain, and then he conducted him into his lodge, and set refreshments before him.

These consisted of nothing more than a few tasteless roots and herbs, a half of a salamander, and a half of a toad. Poor Yah-hah-hajo, whose stomach ached with hunger, looked askance at this pitiable fare, and sighed when he thought of Efa's platters of boiled corn, and hauches of venison; he had half a mind to abuse and beat Kowîkay for his meanness and want of hospitality, but he recollected that he was poor, and did the best he could, and that he would get no good out of him if he did beat him, but would ony hurt himself more than he would Kowîkay.

He therefore behaved like a gentleman, and did not betray any vexation, but devoured in a trice all that was before him.

Kowîkay thought that his own appetite was none of the slowest, but the voracity of Yah-hah-hajo struck him dumb, and he could not stammer out an apology for having nothing more in his lodge, but looked very blank, and got in the corner, as if he was afraid Yah-hah-hajo would eat him up next, from the ravenous eyes that he cast about him.

In his researches, Yah-hah-Hajo spied out something in a corner of the lodge, which he took to be a nest of young rabbits—a dish of which above all others, he was excessively fond. So without any ceremony, or asking Kowîkay's leave, but giving his lips one smack, upon them he pounced, and before Kowîkay could move the length of his body to hinder him he had swallowed nest and all its contents at one gulp but wheu! blood and thunder! who can paint the horror of Yah-hah-Hajo when he discovered that he had swallowed a whole brood of Rattlesnakes! His stomach hissed louder than it did when he jumped into the Hilaka on fire with the bitter waters of Wyhôme, and he felt as though he was at the stake and his enemies were shooting ever so many burning arrows into him.

'The Great Spirit save us!' exclaimed Kowîkay, turning up the whites of his eyes, and trebling all over with fear, 'what have you done, brother Yah-hah-Hajo? —you have eat up all

Chitta-Mico's Papooses—and here he comes—what will become of us?'

And sure enough, the Dread Chieftain who was basking out of doors in the sun, being alarmed by the hissing below, and apprehending some danger to his little ones came walloping down the stairs, sounding his shrill war-whoop, and beating his drum, foaming at the mouth, and his eyes looking as green as the ponds in the moon of yellow leaves.

He was so blinded with rage that he did not immediately perceive Yah-hah-Hajo, but fell upon Kowîkay, thinking he had been meddling with his Papooses.

The wary Gopher, however, shut himself up on his shell tight, and Chitta-Mico struck at him in vain and only gave him a slight wound in one of his paws.

In the mean time Yah-hah-hajo with the gallantry which distinguishes a great warrior, and overwhelmed with reverence for the grand chieftain of the snakes, could not contain himself, but shouted amid the din—'Oh Chitta-Mico, great governor of snakes, great grandfather—do not expend your useless anger upon poor Kowîkay, who will not fight, but hides himself behind a tree. I respect you, great chieftain of the snakes, and to show it, will fight you, skin to skin, and tooth to tooth; how could you Chitta-Mico think that Kowîkay who feeds on mice and little frogs, should have done you this injury? Know that it is I—I Yah-hah-hajo, who in an evil hour, led on by the furious cravings of this cursed belly of mine, have swallowed your Papooses.

'Swallowed my papooses!!' thundered Chitta-Mico,

astounded at the horrid calamity, and at the same time raising his head and neck erect, and glowing with vengeance, out of the coil which he had gathered around him during Yah-hah-hajo's address—'what! swallowed *all* my papooses! —by all the snakes then look out, Yah-hah-hajo,'—and hissing—'Leech-as-tchey' (I will kill you,) and raising his shrill war-cry with re-doubled fierceness, he shot his poisoned arrows, rapid as the lightning at Yah-hah-hajo, who eluded some of them by his agility, but some struck him, and what with the outward pain these occasioned, swelling his joints, and congealing the blood in his veins, and the ceaseless prickings of the lit-tle snakes in his stomach, who were doing their best to as-sist their parent, poor Yah-hah-hajo began to think himself in a bad way; but it was his nature never to despair, and to fight always to the last—so as, soon as Chitta-Mico gave him a chance he seized him by the back, crushed it, and de-molished him at one blow.

As soon as Yah-hah-hajo saw that he had slain Chitta-Mico, he began to repent, and was very sorry and feared much, knowing that now all Chitta-Mico's tribe would be in enmity against him, and that he could never, hereafter hunt in peace on account of them, unless he did something to appease the spirit of Chitta-Mico. So after bowing and mak-ing a thousand apologies to the dead chief for killing him, and having stripped him of his bright war dress, and his drum, he told him that the best atonement he could make to him, was, to restore him to his papooses, and that he would provide him a safe lodge, where they might live comfortably together.

Whereupon he opened his mouth, and requested Chitta-Mico to crawl into it, he lodged him safely in his stomach. Then the little snakes were quiet, and disturbed him no longer; and he licked some of the fat of Chitta-Mico on his wounds, and they immediately healed.

Yah-hah-Hajo having now shaken paws with Kowîkay, and thanked him for his hospitality, without saying a word about the little he had had to eat, proceeded to depart on his way, promising Kowîkay that he would meet him in a few days, with some of his warriors upon the war-path, when they would make an attack upon Hulputta-Hajo's towns; but he must go and pay visit first to Catsha-Tustenagge, who would no doubt join in the entrprise with him.

Though Yah-hah-Hajo meant to keep his word and wampum, he was influenced by private and more important considerations, in going to pay this visit to Catsha-Tustenagge. His thoughts turned to his beautiful yellow speckled daughter, and he saw no better opportunity for him to make a successful courtship, than now when he had two such honorable trophies to show as Huputta-Hajo's tail, and Chitta-Mico's drum. Proud and difficult as he knew Cowowiccohee (such was the name of the tawney daughter of Catsha-Tustenagge) to be, he knew that she would not withstand such high testimonials of Prowess as these, and as he stopped by a glassy pond, to see how he looked with Chitta-Mico's war dress on, he was enraptured with the stately elegance of his form, set off as it was, by such magnificent and glittering attire, and thought himself the handsomest looking fellow that could be.

As he was thus surveying himself, and grinning with delight, and admiration at his pictute in the water, he heard a little way off from him, a great blustering, and looking up, he saw a noted Fop, one whom he despised, of the name of Penwaw* who was dancing, and cutting all sorts of capers before two or three squaws, holding his head up in the air, now setting his arms akimbo, now flapping his sides with them, in an ecstasy of personal admiration and applause, and exclaiming 'Haint-clitz wah-e-sheh—Haint-clitz wah-e-she (very pretty upon my soul—very pretty upon my soul.)

Yah-hah-Hajo looked at him with the most ineffable contempt, but at the same time could not help grudging him his splendid Capa of silk that glittered with gold—the scarlet handkerchief that graced his brow and throat. The beautiful string of scalps that hung from his gorget and the long spurs he wore on his heels. He was vexed to see, at the moment that he was flattering himself that he was the handsomest fellow upon earth, Penwaw assuming such airs in his very presence, as if he was ridiculing him and he felt very wrathy.

'Che-lockse (you lie,) Soole (Turkey Buzzard,)' he exclaimed—'do you dare to say before me that you are better looking that I? and he chased Penwaw, who took to his heels as soon as he heard Yah-hah-Hajo's voice, who, soon catching him, slew him. Then he left him lying on the ground, until he had secured his squaws whom he wished to make prisioners, and

---

*Wild Turkey Cock.

carry as a present to Cowowiccohee, knowing that she would value them highly. This he found no difficult matter, as they were terribly alarmed, and he came upon all three hiding in a bush.

Then stripping Penwaw of his splendid Capa of silk, his scarlet handkerchief that graced his brow and throat, his beautiful string of scalps that hung from his gorget, and the long spurs he wore on his heels, he set out once more upon his journey leading his captives with him.

When Ya-hah-Hajo had got within a little distance of Catsha Tustenagge's town, he turned aside into a shady grove, where there was a spring, to rest, and refresh himself and his captives—just as he was about setting down he heard a great laughing and talking over his head, and looking up he saw Cowowiccohee, and another Hoyden damsel straddling the boughs of a hickory tree gathering nuts—where upon he was shocked, and turned his head modestly down, afraid of offending her, and in a very humble tone first requested permission of her to raise his eyes.

At this speech Cowowiccohee flew into a terrible passion, and sliding down the tree, lighting on all fours, and giving a flirt, she fell upon poor Yah-hah-Hajo and scratched his face well, and almost tore his eyes out, at the same time abusing him and telling him that he was the most impudent wretch on the face of the earth.

After she had thus vented her rage on her lover for his discreetness, she next turned in a fit of jealousy upon the poor captive squaws, and tore their clothes all to pieces, and eat [ate] one of them on the spot.

Yah-hah-Hajo bore his mistress's indignation in good humour, but he could not help cursing in his heart the caprices of women, and blaming himself for his own folly, and for being such a simpleton as not to know that women are offended at nothing in the shape of admiration. He twisted about in his brain what he could say by way of compliment to appease her wrath, and at length bowing and scraping, with a suitable leer of the eye, and with one paw playing with the alligator's tail that hung from his neck by a string, he stammered out, that 'upon his soul he never set eyes upon such lovely whiskers as her's in all his life before.' At which Cowowiccochee screamed out, 'Oh-ho! ha-a-a-ah—mulrowit au-g-h—ha-a-a-h, and walked about, tossing her head up and fanning herself with her tail, and at length she put on an arch smile, and put her paw upon Chitta-Mico's drum that was dangling from Yah-hah-Hajo's belt and asked him in a purring tone, what pretty bauble that was?

When Yah-hah-Hajo told her how he got it, and shewed her Hulputta-Hajo's tail, she gave another scream of satisfaction—'Mulrowit ho-o'—she vowed he was a very clever fellow and to show him how much she applauded his warlike feats she leaped clear over his back, and flirted her tail in his face. She was still more gratified when he declared that he had brought the captives expressly as a present to her; and on the strength of this, immediately devoured another.

Cowowicohee then conducted Yah-hah-hajo to her father's lodge.

During the years that he spent courting, forgetful of Efa, the Dogs, who had multiplied exceedingly, spread over the whole land, and wherever they went, the spirit Wyhôme accompanied them, and filled all the springs and streams with the bitter waters, so that all the tribes which drank of them were poisoned, and as they fell down stupified, the Dogs fell upon them and destroyed them.

But Efa, whose blood flowed in her veins soft as milk, was very sorry, yet she could not restrain the maliciousness and rapacity of her people; the magicians sent all kinds of evil spirits through the land; the blood-hounds sucked the throats of even Yah-hah-hajo's tribe, but they had many hard battles, and the wolves howled so dreadfully, that they generally drove the blood-hounds away; the curs, as they were the most numerous, were always foremost, and squatted themselves down before the very towns of Yah-hah-hajo; and the Terriers, accompanied them, scratching up the trees, and digging up the whole face of the earth wherever they went; and they took squaws from Yah-hah-hajo's tribe, and had children, which are these dogs that we kick about in our lodges, (said the Blind King.)

I have ommitted many other important events in the History and Adventures of Yah-hah-Hajo which the Blind King had notched down, and what I have related, was delivered so imperfectly by Ben, that I have been obliged, in order to connect the raw materials into a tale, to supply some meanings, which perhaps did not belong to the original, and the story ends rather abruptly, in consequence of the defect.

My limits will not permit me to give more

than this one sample, which may serve to show the simple character of the Indian tales.

———

CHAPTER XII.

*Departure from Camp McCrea for Volusia—Wretched nature of the
country—Spring flowers—Escape of a Deer—Arrival at Volusia—
Richland Riflemen—The left wing prepares to cross the St. John's.*

The rest of our regiment not joining us as we expected, after waiting one day, the next morning, 4 companies broke up camp for
Volusia, on the St. John's, leaving behind two with the sick, who
were very numerous, and the horsemen, who were to come as
soon as they could.

The day before, I was attacked with a violent cold, and felt
feverish with symptoms of the measles, but nevertheless resolved
to go on and take my chance of a wagon, when the way was wet,
or I could no longer march.

Our way led through a trail—in some places perfectly
blind—in others, we had to cut down trees, and make a way.
The guide had reported the country as very bad to march
through; but it was horrible. There was hardly a mile of dry
land the whole way—nothing but low pine barrens, flowed
knee deep in many places; low, dismal, boggy, cyprus
swamps, and in one or two places, deep branches or creeks.

The few miserable wagons we were provided with, were
heavily laden, and it seemed impossible that they could ever
pass through these morasses; some tumbled over on the cyprus knee and stumps—others stalled, and the horses

floundered in the bog, and had to be taken out; and while some of the men were employed in dragging them through—the rest were kept standing in water up to their middles for an hour and better.

I had the luck to get into a wagon that was light laden, and drawn by oxen, which got along better than the others, and did not upset; so that I was saved from a wetting which might have cost me my life; but the jolting was nearly as bad, and increased my fever.

After toiling on until evening, we had not made more than 10 miles. The next day, we had very much the same job to perform, and I suffered more, not having taken any medicine, as it was useless and dangerous to take any under such exposure as we were subjected to.

The country was the most dismal, and uninteresting that I have ever seen—transcending infinitely our most wretched pine barrens and swamps in Carolina. It consisted chiefly of a wet prairie surface covered with rank, wiltered grass, and a growth of stunted pines, intersected every here and there with swamps, some of which were nearly a mile in breadth, and characterised by a species of squalid Cypress that grew in them, which Botanists do not distinguish from the taller and finer tree, (Cypressus Distycha.) These did not exceed 15 or 20 feet in height, and had a fir-like appearance. A great part of Florida consists of extensive barren tracts like these, and it is estimated, that, supposing the whole number of acres in the Territory to be 30,000,000, one million or one 30th part, is a very generous allowance for that portion which is capable of cultivation, according to the southern system of cultivation.

A few bright spring flowers enlivened the waste in drier parts; that common, but beautiful and brilliant little gem of the barrens, the yellow *Pinguicula* displayed itself at every step, lifting modestly out of the grass its perfect sided, double-cleft blossom, and attracting the eye in spite of its frequency; the purple species intermingled with it, and also another specious incarnate flower, of the Gynandria-monandria class, which I took to be the *Calopogon pulchellus var. graminifolia* of Elliott, (*Cymbidium pulchellus* of Pursh) with moderate sized blossoms, resupine, on a rather distant terminal spike, and ovate acuminate bracteas; this was in flower in profusion the middle of March—the time of blossoming stated by Elliott is in April and May, and by Pursh in July. Besides these, *Hypoxis erecta,* and *Leptopoda decurrens* (of M'Bride), *Galardia fimbriata* (of Michaux) with deep yellow, semitrifid rays—chaff conspicuously fimbriate, (as it is with all of the genus), and 8 leaved—leaves distinctly decurrent.

In still higher and sandier spots, a species of *Anona* or *Porcelia* (*Asimina,* Elliott) growing from one to two feet high; the flowers appeared to be perfectly developed—the leaves were just putting forth, and I could not determine their exact form; but they were soft and silky—petals not as large as the *grandiflora*, which I met with later in the season, oblong ovate, and not as round; inclining to brown; the interior, smaller petals elliptic, darker, and beautifully barred with deeper purplish brown.

Mr. Elliott describes the Asimina grandiflora

as rarely exceeding 18 or 24 inches in height. Bartram mentions some from 3 to 5 feet. The former describes the petals as yellowish white; the latter as perfectly white. The species I saw, may possible have been the *Asimina grandiflora*, which grew larger and whiter as the season advanced.

To this genus belongs the *Annona Triloba* or paw paw tree.

As we were passing a jungle, or large dried up pond, grown up in tall grass, rush and palmetto, we were suddenly alarmed by the firing of the advance platoons, and the officers behind immediately sprang to their commands, and began to form line to meet an attack. While, for the moment we wondered why the Indian rifles were silent, and all eyes were turned in the direction of the firing to catch the glimpse of an Indian, we beheld a deer bounding off and streaking afar through the woods. It had jumped out of the jungle not many yards from the advance guard, and every man of them had let fly at it without touching it, though many of their cartridges had three buck shot in them, besides ball. They got well laughed at for their bad shooting, and it was well for their credit as marksmen, that it was a deer, and not an Indian, or they would not have heard the end of it for a long time.

We marched about the same distance as the day before, and halted on the edge of a swampy branch, where we expected to meet with trouble, and thought it best to defer till morning the attempt to cross:—this, the guide informed us, was the last bad place, and we would have but seven miles further to go the next day, and a good road. We did not pitch our tents, but bivouacked, as we had done the night before, making large fires at the distance of between two and three hundred yards, outside and around our lines, as Jackson did on the night previous to the battle of Emuckfaw, and on other occasions; by means of which the sentinels could see a good distance before them, and the Indians would be deceived, by taking them for camp fires. But we were not disturbed by them.

The next morning, after some delay in getting over the swamp, we emerged into a high and dry pine barren, and totally different country, rising into swelling hills and gentle undulations, and stretching out into open verdurous lawns, and piny glades, silvered in one or two places with clear, white ponds.

Among the scattering, low, undergrowth, which bordered the road, I noticed in bloom more of the same species of 'Annona,' and the delicate *Ceanothus mycrophyllus*, or Red Root.

We arrived at Volusia before mid-day. The sun was intensely hot, and it was sometime before our tents were pitched. I felt anxious to get into mine out of the sun, as I had a hot fever on me, and the measles began to make their appearance—but to one laboring under fever, a thin tent, under a scorching sun, is as bad as a pair of gossamer breeches in frosty weather, to a Rheumatic; and I no sooner crawled in than I immediately crawled out again.

During this time of my sickness. Gen. Eustis, and some companies of Regulars, arrived in the steamboat: all the horse also, and the balance of our regiment, with the exception of Captain

Quattlebum's company, which remained behind with the sick at M'Crea's, had joined us.

The Richland Volunteer riflemen, under Capt. B. F. Elsmore, had occupied this post a fortnight before our arrival. Capt. Elmore incurred great risks in advancing thus boldly with his single company into the heart, as it was then considered, of the Indian country, and he was told by the people in St. Augustine, that it was madness, and that he would have to fight his way there inch by inch, and be annoyed every day by the Indians after he got there.

The Richland volunteers, however, advanced boldly to the post, and led the van of the Carolina troops in occupying such an important and hazardous station thus early. They were 50 miles from any assistance, surrounded as they had every reason to believe; by the Indians—they had to build them a picquet fort, and many who were youths of the best families, bred up in habits of ease, and unaccustomed to severe bodily toil and fatigue, had to cut huge logs, at the risk of being shot at by the Indians, and carry them a great distance on their shoulders. The provisions also which had been sent them by the steamboat for the depot, had to be taken care of, and they had to go into the swamps and cut down trees and saw planks to make a shelter for them.

The fact that they discovered not a sign of Indians, and remained during this period undisturbed, was afterwards a matter of astonishment to all, especially as it was ascertained by a scouting expedition, which after our arrival here, was made to Spring Garden, 16 miles distant, that a party of Indians had for some time past been living at the latter place, and had removed thence but a few days prior. They were perhaps too much occupied with the movements of Gaines on the west, and the approach of the Carolina force on the east, and had most of them left that neighbourhood, and chose to leave Capt. Elmore's company in possession of the country for the time.

After remaining a few days at Volusia, the left wing commenced on the 22d to cross the St. John's. As the army was ill-provided with waggons, and despatch was all important upon the march, all who were not well enough to march were to be left in garrison with a company to be selected by lot. Among these I found myself compelled, reluctantly enough, to stay.

The lot fell upon Capt. Allen's company, the Barnwell Volunteers.

CHAPTER XIII.

Crossing of the St. Johns—Battle with the Indians—Wounded Men—A dead Indian—A Detachment Encounter Indians—Move of the Left Wing, and plan of the Campaign—Number left in the Picquet Fort at Volusia—A Garrison Life—Mounted Scouts, and Foraging Parties—Florida Cattle.

About mid-day, two companies, Capts. [I. A.] Ashby's and [Thomas] Fripp's, had been put across. Sentinels were thrown out, and they waited for the rest to come over, in the deep low forest, or swamp which bordered the river. As customary on a halt, the men left their places in line, and some were sitting down talking and laughing, some lying down enjoying the cool shade, and others had sauntered a little way off to wash. On a sudden, the crack of rifles sounded, commencing in desultory shots, then immediately ringing in sharp succession, and the shrill war woop followed, until the primaeval forests on both sides of the river sent back the wild echoes of the savage uproar, and there was no telling on which side the foe might next break out.

Now was a scene of confusion, hurry and excitement which would be well worth a representation on canvas. Each company of volunteers headed by its captain was seen rushing to the flatts, without waiting for any orders, each anxious to be first at the combat, and to get first to the rescue. The cool and disciplined regulars were to be seen forming rapidly like clockwork, and drawn up in precise array on board the steamboat, waiting for orders, and ready to act at a moments notice—horses were untethered, and in a moment saddled and mounted, and prancing to the water's edge, and staff officers, and other individuals who were either not attached to any particular command, or who were thrown out in the bustle, were to be seen scampering like mad with the first weapon they could catch hold of, to get over the river to the fight.

Before any had succeeded in crossing, the companies which were surprised and attacked in their unfavorable and disorganised condition, and rallied, and fired two or three rounds, which made the Indians give ground—just after, the

Col. and other officers, and two companies, the Irish Volunteers and Capt. [Thomas] Hibler's of Edgefield came up to the battle ground, and the Indians perceiving their approach, made off. The troops were extended in order to cut them off, but it was too late. In the excitement, Capt. Parker's and Allen's companies, who crossed soon after, met, and in the thick bushes mistaking each other for Indians, both companies fired at each other; but luckily only two men were wounded.

Two companies of U.S. troops also crossed, and some of the mounted men, after some little detention in landing at an unfavorable spot, proceeded to scour the hammock, but being diverted from the trail by the firing of the two companies which had encountered each other, and thinking the Indians were in that direction they left it, and when they returned to pursue it, it was too late, and after going two or three miles, they returned without seeing any thing of the Indians.

In this attack we had 3 of our men killed, and 7 wounded, besides those wounded by accident. One after another they were brought in by the surgeon and his assistants, some shot in the legs; and limping or supported along, others who were more severely wounded, with their heads drooping, and the blood gushing from their necks and trickling down their shoulders.

Our men fought at great disadvantage and were much exposed, while the Indians with their customary caution were concealed behind trees. Several of our men made good shots after they were wounded. Sergeant Grose of Fripp's company received a wound just as he was about to fire. He planted his ball plumb in the tree behind which the Indian was; each then tried who could load quickest and get the first shot. The Indian, with practised dexterity, primed, poured from his powder horn into his rifle, spit a ball out of his mouth into it and, without patch or wadding, gave the butt a slap on the ground, and fired. The bullet struck the Serjeant full in his stomach, but to his astonishment bounded off, it had struck his cross belt. 'Ah! my red rascal,' he exclaimed, 'you did not put in powder enough that time.' Before, however, the pain of his wound would permit him to load and return the compliment more handsomely, and to shew his foe the difference between an Indian chewed bullet and a home cartridge—the Indian had bounded off and vanished, and the brave Serjeant who was unwilling to leave the contest was ordered off the field by the Surgeon.

It was impossible to ascertain exactly the execution done by our fire in the skirmish. A man on board the Steamboat, observed a few Indians get as he thought into the river to cross, some hundred yards above, but he could not see distinctly. The next morning, the body of an Indian was discovered, laid among the bushes at the side of the river, about where the individual had made the observation, and marks were seen where, apparently two or three others had been dragged; some clothing likewise was picked up; if there were any more killed, they must have been sunk in the river. From the blood which their trail showed, they must have suffered not a little.

The Indian found dead, was said, by the guide, and a gentleman who knew him, and supposed to be the chief, Uchee Billy (or Billy Hicks, as his real name was, son of old Hicks) who headed a band of Uchees, that had a settlement at Spring Garden, and made Volusia and the vicinity, the scene of their hostilities—they may have consisted of between 50 and 100 warriors, but it is difficult to say, as they imperfectly disclosed themselves in the woods, and an Indian trail furnishes but equivocal evidence of their number, but from the shots fired, there must have been at least 50. If the body was that of a chief, it had been stripped of any distinguishing marks.

When it is considered that savages are looked upon by some, as little better than wild beasts, that the feelings of our men were excited at the recent loss and injury we had sustained, and that for this and the previous slaughter at McCrea's, we had no revenge, the triumph which some indulged in over this slain Indian (the first victim that the fortune of treacherous war had made an oblation to our arms) which humanity and the sentiment of civilization, that teach us to respect the dead, would on another and a cooler occasion, have arisen in their bosoms to condemn; may be excused perhaps. He was scalped, his body stretched naked upon a pole, and brought into camp for the curious to look at.

I felt myself entrained along with the crowd—nature, philosophy remonstrated—why should I indulge in the vulgar curiosity, to steal a look at the forbidding corrupt clay, to gaze upon the sad remains of a human being?—was it not a petty weakness? was there anything commendable in my acknowledging a feeling of triumph over this solitary slain foe? was there not something shocking and criminal in acknowledging it *thus* over a mutilated, and dishonored corpse? I scouted the idea, but my sterner feelings got the better, and with a real curiosity, which was not objectless and idle, I conquered my reluctance.

A fine specimen he was of the goodly handy work of nature—his limbs were cast in an almost perfect mould, but an evident difference was observed in the upper and lower part of the shoulders and arms, and the rest of the body from the waist down to the toe. The former were small, and by no means remakable for power; but strength, agility, and grace distinguished the latter; the bone straight like an arrow; the compact thews of thigh and calf; the elastic sinews of knee and ankle, and the rounded symmetry that ended in the remarkable high instep, and firm, straight, handsome foot and heel; it was a study for the sculptor.

But the face of that stern warrior, whose red brow so lately frowned with battle's terror; whose parted lip bespoke the bloody thought, and the demoniac cruelty of his race now paled from its natural hue—livid with death—and quelled, scarcely softened into the silent, mute, and petrified expression—here indeed was a model for the artist. I lingered, in spite of my repugnance to the unpleasantness of the scene, to gaze on the beautiful specimen of savage inflexibility before me; I had seen Indians before, and attempted fac-similies, and ideals which endeavored to portray the fierce lineaments of the legitimate savage, but not in any living originals, nor in any attempts of art, have I recognized so perfect a *beau ideal* of that savageness, which we are accustomed to consider as an inherent quality in the unhumanized son of the forest; an element in his nature, single, and whole, of which the Tiger furnishes the aptest type, and which is not incompatible with beauty of phisiognomy, as I realized in the countenance of this Uchee. There was calmness, and a curl, as of scorn, on the divided lip; the muscles were relaxed with a subdued expression, of fierce glee, as though the war yell had been suddenly cut short by the death stroke; and this feature, the compressed brow, and the haughty nose, evinced dauntless daring, resolution, and contempt of death.

It was undoubtedly a noble countenance; the features were regular and handsome, and I wished that I could have seen him when they were animated by the small, black, piercing eye, and heightened and set off by the long raven hair and plume of the warrior.

He was apparently about 50 years of age, as his scalp was sprinkled with grey hairs, and his teeth showed some signs of decay, but with these exceptions his limbs and countenance appeared to have all the freshness and vigour of youthful prime. His head was preserved in the Dr's. cabinet, and afforded a fine subject for the speculations of the phrenologists, of whom there were not a few in Camp, and if in other instances the followers of the science agreed as happily in their results as they did in this, Phrenology would not have to contend against so many opponents. The sconce of the unconscious and condemned Uchee was thumbed and kneaded into one leavened mass of destructiveness, and the basilar region of his brain was so spacious that every other bad quality appertaining thereto found an equal room in it, and merged all difficulties about *Bumps;* while the moral and intellectual organs were supposed too insignificant to merit attention—his forehead, however, though retreating, was strongly marked by the perceptive organs.

I have been rather particular in describing this Indian, as he was one of a tribe, noted as being the most savage and ill disposed of our Southern Indians. Of the origin and native customs of the Uchees, little is known. They are one of the broken tribes, which the Muscogees associated with them, to give their confederacy strength. They still speak a language radically different from that of the Creeks. It is supposed to be the Shawanees [Shawnees], or a dialect of that tongue. They are called Uchees, probably from their town having been formerly situated opposite the Chatta-Uchee River. They have a lighter complexion than the Creeks.

Three or four days elapsed after this rencontre with the Indians, before the left wing took up the line of march for the Withlacoochee. This delay was owing to several circumstances. General Eustis was waiting for more guides, who were sent for from St Augustine, and for the return of a detachment of 200 mounted volunteers who had gone under Col. [P. M.] Butler on a scouting expedition. The weather also was unfavorable for marching, being constantly rainy. Col. Butler not returning, 27 other mounted men, under a Lieut. were despatched with two guides to look for them and deliver the General's orders.

This detachment had not proceeded more

than 6 miles when they fell in with a party of about 16 or 20 Indians, in an open pine barren, some distance from any hammock or thicket. The detachment attacked them, killed one, and wounded another of the Indians, one of the horsemen only, receiving a slight wound in the side. Many more Indians might have been killed, but the officer would not follow them up, and ordered a retreat for a reinforcement. He was afterwards tried by a court marshal found remiss, and sentenced to lose the commission he held at home in the militia, which was that of a Lieut. Colonel.

Col. Butler and the horse having returned, the left wing, consisting of 1,600 men, moved on the 26th. Gen. Scott had already moved from Fort Drane with the right wing, amounting to 2,000.

Gen Eustis was to destroy the towns on his way, and to intercept the Indians would they retreat to the St. John's and his course was to Pilaklikaha. Gen. Scott was to cross the Withlacoochee, and expected to engage them in their strong holds, on their former battle ground—while Col. Lindsay, with 1,000 men, was to approach from Tampa Bay to a point near the Withlacoochee, and intercept them between the Long Swamp and the big Hammock. It was believed that if they were routed by the right wing, they could not escape falling in the hands of one or other of these two forces.

It was a great disappointment to be compelled to remain behind, to find the campaign curtailed to me all on a sudden, and to lose the pleasure of seeing more of the country, but I congratulated myself that I would not have to undergo the disagreeable tedium of a garrison life long, as all confidently expected that the war would be immediately ended, and that the army would return in a fortnight or less.

Our number in garrison in the Picquet fort to which we had removed, amounted, sick and well, to about 300, and Major Gates, U.S.A was in command.

The first few days passed miserably enough the groans of the wounded, and the never ceasing coughs of the measly and consumptive, were the order of the day and night. In the day the hot tents were insufferable, and in the morning and at night, the fogs and damps from the St. John's, were injurious to those suffering from the measles. Then to be cramped up in the garrison with nothing to do, and not to be able to recruit one's strength, except by a turn round and round in the same place, for it was as much as our scalps, were worth to go any distance from the fort, unless in company and armed.

The next few days our situation in Camp was much improved—the sick were separated in hospital tents, and more attention began to be bestowed on the police of the camp, which was highly necessary, as care and cleanliness were essential to health, especially now that the sickly season was approaching.

One great comfort that we had was a sutler and I verily believe he cured as many cases as the Doctor did—one thing is certain; his fee-bill was higher.

As we had about 30 horses, belonging to the sick of the mounted men, now and then mounted scouts were sent about to see if any Indians were prowling about us, and to drive up cattle. On one of these occasions, we were much alarmed at seeing six horses returning at full speed without their riders, with the reins on their necks, and mudded up to the girths —before this we had heard guns fire, and thought that our men must have fallen in with Indians, and that so many as we saw horses must have been killed—if not all, though no blood was perceptible about the horses. While a party were preparing to go in search of them, an express came riding in, who satisfied our fears by informing us, that, in passing through a swamp, they had started two deer, and some of them jumping off of their horses to fire, they got away. Soon after, they all come in, having met with no adventure, except that they came across some cabbage trees which had been cut for provision by the Indians, but the marks of the cuts were black, which showed that they could not have been very recent, or they would have been red.

Only twice in these expeditions, we found a few head of cattle, which were driven up—they were poor and inferior, and appeared to me to justify the remark that it took six of them to make a shadow.

The cattle of Florida differ much in various parts, according to the nature of the range. In the barrens, scrubs, and such like unfertile regions, and where they are much tormented by flies and mosquitoes, they do not thrive; but in the interior, among the rich swamps, savannas, and large grassy ponds, there are remarkable fine droves.

The Diego plains afford very luxuriant pasturage for them. The cattle of the Mickasauky

towns are held in great estimation. Such was the high opinion entertained of them by Gen. Jackson, (says a writer on
Florida) that, in the Seminole Campaign, he offered $100 to
an Indian, for one cow, to be delivered in Tennessee.

Alachua is famous for its fine droves of cattle.

We always managed badly somehow, with our cattle. After shooting one, we generally let the rest go, thinking to
drive them up as we wanted them; but they would make off, and
we would lose them entirely. On one occasion, at Camp
M'Crea, we had 20 head, but we let them all get away from us
the next morning.

There were opportunities to go down the river two or three
times, as there were two steamboats that made occasional trips
between this post and Picolata, but as there was no leaving the
garrison on a mere excursion of pleasure, and the state of my
health did not allow me to go on the expeditions into the
swamps, which was sent to different places on the river, I,
much to my regret, lost the sight of this noble river, fine
woodland scenes, airy groves and bluffs, magnificent lake, and
enchanting islands, which the poetic pen of Bartram, pictured
in such glowing colors, as inspired me with an ardent desire to
visit certain spots, compare them with his descriptions, and
seek out new sources of gratification.

Many days passed with us here, without affording any thing
new or interesting; and my journal was thrown by, in consequence
of the numerous blanks which now filled it. There are, however, a few recollections of Volusia-which I must not pass over
too hastily.

CHAPTER XIV.

No News of the Army—Conjectures—Strength of the Stockade—A Character—Routine at Volusia—Battle.

We expected that in five days after the army left us, some wagons would return for provisions, as they did not carry with them more than a sufficiency for ten days; at the end of that period, however, no wagons arrived, nor had we heard any news of the army, which we expected to receive from Picolata, by the steamboat, which had arrived, and by which we understood that nothing had been heard from them at that place.

This non-appearance and silence gave rise to many conjectures. Some thought it very possible that the guard sent with the wagons, might have been cut off; others feared that a worse mischance had befallen the whole army, and that they might be perishing for want of supplies.

We began also now to consider our own situation a little, and whether it was not very probable that Powell might pay us a visit, and should he have met with any success over our troops, he might come with numbers, flushed with victory, and be daring enough to rush on our picquets; but we thought ourselves tolerably well enough secured, and provided to stand a siege.

Our stockade was made with strong, tall picquets, and we were completing a ditch and breastwork. We had plenty of provisions and ammunition, and a howitzer, which stood ready in one of the bastions, to throw havoc upon invaders.

The mention of this piece of ordinance leads me to the mention of an important character among us, who was connected with it, and whom I should have noticed before.

During the massacre of our men at camp M'Crea, the 4 pounder which was mounted in the fort, was not fired for two reasons, the first was, lest some of our own men might be killed, and the second was that when it might have been discharged with safety at the Indians running through the field, it tumbled down, while the gunner was ranging it.

The gunner had named his piece McDuffie. On one occasion, when a salute was about to be fired, the Col. called out 'Is McDuffie ready?'

'Ay, sir,' said the gunner, 'McDuffie is ready.'

A false alarm had occurred the night before we left the camp, and we formed the line in admirable time—'Is McDuffie ready?' called out the Col. The piece answered for itself— a roaring discharge of grape and musket balls flew over the heads of the sentinels, and before the Col. could make the gunner hear, he had fired another round in another direction.

He was determined to give the Indians a taste of McDuffie this time. After this, the name became transferred from the gun to the gunner—McDuffie was left to be Captain of the big gun here likewise.

He was oddish looking body—a nonpareil, or *sui generis*[81] sort of a good fellow, with a comical mock-heroical figure, being low in stature, with rather narrow but thick set shoulders— a short back which betokened strength, squaring off into the ill-favored profile of a heavy crupper which nature seemed to have clapped on in hasty violation of some preformed idea, as she sometimes distorts the countenance by a pug nose. This conformation was not improved by the fashion of his trowsers which bagged at the seat enough to have served him in lieu of a havresac to stow away three day's rations. This looseness produced sundry ridges or reefs, which ran down his thigh, splicing them as it were, into mock sturdiness, and giving additional effect to a stallwarth pair of duck legs, which had a slight tendency to being knock-knee'd.

His trowsers, like his character, were after a pseudo–military mode—they were black, with a strip of scarlet on the seam, in half-way imitation of Uncle Sam's uniform. Whether he strove to approach this as near as circumstances permitted, or with a dignified independence, wished to preserve the distinction between a South Carolina volunteer and a regular. I cannot say—he invariably wore them rolled up mid way over his boots, Bombastes-like, and they were usually belted around his waist with an old pocket handkerchief when he wore only his shirt sleeves, but when he strutted in his monkey-jacket, he strapped about him a huge leathern belt.

Mac's physiognomy was upon a par with his figure—a pair of small dullish grey eyes, somewhat bloodshot in the corners, were set on either side of a triangular, cocked up nose, his cheeks were a little puffed, as became a man of consequence, and covered nearly all over with enormous coarse black whiskers which met under his chin. The all-indispensable mustachio which thatched his convex lip was a lighter greyish hue, in some shades foxy, for the effects of the sun and contact with viands and liquids of various gaseous qualities. It had been cultivated carefully, and formed a magnificent arch, the ends meeting the whiskers without a flaw.

Over his shock head, he wore a ferocious looking mocknuter, or muskrat cap, the front of which had slackened and fallen from its original shape, and looked not unlike a barn shed.

He had been, according to his account, in the naval service during the last war, and also three years in the Mexican. He was tolerably well acqainted with the management of the piece he had charge of, and very useful by his attention to arranging everything systematically.

Mac professed to be a gentleman of cleanly and refined feelings and taste, and aspired to the dignity of an epicure and cook. 'Now,' he would exclaim, as he fidgetted about his tent, driving a pin in tighter, and carefully spreading the inside, 'now, boys, that we are getting comfortable once more, and out of the way of filth, Ive got something nice just ready, the prettiest bean soup you ever laid eyes on, and a ra'al duff pudding with molasses and vinegar sauce—I made it myself, and I'll warrant it clean—if there's any thing Mac despises in this world, it's fithy cookering. It might have been better for a woman's fist to have been in it, but that, you know we ha'int got. Set to, boys, Mac's a hungry; he'es been nearly all this morning seeing after the gun making cartridges, and getting every thing in its place—I've got one hundred bags, you see, just like this, filled chock full of grape, musket balls, slugs, and buck shot, and as many cartridges to suit them—shells not to be counted, all arranged in their proper place, and the fuses numbered; No. 1 for close quarters; No. 2 for the hill; No. 3 for the hammock; and No. 4 for over the river. Jist let the Injins raise their war-whoop, you'll hear M'Duffie raise a screamer.'

Besides the Howitzer, we had a cannon which the small steamboat we had besides waiting on us, carried in her bows, and which was pointed in the direction of the hammock, whence the attack was expected to be made if there should be one.

Capt. Quattlebum's company had joined us, but the greater number of the officers and men, were sick and unfit for duty.

Every other day now, we began to bury a man; sometimes two would be dying the same day, and the melancholy slow drum and fife, and the minute rounds that startled the sad echoes of the silent forests around, were becoming the routine of the day after breakfast, and getting familiar to our ears.

As the most important event which befel [befell] us at Volusia was consequent to one of these dismal occurrences, I will proceed to mention it. On the 14th of April, Blocker, one of the privates in Ashby's company, who had been badly wounded in the neck, at the crossing of the St. John's, died after lingering some time. A sergeant and four men were detailed to dig a grave, and went with their arms to the burial ground, which was 150 yards from the picquet, behind a hill that hid it from view. While they were engaged in digging the grave, they were fired upon by Indians, who were lying in wait in the adjoining hammock, to the south of us. Goff, who was standing as the sentinel of the party, nearer the edge of the wood, was shot dead in his tracks. Sergeant Holliday was struck to the earth with mortal wounds. The other three ran for their lives; they heard the unfortunate Sergeant exclaim: "Men, fire your guns—don't desert, me, for God's sake". But it was life or death with them; they saw that Holliday was as good as a dead man, and they saw that the bushes were alive with Indians; they did not take time to think, but sped over the hill, the bullets whistling after them, and with the exception of one of them, who received a ball in his thigh, they were unharmed, and all three got into the fort.

Several of us were regaling ourselves as usual beneath the shade of an oak, on the bank of the river, and were fired at; the balls whistled all about us, but only one struck some one's head slightly; the distance was rather great, and before they fired again, every man had got into the fort.

An interval of a few seconds elapsed, after the two first rifle cracks, and then the popping became general on every side of us, except from the river, and the balls whizzing without any intermission thick over our heads, soon informed us they were no small marauding party, who, having contented themselves with winning two or three scalps, would sneak back into the woods, without showing fight, as they had done at M'Crea's, but as we had reason to believe, a large body of Indians, either a detachment of Powell's army, upon the retreat, or sent hither to cut us off, and take the ammunition and provision left for the support of the left wing—or, perhaps, the great Oseola himself in propria personâ, who had managed by his wiles to elude Scott, and had marched this way in Indian double quick time, at the rate of four miles a day, with the intention of defeating us, eating up all the provisions of the army, and breakfasting the next morning in St. Augustine—now that all the troops had left this part of the territory unprotected.

Every man who could stand on his legs lost no time in occupying a station where he could fire through the picquets—the disciplined coolness displayed in observing the places which had been assigned to each one, was, upon the whole, commendable; but some could not refrain from leaving their posts on that side where they thought the attack was least, and rushing to that where it seemed hotter, and where they could draw a fair bead upon a red skin.

The stockade enclosed about three fourths of an acre—the picquets, as before observed, were high and strongly dropped in the ground, the spaces between allowing sufficient room to shoot through. A ditch and breastwork made it pretty secure; but at this time there were none on one whole side where the stockade had just been enlarged.

Our number, including servants, amounted at this time to 292, 20 of whom were absent on a foraging expedition in the steamboat, about 30 were incapable from extreme sickness of turning out of their tents, and upwards of 150 were more or less sick or convalescent. The alarm occurred between 9 and 10 o'clock A.M.

The positions occupied by the Indians, were a peninsular piece of pine wood, on our north west side, bordering upon the river, and about the distance of 180 yards from us. An open plain intervened between this and the next covert, which was a branch locked up by a close growth of bays and other small trees, brush-wood and vines, and nearer to the fort. This thicket extended back, bounding the plain in our rear on the east—on this plain, arose the hill before mentioned, from behind whose brow, which was not much over a hundred yards, another party were firing over. This and the hammock were the most dangerous points, as our ground in the picquet, fell with a considerable slope in that direction, and from their vantage on the hill, they could fire down upon us over the piquetting.

Having like a good Historiographer given this small sketch of the battle ground, in the first place, I will now attempt to describe the battle, if it may be dignified with that term.

'Pop-pop-pop-pop,' cracked from every quarter of the welkin, the quick sharp, murtherous-sounding rifle—'whoop—whoop—Who-lu-lu-lu-lu,' echoed through the woods, the shrill, savage, animating war-yell—there a tall, striding half naked warrior, might be seen rushing from behind a bush, planting his left legging in advance, firing, and disappearing as suddenly as he stept out, or a glimpse might be caught of him, pouring his horn into the palm of his hand, spitting the ball from his mouth into the muzzle of his rifle, and knocking the butt against the ground—here a grim red visage peered from behind a tree, or a dark plume waved over a bush.

Bang—bang, went the musquets—our boys got at work—'I've hit one'—'I seed another reel'—and 'I can't see e'era one, but I'll make a shoot any how,' were the several exclamations—the last was, I believe, the truest and most general. The men were too anxious to discharge their ball and buck shot, and many fired chance shots into the woods. Had they reserved their fire and allowed the enemy to become a little bolder and advance, they would perhaps have done better—but as it was, after the first few discharges from the fort, they retired a little on our right quarter—but continued a hot firing somewhat higher up the branch, concealing themselves more in the thicket.

Major Gates, after the lapse of two or three minutes, got the Howitzer prepared to throw a shell in among them there. This would have been sooner done, had not some one mislaid the Linstock, port-fires and cartridges, and the dampness of the weather prevented the powder from taking fire after two attempts. However, at the third, off she went—and now after the manner of all writers of great events, who, when they come to any thing which surpasses the minor details of narrative, anything which smacks of the grand, the terrible, and the awful, creating a pause of expectation, like the hush of nature before a Thunder storm, halt to take breath, and send that jaded pack horse of the muses, poor Fancy, a puffing and blowing, to scour the regions of the earth and air, in search of some valuable comparison—so will I, kicking off the buskin and putting on the sock, stretch out my legs, throw my head back, shut my eyes, and dream out this period and chapter until fancy nudges me in the temple and wakes me with the julip ot a simile, by which I may adequately illustrate the wonderful effect which followed the discharge of this dread compound of Heaven and Hell, for which our enemy had no name, but which we simply denominate a Bomb and a shell.

———

CHAPTER XV.

The Battle continued—A simile—A stratagem—M'Duffie's account of the battle and the big gun—The Project.

As when in the flat and gloomy barrens of Carolina or Florida, the bell frogs, and the lesser tribes of shriller clamorous frogs, hold opposite discourse on either side of some fenny pond, if suddenly a hoarse-mouthed bloated bull frog, mounts the brink and bellows out 'Blood and Ounds,' the little frogs suddenly pop into their holes and cease their chirping, while the bell frogs stand listening, and occasionally utter a 'clink clang;' so in like manner, there was silence for a space between the contending rifles and muskets; our red visitors hopped behind their trees, struck with mute wonder, and not knowing what to make of the doubled tongued herald we had sent to parley with them; while with the exception of one or two scattered shots, a pin might be heard to drop among us, as we waited anxiously to hear the shell explode, and see what effect it would have. It took its curved flight through the glassy tranquil air, like some dark demon sailing the concave of Heaven, and lighting slant upon the globe. It burst just over the branch; we gave them a yell from the fort; the echoes came back unanswered to us—they were as silent as the grave. What had become of them? Were they all blown up? Or was the ground too hot for them, and were the foe "sullenly retiring?" The devil a bit of this—they did not leave us long in suspense, but pop-pop-pop-pop-pop-pop, a volley of at least 50 rifles greeted us. It was difficult to say whether they fired only powder or balls, for not one struck any where near us. It was evidently an empty explosion of vexation, disappointment and puerile bravado—it shewed that they had removed much farther off. The firing still continued from behind the hill and hammock, and had they come out more boldly, some of their shot could have taken effect among us on the more elevated part of the encampment; but they contented themselves with firing over the hill over our heads—only one ball struck through a tent, and another spent one hit one behind me. A fuse was now gauged for the hammock and a shell jerked in among them there; as it sailed through temptuously or superstitiously fired at it; when it fell and burst, it was seen to tear up the ground and branches of the hammock in handsome style. The savages gave a yell and fired another scattering volley.

Another shell was cast just over the brow of the hill. After this the firing centered more in the direction of the distant wood that bound the plain on the north east. The Major had three or four more shells thrown, and the action was over. I think it was for about ten minutes that the firing of our muskets lasted—but thirty minutes must have elapsed during which the

Indians continued their useless expenditure of ammunition.

Some little time after they appeared to be gone, while we were yet standing to our arms, in ease they should recommence, we heard another volley about half a mile in the woods, in the direction towards Spring Garden, whither they seemed to have taken up route. We could not conceive what they meant by this, unless it was for a triumph over the two scalps that they had taken, or a bravado, to induce us to come out of the Fort and pursue them. This the Major thought he could not do consistently with his duty, which was to protect the depot of supplies, and the sick, and while we were here in a defensive, and not an offensive capacity, and could gain every advantage by remaining in our strong position, it was not incumbent upon us, as a matter of duty—nor would we have been justified, if, for the sake of gaining a few doubtful Indian laurels, we had rushed out where we should have been exposed to ambuscades on every side, and if they had succeeded in drawing out a part of the garrison, which might have been their object, a portion of them might have waylaid these, or led them in pursuit too far from the fort, and the main body meanwhile, might have had sufficient boldness to make a rush on the weakened garrison, which, effected suddenly and simultaneously, the contest at the picquets, supposing their force to be greater than ours, might have been doubtful. It would not have done with our ignorance of their force, to have sent out less than one hundred men, and of those who would have stayed to protect the fort, more than two thirds would have consisted of sick and weakly convalescents.

That an assault upon the stockade was intended, there was some reason to believe; their spies must have informed of its exposed state, on one side, while we were enlarging it, and seeing the steamboat go off with men, they might have thought our force more reduced than it was and it was probable that they had collected to try by force or stratagem to take the fort, with the provision and ammunition. Had it not been for the men who were digging the grave, whose scalps they were too eager for, they would probably not have given the alarm as they did, in the first instance, on that side. As it was, until they saw that the horned guns* were ready every side, and that we had the big gun in that direction, they did not fire much on that side, though it was evident afterwards that the largest body was secreted in the hammock there, and there appeared to be, the nucleus, on which, when they began to retreat, they rallied from the opposite sides, after endeavoring to draw our attention thitherwards.

Had a sortie been made, (and the garrison were willing, and even anxious for one, had it been ordered) more honorable mention, it is true, might have been made of the Battle of Volusia, and the effect it might have had upon the Indians, in the contingency of its being fortunate, would have been, perhaps, better than as it was, but that such a sally would have been made under the worst possible disadvantages, and at great hazard, ending perhaps in great loss, without any gain on our side; and perhaps,

---

*So they call musquets with bayonets.

in the eventual destruction of the whole garrison, the unfavorable nature of the ground at Volusia will, in part, show. The troops would have had to act in an open defile between a thick hammock, which they could not penetrate, and the Indians, who could have poured a destructive cross fire upon them, the moment they moved out of the Fort.

From the manner in which they surrounded us, and their constant firing alone, we were under the impression that their number was considerable. But up to this late date, we had received no intelligence of our army, and consequently knew nothing of the movements of the Indians. It was the general impression in camp, that the main body, or a portion, had retreated, or had been driven this way, and would make a desperate attempt upon us. This impression was afterwards in a manner justified—at that time, the Indians *had scattered* in different directions.

Immediately after they left us, there was strong reason to believe that there was an attempt to play off a stratagem upon us. A smoke was seen some distance off in the direction they appeared to have taken, and about the same time, we heard groans, which at first some thought might proceed from one of our men, who had been shot. It seemed singular, however, that we should just then have heard them, and not before—upon listening attentively, the general impression was, that it was the accent of an Indian, and further in the woods than where these men were shot. This impression was strengthened when some one, having volunteered

to go to the edge of the hill, and call the names of the unfortunate men, he saw Holliday lying dead, and calling the other's
name, he did not answer. It was not at all likely that they would
have left any life in their victims—neither was it very probable,
that it was a wounded Indian, for their stubborness in enduring
any suffering, rather than subject themselves to be taken alive by
their enemy, is well known.

The Major, after going once himself to reconnoitre whence
the sounds proceeded, concluded that it was a lure to obtain more
scalps, and a shell was thrown to rout them out, after which the
groans ceased.

As it fell and exploded, and all was still as death after, the
thought flashed painfully through my mind; if this were really one
of our dying men what must have been the mental agony of that
awful moment; the horrible conviction that he was deserted, mistaken for an enemy, and his groans entreating for help cut short
by so cruel an answer! but this supposition had so little evidence
to support it that we remained persuaded with the other belief.
The bodies were not brought in until the second day after the
attack—the reasons for which were, that the commander
thought that the Indians would lie in wait in the hammock, expecting that we would soon send out a party to bury the bodies
and they would fire on these and retreat, and get off as usual, and
he did not see the necessity of exposing many lives for two dead
bodies—and as the coffins were not ready until then, it was
thought better that they should lay where they were, than be
kept in the garrison, where they would be offensive.

A strong party was sent out to bring them in—the bodies presented a shocking scene—the buzzards had already held their carnival there—the features mangled by them, distorted by a two days' suns; and the scalped gory heads looked frightful!

The first thing that was done after the Indians appeared to have gone, was to complete the ditching before night, and all the garrison who could do duty turned out with their arms, and it was effected. That and the following night half of the force remained during half of the night on guard, and were relieved by the other half, and after this, always from 4 or 5 o'clock until sun rise, the whole were out, every man at his post ready to meet an attack.

Our friend, M'Duffie, was always the first to be seen on these occasions standing with erect importance by the side of the Big Gun, the linstock in his hand, his shaggy cap cocked over one eye, and the dew drops glistening on his formidable coal-black whiskers and foxy mustachios. The second night after the attack, I was listening to some of the usual rodomontade of our miles glorious, in which he gave the following account of himself, and of his exploits with the Big Gun to some questioners who were standing about, who wanted to know the particulars of the share he had in the action, and the reason why the howitzer was not fired sooner—'you see,' said M'Duffie—'now listen—the first thing I heard was 'crack—crack,' and the next thing I heard was – 'Mac—Mac'. The Major, he had started for M 'Duffie, for he could do nothing without me—I he'ered him holla—'Mac the Fusier—Mac, Captain of the Big Gun'—'Ready, sir, ready' says I.'

'But you happened not to be ready that thar time Mac,' interrupted Crocket, one of his listeners.

'Who says that tells a—but you go to grass—I was side and side with the major from the jump—there was only one thing kept me, and that not a second—you see, as I ran into the fort, I saw our flag, our Star-Spangled Banner—that glorious banner, under which we live or die, hanging at half mast high for our lamented Dead,'

Here Mac was again interrupted, and reminded that he spoke of a circumstance, which did not happen until the next day; but the military enthusiasm of our Thraso was not to be damped by the discovery of this Irish anachronism, and taking the bull by the horns, he proceeded in his rodomontade, with all the gravity and importance, worthy the narration of some veritable and heroic action.

'Ha! the thought inspired me—the enemy shall see that we are not disheartened at what they have done—South Carolina shall not fight with the banner of the dead—and I pulled the cord, and the gallant little handkerchief flirted up to the sky, its stripes and stars once more waving over our heads. The next moment I was at my post—the port holes thrown open—the linstock ready a burning—the port fire in my hand.'

'Touch her off,' cried the Major.

I gave the port fire a flourish—phiz—she would not go; I tried again—another phiz; she drivelled at the mouth like a young sucking babe, and the cartridge was as wet as an old cow flatt.

Well—after a bit, we got her to rights, and made the old woman hollow, and didn't we deliver her of a beautiful pair of twins!

'Point her the other way now, Mac,' cried the Major.

And I took the old woman up in my arms, and raised her head so that she could just see over the hill—she went off by herself this time, I believe—I must have overdosed her; for it was a rowser; and she keeled back and kicked the Major clean head over heels—at the same time, I saw the legs and arms of a dozen Indians cutting capers in the air.

But boys, I've got business on hand, and must not be talking here—I must go and see, and get things ready'

'What now Mac?'

'Why you must know I told the Major of a project of my own for killing these rascal Injins and clearing the ground of them; I'm going to fix up a tent on the hill yonder, to look like a guard tent, and put some shells in it, then I'm going to strew powder all the way from the magazine up to it.'

'Well, what then?'

'Why when they rush upon the tent, I'll touch off the train, and blow up the villains sky high.'

'Yes, and first blow us up.'

'Oh I'll take care the powder don't run the wrong way— but if we should be hard pushed, Mac says, let us die an honorable and glorious death.'

Accordingly, the next day, the Major and officers not objecting to the plan of keeping the

Indians from prying about and molesting us, providing it could be put in safe execution, the trap was set—a string being fastened to the trigger of a pistol inside, and drawn rather tight around the tent on the outside, so as to intercept the feet of any one approaching it, and set the pistol off in some powder, which would fire the shells—and M'Duffie could not sleep the whole night, thinking of the glorious explosion which was to take place,—which was to blow out the brains of at least fifty Indians in his estimation, like 'the rinsings of Belzebub's porridge pot' and immortalize him as the inventor of a scheme, by which he would vanquish more Indians than any general on the campaign, with the least trouble and risk.

But fortune did not favor the scheme; and after the trap had remained three or four nights, and we expected momentarily, as a stray horse galloped by it, or a dog barked in its precincts, to hear it explode, it was taken away.

CHAPTER XVI.

Volusia—Growth around—Singular Foundation of Soil upon Shells—The St. Johns—Aquatic Plants—Other Plants, &c.

There was every inducement here; want of occupation and exercise; the delightful country and season of Flora, to ramble about the vicinity, but the pleasure of such excursions was very much damped, by the thought that an Indian might be lurking in every bush, and by having to go along always 'with the beard on the shoulder.' There was no knowing how soon, while I was stooping to pick a flower, one of the sneaking villains might pick off my scalp. I saw little therefore of the surrounding country, and the observations I have to make are consequently limited.

'Volusia, ' says Dr. Simmons, 'is about 65 miles to the south of St Augustine., and is a very fine tract, lying on both sides of the St. Johns; the greater portion being on the western side of the river. A good part of it is suitable for cotton, and the rest is highly valuable from its adaptation to the culture of the sugar cane. The settlement was made nearly three years ago, under circumstances of great difficulty and danger, by Mr. Horatio S. Dexter, its present proprietor. (1819).'

Mr. Woodruff, who was killed by the Indians, among the first victims of this War, was the late proprietor.

Our picquet was pleasantly situated upon the river, commanding a reach and beautiful bend above and below the magnificent stream, which here is narrow, and not above 200 yards in width. On the opposite side was a continued forest or swamp—the trees moderately tall, and consisting principally of Querci, Acer rubrum, Acer negundo, Ulmus, Hickory, Nyssa or black gum, Liquid amber or sweet gum, Ash, Morus rubra, Cyprus, some Pine, &c. &c. I saw but few Palmetto, and these were scattered on the bluffs. On this side on our left a similar wood of some depth bounded the river—the edge of this hammock was grown up with brush wood, low gum and tallow nut bushes which extended out from it. These forests and bushes were clothed with the most brilliant verdure.

Two or three moderate sized live oaks grew on the eminence and the brink of the river, and in the plain to our rear about the same number of beautiful Quercus Laurifolia, or Water Oak. These were singularly fine trees. They grow to a considerable size, and their ample compact foliage spread into a perfect globe of shining green, reaching so low to the ground that one had to stoop to enter their vast amphitheatre of shade. The sod here is very favorable for these oaks, and, also for the lordly Magnolia, but it was probably too far from the sea coast for these latter—there were none. It is fine for the orange. The mould here and for the most part along the banks of the St. John's is based upon a singular formation of shells. In digging our ditch, the spade, after leaving the surface, encountered nothing but this mass of testaceous deposit, closely imbedded in loose sand, and as we dug deeper, in blue clay and decomposed testaceous matter. The shells near the surface were chiefly periwinkles of different sizes, some very large, (Palludina?) and fresh water Cochlea. At a lower depth appeared to be some sea shells. We found some human bones and some of large fish. The eastern side of the St. John's is distinguished from the western by these shell and sand bluffs. The western is bordered by low hammocks principally. In many places about us the top soil was washed off and left bare, and the shells appearing, gave the surface a singular white and barren aspect. Immediately after the hardest rain the ground would be only damp.

There were two Indian mounds, with a quantity of pieces of pottery, and some fragments of bones about them. One of them appeared to be the site of an Indian town-house or temple; and it is difficult to say, at this time, whether much of the varied rise and fall of the ground here is to be attributed to natural or artificial causes.

Bartram mentions having seen in his tour, similar elevations, and spacious avenues, 100 feet or more in width, and cut some feet deep. The eastern shore of the St. Johns is said to be much higher than the western, and its waters higher than those of the sea on either side and supplied by subterraneous channels and reservoirs. It appears to have connection with the sea, as the water is both salt and fresh, and as high up as Lake George, salt water fish have been taken. We found the water disagreeable and did not drink it. We observed, the day after a hard rain, the surface of the stream caked over with a yellowish red substance, which, at first, at a distance, our imaginations might have conceived to be blood, and in vulgar apprehension, it would seem that a sanguinary battle had taken place above on the river. Our impression was that these cloudings were occasioned by the washings of the filth of the swamps. They may be produced by the sulphur springs, that are found in different places on the river and render the water putrid and unwholesome.

The margin of the river at Volusia is bordered with many aquatic and amphibious plants, among which, the large bonnet leaf, (*Cyamus lutea*,) is most conspicuous; it was not in bloom; the large orbicular leaves of this plant, float on surface of the water, sometimes rising above; it grows in very deep water; they form a shining carpet for the Naiads to dance upon, and the little water birds are often seen tripping over them, while the silver trout and the golden Bream disport beneath their contiguous umbrage and find a shelter under their dark covert. They have the faculty of repelling water in a great degree; the large roots are frequently seen strewed on the surface, cut up by the alligator, either for food, or in his chase after the many tribes.

The Wampee (*Pontederia*) formed also extensive tracts; it was flowering about this time.

That singular plant, the mystic *Pistia Stratiotes* (Bartram) *Spathulata* (Michaux, Pursh; Nuttall, Elliott;) Indian or wild lettuce, struck my attention. Bartram is the only one of these Botanists who has described it fully; Mr. Elliott never saw it; (I should perhaps except Michaux, whose work I have not seen.) It resembles garden lettuce very much; the radical leaves are opposite and expand in a circle forming a regular head—they are orbicular, abrubtly spathulate, strongly nerved—the nerves centering in the spathe, like the sticks of a fan; their colour is a bright green yellow. They float on the water, and the plant is nourished, and kept in its horizontal position, by the long fibrous, hair like roots, which descend to the muddy bottom, and collect particles of mud around them. The term *Stratiotes* is applied to them, from the number of individuals of these plants, which congregate together, forming extensive green pastures for miles on the water—they are sometimes driven by winds from their hold, and are seen floating down the current. When the winds subside, they settle again, take root, and

form new tracts; they are said never to be found to the North of
Lake George, owing to the violence of the Lake, which uproots
them. It bears a small white flower; It was not in bloom at this
time.

Besides these amphibious plants, I saw *Rumex brittanicus*, Water Dock; *Hydrocotile fluitans*, and a kind of aquatic moss, suspended beneath the surface of the water.

Of small plants growing in the fields and damp pine barrens
around, I observed in bloom, (April) *Salvia lyrata*, *Hypericum angul.*,
Polygala viridiscens, flowers in an oblong head, greenish, tinged
with yellow; plant very small. *Pinguicula pumila* scapes many, in
clusters, a little viscid, each one crowned with a different colored
little blossom, azure, purple, white and intermediate shades,
marked up to the summit of the tube with blue, purple or yellow veined with streaks of bright purple and red. A species of
Physalis growing in the sand a few inches high, leaves repand,
somewhat angular, reticulate, silky; flower of moderate size,
dusky yellow, beautifully marked inside, half way with five greenish leaf-like shades with dark purple midrib and veins—
nodding.

Vicia acutifolia (*Paucifolia?*) it appears to be distinguished mostly by its few pair of leaves and their distance.

Of other plants and shrubs and small trees: an elegant
species of Feru that grew from an old stump at the side of the
branch 6 or 8 feet high, the stem conspicuous for its smoothness
and greenish white color, tinged with red—very branching.

Clematis ovata, a beautiful species, climbing high over gum bushes, &c.; flower solitary, large

rugose. Nothing can be fairer, fresher looking and more templing to the eye than the beautiful bell blossoms of the Virgin Bower; the snowy whiteness, and crispness of the inside of the revolute petals; the crowded golden stamens which enrich like fairy work this mystic Penetralia of the Sylphs, and other little winged spirits of the air, and the fleshy, purpled carnpa-nulate and waved exterior. The leaves of this species were ovate, acuminate, reticulate and on short petioles. *Bignonia capreolata, Zizyphus volubulis, Smilax, Vitis labrusca* (in bloom,) *Cissus bipinnata, Cissus hederacea,* (not in bloom) *Itea, Aesculus pavia, Ilex opaca, Prinos, Styllingia sebifera* or Tallow nut, and a small tree growing horizontally at the edge of the river, the branches flowering in the water, roughened—Calyx 4 part, very small. Cor. 4 clft. pet. lanceolate, white, flowers in paniculate cymes, leaves oval lanceolate, acuminate; a little scabrous on margin, veined.

CHAPTER XVII.

Alligators of the St. John's—Time passes more and more tiresomely and disagreedably—A stirring incident—Horsemen seen on the opposite landing—The arrival—A tall and important personage—Breaking up of a Campaign.

The St. John's is famed for its Alligators—they grow to a great size, and are very bold here. They would approach close up to the shore to take a bait in the presence of a crowd of us whooping and halloing at them, but they appeared to be not at all frightened, and would only move slowly away or turn a summerset in the water, and immediately again the big head was seen floating up to the bait. We succeeded in hooking one fellow; he was not a large one, being only 12 or 14 feet in length; they grow to 18 or 20. At night they would make a thundering noise, with which the earth would seem to tremble. The horses which were tethered close by the river bank, would be kicking all night against the attacks of these formidable monsters; which at first were mistaken by the sentinels for canoes, as they were seen moving along close under the shore, and heard splashing in the water. The blow of the horse's hoof ringing against their hard mail could be distinctly heard, and they were constantly breaking their halters, and rushing away from their fastenings to get rid of their tormentors.

More than three weeks had now passed, and still we knew nothing of the army and the Indians. Our time passed more and more irksomely. Disease in another shape was making its progress among us. Many who had been sick of the measles had got nearly well, but the system was predisposed to fever and some bilious cases, which our doctor expected to take a typhus type, began to make their appearance. That in a short time it would be very sickly here on the rivers and swamps we did not doubt, and the question began to be mooted, what should be done, in case the army did not return by the time the term of service of the volunteers had expired. Some thought they would be at liberty to return home, without waiting for any orders or discharge; but generally, we were disposed to wait a week or two after the time, as we did not know but what the army might be delayed over the period and might be in want, and would expect to meet supplies here, and we would not be at liberty to break up the depot. There was one reflection also which seemed to render our stay a matter of necessity; that we did not see how we were to get away until the commander in chief should send another steamboat—-the one that we had with us might take us all in several trips—but the lives of those who would be last would be jeopardized—and there was no guide to show us the direct route to St. Augustine, and the indirect one by which we had come, was through such a miserable country that the chances of loss from sickness would be greater than if we stayed where we were. What, with such contemplations and prospects before us—our daily deferred hopes of seeing the army return— the spiritless inaction—the approach of disease—the mournful daily burials—the constant expectation of a midnight attack—the awful roaring of alligators—the melancholy howling of wolves— the hooting of owls, and the disagreeable miasmatic grunting of bull frogs, and nightly clamour of other odious reptiles about us, our situation was upon the whole a very gloomy and unpleasant one.

Since our two men had been shot and scalped, our bounds had become still more narrow. It was not safe to be more than 30 yards from the Fort, and in fact, every where outside of the picqueting, a shot could take effect. Even from the hammock, on the other side of the river, which was perhaps not quite 200 yards wide, where we did not anticipate any danger, a well directed fire of rifles, and a few muskets, some of which the Indians were known to be in possession of, into a crowd of us, would have done considerable execution.

I always observed, however, that the lessons we had learned by experience, were soon thrown aside. The men soon lost their caution, and in a few days after such occurrences and warnings, were just as venturesome as before.

For a few days after the attack, an order was observed, that not more than a few at a time should go out of the picqueting, as, the gate being very narrow, in case the Indians should attack us suddenly, if half the garrison was out of doors, without arms, much risk and loss might be incurred. Scarcely a week had elapsed, however, when this order began to be neglected, and we were one evening standing, a great many of us, in a crowd, on the bank of the river, looking at the attempts of some one to catch an alligator; others were fishing a little farther down the river, where they would not have thought of going the day after the scalping of Holliday and Goff; and others were rambling about, almost as much as they ever used to do. More than two-thirds of the garrison were thus out, without arms. Suddenly, half a dozen rapid whoops pierced the air, apparently close in our vicinity—almost in the midst of us.

The effect was electrical. Not a word was said; but there was a rush; with a panic, for the gate. The impression was universal, that Indians had observed our disarmed condition, had crawled up within a few yards under cover of the river bank, and were already upon us.

I happened to be standing near the gate; the individual, with whom I was talking, next to me, was the first to get in; but I was more unlucky. The dense crowd, passed, like a whirlwind, over me, and I found myself precipitated from the draw bridge into the ditch, with two or three others tumbling over me. In this discomfitted situation, with a blow on the head I received, in falling violently against the picqueting, which stunned me into the belief that it was a rifle ball, the thoughts, for the instant, whirled through my brain in the shape of tomahawks and scalping knives. That I was 'a case' seemed as clear and vivid to me, as the fire that flashed in my eyes from the blow I received. I instinctively felt for my knife, the only weapon about me, and there was but one thought more, besides the vague one of dying resistance, and that was the only feeling of destruction; of slaying those whom I grappled, whose efforts to get in proved more successful than mine, and who trampled upon me. The sight of us in the ditch only increased the panic of the rest, who thought, as they were whirled along in the mass, that we were dead bodies; yet no one heard a rifle, and as time sufficient had elapsed for the half of us to have been slain, if there had been Indians as near as we thought, a simultaneous re-action took place; and countenances, pale and compressed with excitement, began to show a flush of foolishness, and to relax with a haggard smile. A feeling of the ridiculous came over us all, and I commenced to rub my shins, to clear my eyes of dust, and look about for my spectacles. I felt excessively rueful and mortified, and my first thought, when I could look about, was to catch the eye of an Indian laughing at me.

A poor rabbit had been the cause of the alarm and affright, which some one had startled near by, and unthinkingly commenced whooping after. The individual ran himself, when he saw the crowd pushing in at the gate, thinking there was some other cause of alarm, & when the panic was about subsiding, he explained the circumstance. He was severely reprimanded by the Maj.

At length, after a month had elapsed, some horsemen were descried, one afternoon, on the opposite landing place. We made the woods on the still St. John's lively with our glad cheers at the long anticipated sight of those, of whom we did not know what had become, and great was the curiosity and anxiety to know whether this was only a remnant, or the advance of the army—how our more particular friends had fared—whether we should find them all alive, or hear that they had found honorable graves in the desert with the lamented Izard, and Dade's unfortunate hundred.

A towering and portly personage, with a rather florid complexion, an air of great nonchalance and military affectation, with somewhat of a stooping gait

> "And goodly to the sight
> He seemed a son of Anak for his height"

was among them. He was now inside the picquet, and the sutler having, instanter on his arrival furnished the Major's marquee with a few bottles of *Champagne*, while that was discussing, they discussed the *Campaign*. It did not take longer to dispose of one topic than the other—and the tall personage was now in the midst of the throng, who had assembled about him to look at him, and to hear the news, and in less than half an hour, he had shaken hands with, and spoken half a dozen sentences to every man in the garrison. By this courteous and half-fellow-well-met address, he in that short space of time, completely won the good opinions of all our soldiers, who swore that he seemed a 'mighty clever sort of a man—all sorts of a clever man—no fal-la about him, &c.'

It is almost needless to acquaint the reader, that this was Gen. Scott—who had come with an advance body guard.

The next day about noon, the whole army arrived and began to cross.

The men presented truly a squalid and warworn appearance. If they had no wounds to shew, they had dirt and rags enough to prove they had suffered all the toils of a campaign. At any distance, they would easily have been mistaken for Indians.

The return of the Troops, and breaking up of the Campaign, was a scene, which, had I been a limner, I should have thought an interesting subject for a sketch. There was the torn and tattered, embrowned and black visage crowd on the other side of the river, waiting all day anxiously, but patiently, to get across.—There were the heavy wagons, with their lean horses, one by one pushed across in the flats, and groaning their way out of them—an endless train, which it took nearly the whole day to get over; and brought to mind the vast trouble and expense that had been put in demand to conquer the Indians, all of which had proved so utterly vain. Here, on this side, was a U. S. Colonel, or an aid-de-camp, strutting about and giving orders, looking like a regular campaigner, and though as much soiled as the rest; preserving in his dress an appearance of greater show and care, and maintaining an air of military importance. Here was a company drawn up which could now scarcely be distinguished by any uniform, except, that of dirt, from the common militia; but that their upright heads, and close touching elbows showed that they were regulars; their blue suits were bemired out of recollection, and their brightened belts were now all tarnished—what had become of all their neatness and cleanliness? Now a rusty, ragamuffin Captain or Lieutenant might be seen indulging at the sutler's stand devouring a piece of cheese, or dipping up with his dirty fingers sugar or molasses, with which he gaumed his hairy lips that had not seen a razor for better than a month. Tents were moving and pitching—wood was cutting and hauling—horses were feeding and tethering—and groups were shaking hands, and listening to the adventures of the 'finished campaign.'

Some of these I will relate and devote a small chapter to, as my limits will not permit me to he more prolix, and not being a partaker in them, I shall only mention a few detached events from my memorandums.

————

CHAPTER XVIII.

Crossing the Oklewahaw—Gen. Shelton and an Indian Chief—Battle of Oakihumky—Fort Alabama—Indian Express—Embarassments and hardships—Failure of the Campaign—Indian Ponies.

On arriving at the Oklewahaw, the mounted men crossed first. The scene was a picturesque one—the wild riders plunging their horses into the black deep stream, swimming them across, to plunge into the dark Hammocks that awaited them on the other side. The foot had to construct a bridge; the wagons were unladen, and the volunteers had to carry on their backs all the provisions, &c. as the bridge was too slight to bear much weight. They did not all get over until near midnight.

The mounted men came upon a camp, and beheld the Indians at a distance, dancing the war dance. The Indians made off, after firing upon the mounted men. It was on this occasion that Gen. [Joseph] Shelton of Newberry, who had come out upon the campaign as an independent volunteer, and was not attached to any particular command, descried an Indian chief, who was separated some little distance from the rest. The General galloped after him, and the two foes were in collision, both alone, unattended, by any one of their party. Gen. Shelton fired his double barrel at the chief, who fell on his knees, mortally wounded; but in falling, he dropped his rifle on his palm, and with a dauntless air and determined countenance, leveled at the General, and wounded him in the thigh. The General's other barrel missing fire, he presented one of his pistols, and was in the act of firing, when the advance Guard rode up, and the Indian chief was immediately riddled with two or three balls at the distance of five paces—This was Yah-hah-Hajo, or Mad Wolfe.*

In some huts they found a string of scalps, which consisted of small shreds about the size of half a dollar, strung together, intended probably

---

*See Vocabulary—Names of Chiefs.

as a decoration to some part of the dress. When not far from the village of Oakihumkey, the advance guard of the army, about 12 o'clock, was fired opon by Indians who crossed the road some distance before them and passed into a large hammock on the left. The hammock was flanked, and the horse disposed so as to cut them off—while the regulars and Richland riflemen made a charge. A contest, which lasted, off and on, about two hours, now ensued—the Indians all the while retreating farther into the hammock. They could every now and then be seen at a great distance off, dashing from behind trees and leaping from one to another like so many squirrels, and as some furious warrior stept forth, he would in the most martial and valiant style throw back from his shoulders his blanket mantle, give his rifle a flourish up in the air, stretch himself erect with the most haughty and braggadocio air, and fire up into the tree tops at more than 300 yards distance. Only three or four of our men got wounds. What execution might have been ascertained; but it was subsequently reported by a Spanish half-breed Indian, who was taken prisoner at Tampa, that the Indians lost in the fight eight killed, and fifteen wounded.

On this occasion the manner in which the Indians fight behind trees was remarked. The prints were seen where one lay down while another stood behind a tree, so that when one fires the other is ready to pick off the incautious enemy who thinks there is only one.

This was the only important meeting the left

wing had with the Indians on the route to Tampa.

After burning Pilacklikaha, the flames of which attracted the inhabitants of the surrounding hammocks, and those who were engaged were assaulted on all sides with deafening shrieks and yells by more than a hundred—Parakeets; they proceeded to Fort Alabama on the Hillsboro river which was garrisoned by some Alabama troops. A week before, the garrison had been attacked by a large body of Indians who had fought very boldly, at one time coming up very near—a great many rounds were fired on both sides. The Fort was a close stockade made of timber, and the only chance the Indians had to shoot into it was through the loop holes—only one man was wounded. 1700 bullets were counted in the timbers after the battle.

At 10 o'clock an Indian was seen approaching the Fort with a white flag hoisted. He proved to be a chief of the friendly Indians who had accompanied the right wing—an express from Gen. Scott sent to inform Gen. Eustis that he had left the Withlacoochee some time ago and was now at Tampa Bay. This Indian ran great risks in coming upon the errand, and had it not been known that Gen. Scott had 50 friendly warriors with him, our troops would not have been persuaded to trust the peaceful overtures of the red messenger—a real friendly Indian?—our troops were not disposed to believe there was such an entit under the sun; and when the question was repeatedly asked among us, whether we should put faith in the friendly demonstrations of an Indian who should appear in this way it was always answered—rather put cold lead in him, and our sentinels were very apt to do so.

Gen. Scott had given him very particular instructions how he should approach our army with caution—that if the army were on the march, he should approach it by the rear, and not in front; and should ride up as near as he could, out of gunshot, waving the flag in one hand, and holding up the dispatches in the other. The General gave him the best horse he had, and urged him to use the whip the whole way, so as to pass speedily, and avoid the hostiles.—The Indian would not take the whip, dryly observing that if he was pursued, he would put his horse to speed, that he would not have time to use it. The General then asked him if he was going to take a rifle, but this he likewise declined encumbering himself with, and asked for a pistol, which was given him.

On the way, the army was much encumbered with the wagons which they had to lighten, by throwing away some of the provisions; the pork, beans, candles, soap, &c. were scattered on the road, and rations issued every day. There were many sick, who suffered severely; some who could hardly support themselves, being compelled to walk for want of transportation. Expecting to return in ten days they carried very little clothing—many only one shirt. Each horseman carried a bushel of corn in his saddle bow, which he had to drop when any Indians made their appearance, as he could not charge with such an encumbrance, this way, once or twice they lost their corn, for while they would be dashing far ahead after a few scattering Indians, the greater body of them would sneak up behind, and carry off the corn, hiding it as well as they did themselves. They found before they had proceeded half way, that they had not brought corn enough. For six successive days, the horses had not a mouthful to eat, but what scanty herbage, and hard palmetto leaves they could pick up around their stakes, and at last they actually became desperate with hunger, and 150 of them eat up their halters and rushed madly into the woods and were lost.

The three divisions of the army met, neither having accomplished any thing more than killing two or three Indians in one or two scattered skirmishes. When Gen. Scott got to the Withlacooche, where he expected to find the Indians, the birds had flown. They had stolen off in different gangs by different routes. That great credit is due to the cunning of the master spirit which conducted the Indians on this occasion out of the trap which had been laid for them, there is no doubt. The failure of the campaign, however, is attributable to some causes else. Gen. Gaines, who certainly acted right in going into Florida with an army, though he had received no orders to do so, not knowing at the time of any contemplated movement against the Indians, only unfortunately did not accomplish more than bringing the Indians to a parley, and too hastily concluded and sent abroad the intelligence that they were beaten and had come to terms, when they were only seeking a little delay to outwit him—they were informed that they had better give themselves up as a large army was coming against them. They took advantage of the information, and if they did not break up at that time and go and hide, they kept their spies about, and no doubt were aware of the approach of the three columns even before Gen. Scott was kind enough to inform them by firing minute guns every morning. When the last mentioned General got to Tampa Bay, he found that the report of the Indians having been defeated by Gen. Gaines had prevented the supplies which he expected from being sent there. He was consequently obliged to hasten the return of the army, and instead of using exertions while on the spot to hunt the Indians out of their retreat, after Col. Goodwin's horse had without success performed an expedition to the Pease Creek, where it was reported by the Spanish Indian prisoner that the Indians had concealed their women, and children, and plunder, the army returned by the same route back again. The term of service of the troops being nearly expired was another reason why the campaign could not be prosecuted any farther. The great error was in bringing these troops so late into the field—two months were consumed in preparations and in effecting nothing, and the third in marching to Tampa and back again.

On their return they caught some Indian ponies. The Seminole horses are a lively, sprightley little breed, descended originally from the Andalusian stock brought over by the Spaniards, but now much degenerated. One or two of those what we saw were tolerably good looking, fine limbered, agile little animals—but for the most part they had not much to recommend them. All had rough coats of a light dingy color—foreheads arched to the nose—short necks, and active limbs. The individual who succeeded in running down and catching one of these ponies, claimed it. One man told me that his poney had given him more trouble in catching than he was worth—"That he was little, old, and ugly, hard to catch, and when caught, good for nothing."

———

CHAPTER XIX.

Return of the Volunteers—Pine Ridges—A Phenomenon—Clear Water Pond—An Encampment Scene—Wet Barrens—Botanical Notices— Birds—Arrival at St. Augustine.

On the 28th April, our regiment, with the horse, took up the line of march for St. Augustine. about an hour after sun rise. We amounted to more than a thousand men, the horse constituting the larger portion, as many who had been unwell, or worn down on the march, provided themselves with the horses of the mounted men, who were sick and went in the steam boat. The order of march was the same as usual: the horse on the flanks, the foot as advance and rear guard to the wagons in the centre; of these there were about forty lightly laden. The road as far as the eye could see was lined with troops. It was an animating sight— all life and joy—the quick forward step—the occasional cheer and shrill wild wood whoop of gladness and freedom piercing the forests and telling the savages good bye; and this violation of the restraints of military decorum denoted how buoyant each heart was at the thought of the return. The spirit of the volunteer which erst had warmed itself with the fervor of enthusiasm in the cause of the distressed, and welcomed not coldly the requisitions of duty and patriotism; which nerved his hand to take a stern, untrembling, nay, seemingly unfeeling adieu, of the one which grasped it, perhaps for the last time; which proudly triumphed over the enticements of ease and gain, which caused many a sturdy woodsman to throw aside his axe and take up the hatchet; that spirit had carried him fearless and unflinching, on through the perils and hardships of nearly three months tedious service, and its relaxation now for the elate and virtuous hopes, and tender longings after "sweet home," was natural and becoming.

There might have mingled with the general expression of joy, an occasional murmur and complaint of the unmannerly treatment of Uncle Sam's officers in sending the Carolina troops by land a long and tedious route, while the pet regulars were to be transported at their ease in steam boats, but it was drowned in the acclamation of joy, and the reflection that a few days now would deliver them from their hard task-masters, and restore them once more to their original independence, and so that they were on their way back to Old Carolina, it did not matter how—they were ready to foot it to St. Augustine, and go from thence in a fishing smack. The men shouted—the waggoners cracked their whips—the horses neighed—the merry little Indian ponies scampered about, and intermingled their shrill, colt-like whinnying, and a few dogs of a species between hound and cur, and a bull terrier or two, completed the scene.

Our road for a few miles was the same as that by which we had come from Camp McCrea, and after we left it for a more direct course to

St. Augustine, there was but little variation in the features of the country. The first day we passed over some pleasant pine ridges, where we saw a curious phenomenon; the pine logs on the ground bore recent marks on them as of glancing shots, and at first we thought there had been a battle there; but it was the effect of a violent hail storm, the situation being high and exposed.

In the part of Florida I have travelled through, the barrens are monotonous enough, but differ from those in Carolina having, in some measure, prairie features. The growth is scattered, and the eye is often delighted with the extensive reach of verdurous plains, piny vistas, and glades, with here and there an undulating green mantled hill. Towards evening we came to a beautiful sheet of water covering a considerable space. It was one of the 'clear water ponds,' which make a distinguished feature in Florida scenery. Its smooth shallow waters laved on one side, the cheerful green of the sloping margin, and on the other, far beyond, the forest lay, even and regular as a park; the sun light glanced and reflected as from mirrors on the still, suspended, round leaves of the white water Lily, whose imperial, silvery crowns of flowers, rising erect half-way out of the surrounding Lymph, would have been likened by the poets of mythology to the crests of water gods just rising to take a peep at the earth. Over the fresh emerald meadow sides the clean and tidy white crane walked, or sailed along with dangling feet, eyeing her finny and froggy prey; and from the verdurous hill the evening lark sent her clear voice abroad to mingle with the chidings of the April gale.

I observed a belt of saw palmettoes around one edge of the pond, jaundiced and withered by the influence of the water; their drooping deflected leaves struck the attention immediately, as strangely contrasting with their natural erectness and stiffness.

Here I first saw, growing in the water, near the margin, a conspicuous plant which is common in the wet pine barrens, having a tall stem 3 or 4 feet high, remarkably smooth and transparent, and of a glaucous green, with a few subulate leaves growing regularly on it, and a racemose corymb of citron colored flowers. It was *Polygalac orymbosa*. This tall and different flowering plant would scarcely seem to belong to the same genus as the low round bachelor's button, or that minute species the *Polygala viridiscens*.

We reached our camping ground early, having marched 18 miles. It was in a dry and open pine barren with a small thicket on one edge. The scene on these occasions was romantic and picturesque. Here was a whole state, as it were, assembled in the compass of a hundred and fifty yards square, in these wild woods. So many knight errants who had come out to have a passage of arms with the fierce barbarian arid were returning adventureless. The forests begin to resound with the axe, trees are crashing and falling in all directions—the white tents are spread and numerous fires blaze up before them evolving volumes of smoke, through which the round moon looks dark and red like a dried pumpkin, and the tall pine tops wave shadowy, mingling their fresh aromatic odour with the warm resinous fumes that curl over them. The busy cooks are seen with their sleeves rolled up over their arms, some parching and beating coffee; others up to their elbows in flour, manipulating, and patting and roasting enormous cakes—each fire is circled by a throng, some are setting down watching in anxious silence the gradual embrowning of the coffee and dough, and others are whiling away the tedious hour in boisterous mirth and talk; the neighing of horses, whinnying of Indian ponies, and greedy mastication of corn is heard on every side. All is busy animation, life and satisfaction—all but yon dark and haggard squad, that stands separate from the joyful crowd, inhaling the damp mists of the hammock side. They look most condemned and uncomfortable; like poor ghosts waiting by the river Styx— see how they move off with laggard steps, and the broken down gait of tired hacks; their shoulders crimping beneath their muskets, the bayonets straggling, as do their legs, in every direction. They are the guard—the essential entity—the vital principle— the eyes and ears of the Camp; but in reality, they look more like school boy culprits, sent to bed without supper, then men appointed to watch over the lives of an army, who are about to resolve themselves, body and soul, into simple automatons of sight and sound. They are pitied by all, but their tour has come, and the duty must be performed; and after marching all day through boggy hammocks and prairies with water up to their knees, they are not allowed an instant rest, but are mached off again immediately, to parade before the stiff adjutant, and then to the guard house, which is no house—seldom a tent, and they pass the wakeful, tedious, interminable night, beneath the sky and the high pines around a few embers.

They are not permitted the solace of the laugh and jest to while away the lagging hour, but must keep a dead silence, or whisper like the crickets around them, until they become so drowsy that nature can no longer support them in their efforts to keep awake, and in spite of the officers commands, and threats, and joggings, they begin to snore, and fall into a gentle oblivion, forget where they are, the duty they are upon, and that the rifle of the Indian may be within a few steps of them. Suddenly, just as a sweet dream begins to delude them with the belief that they are snug at home, sitting around the family fire-side, or locked in the dear one's embrace, a harsh, loud voice, dreadful as the trump at the last day, startles them from their doze, 'Turn out, third relief—fall in'—Up they jump, and the first idea, before the scattered senses collect themselves, is that of Indians:

'Where's my gun?'

'This is mine.'

'Give me mine.'

'Some one's got mine—I've got some one's,' they exclaim in momentary confusion. But the grim sergeant of the guard stands before them, and they hear his gruff voice repeat, 'Come, fall in—fall in your places, third relief'—they grumble about the time being so short, and are marched off to pass two weary hours in the very teeth of a frowning hammock, where they expect every moment a ball to be put through them.

The next day we marched over a more level and wet country. The soil of these wet barrens is mostly covered with grass, growing about a foot high, and generally presenting a withered and uninteresting appearance.

A feature peculiar to these prairies is the coppices or dry ponds of cypress which constantly recurring with their regular angled boles, monotonous, upright, stiff leaves, and deep green foliage mingle their scenery with the tedium and gloom of the waste, but are not altogether unpleasing to the eye, which naturally reposes upon their verdure, as a relief from the wiltered waste of grass, and dull dwarfish pines. In some places, these highland islets or coppices may be called hammocks and with the cypress you see united clumps of tall and flourishing Bay trees.

Occasionally the trail was crossed by larger and more extensive hammocks or swamps, consisting of a variety of forest trees and shrubs.

A beautiful tall shrubby *Hypericum* covered whole acres of these cypress swamps, so thick in some places, as to impede us—3-5 feet high; leaves crowded, small, linear, revolute. (*Hyper fasciculatum*).

The openness to the sun and air promotes vegetation in these barrens. The humid soil was spread with a rich carpet of flowers. The *Saracenia*, or Trumpet, with its mystical cowled leaf distilling from the sun nectar, to delute unfortunate insects with—accompanied by its conspicuous yellow flower, was very frequent.

The *Prenanthes simplex* is a very engaging flower; its pale purple ligulate rays converging into a bell and nodding; one or two only on the virgate branches. It was not very common.

Another very common and tall flower, in these damp grounds at this season, is the early white aster (*Aster obovatus*) the branching corymbs very conspicuous.

Aletris aurea—yellow flowered star grass-beautiful pale saffron flowers—very viscrid—rather rare.

Helonias erithrosperma—covering large patches with its singular pompon flowers, white above, terminating in pink at the lower end of the plume.

Helonias dioica; Sabbatia white, and rose; a white *Orchis; Leptopoda decurrens*, very numerous, &c. &c.

On the third day we arrived at the sandy region, and struck the main road to St. Augustine., which we had travelled on our way to Gen. Hernandez's, at the commencement of the campaign. It was not then the season of flowers, and there was little worth of observation, but now the trees were clothed in their perfection of foliage, and every mile presented attractive and new embellishments on the tapet of Flora.

We now came to tracts covered with the delicate leaves, and purple, saffron-powdered buttons of the sensitive briar. Here too in stronger spots was frequent the blue and pink *Tradescantia*. In damper spots *Asclepias paupercula;* flowers white beautifully tinged with purple.

In the driest and most sandy *Asclepias amplexicaulis*—*Ceanothus mycrophyllus and intermedius*. The dark stemmed *Physalis*—*Onosmodium hispidum*—*Annona Grandiflora*, &c.

Other tracts were engrossed by low undergrowth,

such as Saw Palmetto, *Andromeda*, the heath of America, *Quercus sericea* or running oak, &c. From this last, which grows plentiful in Florida, are obtained the Nut Galls, which are an article of Commerce.

In such bushy spots, particularly among the Saw-Palmettoes, the Florida Jay is to be met with. This bird differs much from our Blue Jay (*Corvus Cristatus,*) being rather smaller, having no crest, nor any black on the head and collar, the former in the Florida Jay is a bright azure; the latter cinerous. Its back is a beautiful light yellow azure without any white feathers like the Blue Jay. It resembles more the Magpie; its notes are not as loud as those of the Blue Jay, but noisy, quarrelsome and more frequent. Its flight is low—it sails or sweeps from bush to bush— sometimes with flapping of the wing. Its motions are abrupter and quicker than the Blue Jay's. It is not very frequent on the eastern coast of Florida, and is not found in any part of Georgia or Louisiana.

This morning we saw some Whooping Crane flying over our heads. Our eyes were attracted to them by our hearing their loud croaks far off. The whole army shouted ridiculously at them as they passed slowly on heavy wing. They veered away and lit on some trees, where their erect forms appeared singularly tall, fully 6 feet high. The frequent the savannas, but are said to come to the barrens and high grounds to get gravel, from which circumstance it is called also the sand-hill Crane. One of the Indian names for it is *Soleta,* which means, likewise an army or troop.

I should not omit to mention that Doctor Strobel had brought along in a box, from the other side of Camp King, two live birds of a singular and new species—the Carracara, or Brazilian Eagle, (*Polyborus vulgaris*). This bird is described in Audubon's 2d vol., who found a specimen at St. Augustine in 1831, and was induced by its novel character to make it a separate genus. In its head and beak it resembles the Vulture—in its talons the Eagle—in its habit of breeding on trees, it approaches the nature of the Hawk—but in laying only two eggs it again is likened to the Vulture. The first time Dr. Strobel saw one of these birds a few years ago, it was feeding with a flock of buzzards, on the offals of fish, and experiments have since proved that it feeds on both live and carrion food. The natives call it 'the King of the Buzzards;'* as it will drive buzzards away from carrion and eat before them.

These were two young ones, which were discovered in a nest on a pine tree while felling trees at an encampment; they flew out and were caught—on being approached they were very wild, erecting their crests and the feathers on the back of the neck, screaming and falling backward and defending themselves with their claws like the Eagle. They are of a brownish yellow colour, and have a black cap which terminates just above the eye and gives the head a very marked appearance. The fact of their breeding in Florida, which was not previously ascertained has been established by this discovery of Dr. Strobel.

The next was about 15 inches in diameter—

---

*Soole-Micco.

of an oval shape, rather shallow in proportion, composed of dry sticks, pine tops and leaves, and in the crutch of the tree.

The Carracara Eagle is not uncommon in Mexico and South America.*

CHAPTER XX.

Posy Balls—Anastasia Island—Light House—Quarry of Shell Rock—Plants—Shells—Drumming—Conclusion.

The Campaign, with all its hard accompaniments of fatigue and coarse fare, was now finally at an end, and we were once again among the abodes of civilization. Our stay in St. Augustine while we waited for vessels, was during a happy era. It was the season of a kind ol Carnival, and the 'Posy Balls' had commenced.

'Do you go to the Posy this evening?'

'Who is the King; who is the Queen of the night?'

'What is a Posy Ball?'

I was informed—These simple celebrations, which of course partake of nothing of the magnificence which attends them in the old Catholic countries, begin on the third day of May, and last for nine nights. The custom is commemorative of the finding of the cross. Several houses are thrown open on the same evening, and there is free admission for all who feel disposed to go and look at the 'Altar of Flowers;' and put in a claim for the 'Posy.' The Altar is in a recess hung round with white curtains and muslin festoons, and garnished with wreaths of real and artificial flowers, evergreens, and paper fancy work. At the head of the alter is a small mirror,

---

*These birds are at present alive in Charleston, in the possession of the Rev. Mr. Bachman. The above account is almost verbatim from the Charleston Courier, 27th May.

and beneath that a figure of Christ on the cross—above are disposed strings of beads and other ornaments—Bouquets of the gayest flowers of the season are arranged in vases on the steps, which are covered with spotless white drapery and lit up with numerous wax tapers, white green, rose, &c., in highly burnished candlesticks. The picture, on entering the room, is brilliant and striking—I had conceived of a 'posy altar' a mere something of wood or stone resembling a wash hand stand with a few nosegays on it. I had no idea that it was so large and important an affair. There is more fuss, preparation, and solemn care bestowed upon a Posy Altar than upon a bridal bed-chamber. Little boys and girls are seen employed all day in fetching baskets of flowers; the utmost attention is paid in adding nightly to the flowers—in removing a drooping one or putting a fresh one in its place, and a little girl is seen occupied every half a minute in retouching and arranging something, and snuffing the tapers.

But now for the ceremony—it is a very simple one—the company assembles—the mysterious Posy—the subject of so much consequence, of daily and nightly chit-chat among the beaus and belles—the object of contention to some, and to others of fear—is in the mean time kept concealed from vulgar eyes and hands on the mantelpiece or bed, in a separate apartment, with as much zealous care as an Indian Calumet is wrapped up and set upon the forked sticks, or it is shewn as a matter of favor only to a few. It is not by strict law to be removed from its sanctum sanctorum until the queen of the proceeding night arrives, who chooses some one who is to be King, and he who is chosen divides the Posy with some black-eyed beauty whom he selects for his Queen.

The King has to bear the expense of the next ball as a condition or the honour of reigning over so many fair subjects. The Queen appears on that evening dressed in white—her head adorned with flowers, and the Posy in her hand. After her Majesty appears, the Ball opens, and now dark floating eyes and tender dream-like forms are seen languishing through the majestic maze of the Spanish dance, or the voluptuous whirl of the Waltz.

At a certain hour the following day, the King of the next Ball meets his Queen to assist her in decorating the altar afresh for that evening, and while this is doing they have a fine opportunity for a delightful Tête à tète.

There is another similar custom called *Patgo*. The young marksmen shoot at an imitation bird, and he who is successful is elected King of the entertainment.

While we were thus dancing away at these merry meetings, and grim-visaged war appeared to have smoothed his wrinkled front, and the Campaign seemed like a dream, it was singular to think that we were still in the vicinity of savages, whom we had left victors and flushed with success, and who daringly followed as the moment we quit the country, until their tracks were discovered a day's march from the town, and they had committed depredations and murders within a few miles of us. In the midst of our revels we might have heard the sudden war whoop at the gates.

Made an excursion to the island of Anastasia,

which lies opposite to St. Augustine. After some trouble in getting a boat in consequence of the demand there was for them for similar excursions, and the *punica fides* of the Minorca fishermen who after engaging a boat to a party would take the first who were ready, and who in the mean time offered a trifle more, I succeeded in getting into one with an agreeable company.

The day was not as favorable as we might have wished, and before we reached the beach the heavy clouds portending a soaking rain, began to circumvent us, and threatened soon to canopy our heads with their invidious gloom and shock our fever-apt frames with an anguish shower bath—the town and fort were lost in the dense shade of the dark indigo heavens, and already on one side the commingling of the waters of the sky and sea roared out their dismal greetings to our ears not more than a hundred yards from us—happily our course lay in the opposite direction to their din, and our Minorcans tugged their oars with spirit; we steered for the blue heaven that lay temptingly before us, just large enough, as the saying is, to make a Dutchman a pair of breeches, and effected our retreat in handsome style defying the enemy and fairly outrunning him, and having received but two or three scattering spent shots, which did not penetrate the skin.

We landed and walked to the Light House to wait until the rain was over. Here a Spaniard, whose name was Andro, with his family, the eldest of whom was a beautiful, modest, dark-eyed little Muchacha (young girl,) just budding into her 14th year, held his desolate abode, defying alike the tempests and the Indians in his fortified castle. Having spent an hour or two beneath the hospitable tower of Signor Andro and made a delicious repast on dried fish which garnished his hall from one end to the other, eked out with cheese and crackers, brandy, fruits, and a bottle or two of Frontignac, and after exchanging soft words and glances for rosy blushes, and sweet Magnolia flowers with the pretty Isabel, we left the Light House for a tour on the island to go 'Drumming.'

The sun had come out, and shed all his glory upon a mild and lovely afternoon. The sky had changed its sullen darkness for the soft bright blue of the tropic summer, and the green brushwood, spangled with the spray of the showers, the shining white and hills, and the azure glassy ocean trembled to the eye, beneath the effulgence of the glorious orb.

Fair Anastasia!—how delightful is thy sunny beach—thy palmetto and rock-girl hills, and the calm blue sea that surrounds and kisses buxomly the lonely shores—how soft is the landscape around! Like the mellowed painting of the camera obscura—yon pale gold streak of desert beach that laces the blue mantle of the waters, and close to it the white ridge of chafing billows, which dispute the entrance of the quiet harbor.

The eye reposes next on the ever rolling sand hillocks, and the little valleys scrolled, here and there, with a few scrubs and marks of verdure, of the far coasting north beach. Before me rolls the Eternal Ocean—mighty Architect of the curious masonry on which I stand, the animal rock which supports thousands of acres of vegetable soil. How many millions upon millions of these shell fish, must have been destroyed to form a substratum for one rood of land. How strange a metamorphosis! What a circle of design! Life turned into Death, and Death recreating Life! This testaceous composition lies in horizontal masses, not deep beneath the surface. There is a quarry on the island, which suppled the stone of which the castle of St. Augustine and Fort Picolata were constructed. Some of this stone is of a light brick colour. I saw hewn slabs lying on the ground, which were white, and looked at a distance like granite.

Here is a high bluff washed by the sea, with projecting shelves of this curious rock, and grottoes, raftered over with the fantastic decumbent stems of the saw palmetto.

Behold through the vista of hills, and over yon little meadow valley, the small smiling town, with its curtain wall, and two or three empty quays, its white stone buildings, somewhat dingied by age, with large doors and balconies—at one end the light architecture and pinnacle of the New United States barracks, and at the other, the heavy, broad quadrangle of the stern, inquisitorial looking Spanish Castle.

I spent but a short time examining the vegetable treasures of the Island. The glorious Palmetto royal (*yucca gloriosa,*) was just beginning to show its pyramid of silver tulip flowers.

Afar before me, I beheld a shrub—its coal red flowers fired the white sand hills—it was new to me, and I gathered it with transport—it grew two or three feet high, the flowers were in clusters on opposite branches—deep red, scarlet; orange, and yellow intermingled—pungently aromatic. I afterwards found it to be the *Lantana Camara*. Bartram mentions coppices of the *Lantana* among other curious shrubs on an Island in Lake George. It is a native of Florida.

The Sea rocket, with its fleshy, glossy, green leaves, and white flowers. (*Cakile Americana*) was in plenty.

After picking up a few shells on the golden beach (which was literally nothing but shells) *Arca* of various sizes—red, yellow, and white; *Tellina; Ligaretus; Donax; Pholax;* a beautiful *Mytilus* white, waved with iodine purple, &c. &c., it was time for 'Drumming' the magic hour, between the 'fall of the ebb, and the rise of the flood'—for this delightful sport, whose praises and superior enchantments over all others in the Walton line, I had so often heard spoken with such rapture by the mouth of a North Island and Beaufort-man: the noble nature of the fish— his size and strength, the slow approach which he makes at first to the hook, like a crab—then the sudden overwhelming transport, that comes over you when you feel him dashing boldly off with the line, threatening to drag you after him, and upset your frail boat—how charming his resisting weight, comparable only to the intoxication, and gentle rapture one experiences, when pulling along a buxom lass through a Virginia reel—the art required to play him properly, so as to soon conquer the bright foe and lay him along side of the boat, when you feast your eyes upon his upturned white stomach, and lay your fingers trium- phantly upon his soft, heaving throat, and hurl him into the boat like a bleating sheep; the sweet pastime, the while, attended with the enchanting magic music of the sea caves, which strikes the azure surface and fills the air around.

Our party consisted of five—there were only three drum lines, and two of us had to be contented with baiting for the insignificant cannibal whiting, instead of the lordly dainty. Drum, until their turn came for an exchange. It fell to my lot to unwind a fine line, with two hooks, that I felt assured were just of the right size, and strong enough to hold a shark. When we had seated ourselves with all the convenience necessary for the import business in hand, the process of baiting began. Partly from a principle of modest deference to my superiors in any art or science, which I have always carried along with me, and partly from an innate abhorrence I have ever had to touch a crab, save when cooked, and divested of its clawing propensity, I resigned this delicate affair into the hands of one of the fishermen, who forthwith, and in the twinkling of an eye, stabbed an unfortunate crab with his knife, seized upon one fierce, threatening claw, then the other, and snapped them off, next quartered the body, and ran too pieces of the oozing, rich, white and red morsel through each hook close up to the shank; then cracking up the shelly integument of a claw he affixed the exposed meat to the barb.

Our *Cicerones*[82] of the depths and shallows of the briny element having now drawn in their oars and cast anchor over a spot which they assured us was rocky and just the place; we heaved our lines and sat in profound, silent expectation of a bite, but bite there came none—almost an hour elapsed—we had not the satisfaction of even 'a glorious nibble.' We began

To get provoked and talkative; to mend the matter there were a dozen boats, some almost within arms length of us, in which the fishermen were pulling up the fat drum every five or ten minutes—sometimes two at the same instant would be hauling in their prize, and the boat would nearly keel over with the weight, as they turned the floundering in. Our ears were dinned on every side with the constant repetition of the singular mellow sounds which these fish make as tho a regiment was approaching on the water. Another hour passed, and we had maintained the spirit and philosophy of true fishermen, but it did not avail—our luck had amounted to nothing more than a few ignoble whiting—in vain did we, with the most fishermen-like precision, gently draw our lines towards our breasts, to feel the bottom, and to attract some squeamish drum with the motion—in vain we sought the choicest fat and corally morceaus and concealed the points of our hooks in the flesh of the most specious claws; it served us nothing; we began to think that the Minorcans were leagued with the drum to disappoint us, but when we hinted our suspicions that something must be wrong, and demanded of them why fish were caught in every other boat but our's, they only shrugged their shoulders, and persisted that 'it was luck,' and that very often several might be fishing in one boat, and the fishes would all come to one line; and as if to prove the assertion, just as one of them said, a ripper of a drum seized his hook—we hailed the omen and trusted that luck was turning in our favor, but it did not, and after spending nearly another hour, we returned to the town.

THE END.

Books Published by the Seminole Wars Foundation

The Origin Progress and Conclusion of the Florida War, by Capt. John T. Sprague.

Reminiscences of the Second Seminole War, by John Bemrose.

Amidst a Storm of Bullets: The Diary of Lt. Henry Prince in Florida, 1836-1842, Frank Laumer, editor.

Fear and Anxiety on the Florida Frontier: Articles on the Second Seminole War, by Joe Knetsch.

The Fort King Road: Then and Now, by Jerry C. Morris and Jeffrey A. Hough.

This Miserable Pride of a Soldier: The Letters and Journals of Col. William S. Foster in the Second Seminole War, John and Mary Lou Missall.

This Torn Land: Poetry of the Second Seminole War, John and Mary Lou Missall, editors.

The War in Florida, by Woodburne Potter. Enhanced Edition. Introduction and Enhancements by John and Mary Lou Missall.

Efa, A Seminole Dog (Children's), by Jerry Morris.

Available from our website: www.seminolewars.us

Notes

1 https://south-carolina-plantations.com/dorchester/wraggs.html; https://www.findagrave.com.

2 https://www.wikitree.com/wiki/Smith-74923.

3 https://en.wikipedia.org/wiki/William_Wragg_Smith; David Taylor, *South Carolina Naturalists: An Anthology, 1700-1860*, (Columbus: University of South Carolina Press, 1998), 202 [Available at https://books.google.com]; Charleston Library Society, *A Second Supplemental Catalogue, Alphabetically arranged of all the Books, Maps and Pamphlets, Procured by the Charleston Library Society* (Charleston: A. E. Miller, 1835), 73, 75. [Available at https://books/google.com].

4 https://www.findagrave.com; "The Baronies of South Carolina," by Henry A. M. Smith in *The South Carolina Historical and Genealogical Magazine*, Vol. 11, No. 2 (April 1910), 86-87. [Available at https://www.jstor.org/stable/27575263?seq=13#metadata_info_tab_content]

5 Melody, written by William Wragg Smith in William Gilmore Simms, *The Charleston Book: A Miscellany in Prose and Verse* (Charleston, S.C.: Hart, 1845), 241-242 [Available at https://catalog.hathitrust.org/Record/00142155].

6 *Niles Weekly Register*, September 3, 1836, published an article from *Sketch of the Seminole War* and identified W.W. Smith as the author. David Taylor, *South Carolina Naturalists: An Anthology, 1700-1860*, identified William Wragg Smith as the author of *Sketch of the Seminole War*, 202.

7 Treaty of Payne's Landing (1832), called for relinquishment of Indian claims to land in the Florida Territory in exchange for land west of the Mississippi; John T. Sprague, *The Origin, Progress and Conclusion of the Florida War*, a Reproduction of the 1848 Edition (Tampa: University of Tampa Press, 2000), 74-78.

8 Col. James Gadsden, commissioner to negotiate Treaty of Fort Moultrie; Sprague, 20-24.

9 Fort King, Indian Agency, built in 1827, future City of Ocala; Sprague, 21; John K. Mahon, *History of the Second Seminole War, 1835-1842*, Rev. ed. (Gainesville: University of Florida Press, 1992), 88. Today the site is a city/county park with a reconstructed fort and visitor's center.

10 Capt. Gustavus S. Drane, supervised construction of fortification that was given his name; John Bemrose, *Reminiscences of the Second Seminole War* (University of Tampa Press, 2001), 36; Francis B. Heitman, *Historical Register and Dictionary of the United States Army, 1789-1903* (Washington, D. C.: Government Printing Office, 1903), 382.

11 Bvt. Brig. Gen. Duncan Lamont Clinch, in command of troops in Florida Territory (1827-1836), resigned Sept. 1836; Heitman, 310; Mahon, 65-66.

12 Gen. Wiley Thompson, Seminole Indian Agent at the commencement of the Second Seminole War Former Georgia Militia officer (1817-1824), Georgia Senator (1817-1819), and United States Congressman (1821-1833). Killed by Osceola and others on December 28, 1835 at Fort King; *Biographical Directory of*

the United States Congress, 1774-Present [Available at http://bioguide.congress.gov/scripts/biodisplay.pl?index=T000222].

[13] Volusia Marker is located just east of the St. Johns River Bridge, under the "Volusia Oak." The town was a major port on the St. Johns River, supplying men and material to posts further inland and south along the river.

[14] Jumper (Ote Emathla, Otee-Emathlar), influential Seminole leader, Chief Micanopy's brother-in-law; Sprague, 97; Mahon, 127.

[15] Micanopy (Sint Chakkee), Head chief of the Seminoles at the war's commencement; Mahon, 125-127.

[16] This is in reference to General Andrew Jackson's 1818 campaign into Spanish Florida in what became known as the First Seminole War; David S. Heidler and Jeanne T. Heidler, *Old Hickory's War: Andrew Jackson and the Quest for Empire* (Mechanicsburg, PA: Stackpole Books, 1996), 135-158.

[17] Assiola (Osceola, Asi-Yoholo, Tallahassee Tustenuggee, Powell), member of the Red Stick branch of Creek Indians, influential leader during the Second Seminole War. who most represented the war spirit and symbol of Indian resistance to emigration, captured under flag of truce (1837), imprisoned in Fort Marion at St. Augustine then transferred to Fort Moultrie, Charleston, SC where he died; Sprague, 100-101, 214-217; Patricia Riles Wickman, *Osceola's Legacy,* (Tuscaloosa: University of Alabama Press, 2006), 17-19, 24-29,134-151.

[18] King Philip's War, also known as Metacom's War, or the First Indian War. It was an armed conflict between English Colonists and the American Indians of New England in the 17th century. It was the Native American's last major effort to drive the New England Colonists out of New England.

[19] Tecumseh was a Native American Shawnee warrior and Tribal chief, who became the primary leader of a large, multi-tribal confederacy in the early 19th century. Born in the Ohio Country, growing up during the American Revolutionary War and the Northwest Indian War, Tecumseh was exposed to warfare and envisioned the establishment of an independent Native American nation east of the Mississippi River under British protection. He worked to recruit additional members to his tribal confederacy from the southern United States. https://en.wikipedia.org/wiki/Tecumseh.

[20] The Black Hawk War, or Black Hawk's War, from 1865 to 1872, is the name of the estimated 150 battles, skirmishes, raids, and military engagements between primarily Mormon settlers in Sanpete County, Sevier County and other parts of central and southern Utah, and members of 16 Ute, Southern Paiute, Apache and Navajo tribes, led by a local Ute war chief, Antonga Black Hawk. The conflict resulted in the abandonment of some settlements and hindered Mormon expansion in the region. https://en.wikipedia.org/wiki/Black_Hawk_War_(1865–1872).

[21] Col. John Warren, from Jacksonville, commander of the FL militia, supported regular troops at Battle of Withlacoochee (December 31, 1835); Sprague,

92, 163-166, 230; Mahon, 101, 179; *Army and Navy Chronicle (hereafter A&NC)* V (December 21, 1837), 387.

[22] Referring to the battle of Black Point in December 1835. Smith goes into detail about the battle on pages 15-16. Wacahoota, Florida is an unincorporated community in Alachua and Marion counties, Florida. The name "Wacahoota", spelled Wacahootee or Wacahootie on early 19th century maps, is believed to derive from a combination of Spanish vaca, "cow", and Muscogee hute or hoti, "cowpen".

[23] Referring to the Battle of Withlacoochee, not the river.

[24] Maj. Gen. Edmund Pendleton Gaines, bvt. Maj. Gen. (1814) for gallantry in defeating the enemy at Fort Erie, in command of the Western Department of the Army; Heitman, 442; Mahon, 144.

[25] French phrase: war stratagem. https://www.merriam-webster.com/dictionary/ruse%20de%20guerre.

[26] Charley Emathla, Seminole chief who favored migration, Sprague, 88-89.

[27] Lt. John Graham, graduated Military Academy (1834), promoted bvt. 2nd Lt., 4th Inf. (1834), 2nd Lt. (1836), 1st Lt. 2nd Dragoons (1836), Capt. (1837), Adj. Gen. of Territory of Florida (1840-41); Heitman, 468; George W. Cullum, *Biographical Register of the Officers and Graduates of the United States Military Academy ... 1802-1890*, 3 vols. (Boston, 1891), 1:585-586.

[28] *Rara avis*, Latin for, Rare bird. https://www.merriam-webster.com/dictionary/rara%20avis.

[29] Lt. Constantine Smith, 1st Lt., 2nd Art. (May 30, 1832), killed Dec. 28, 1835 by Seminole Indians near Fort King; Heitman, 895.

[30] Brig. Gen. Joseph M. Hernandez, Florida Territorial Delegate to U. S. Congress (1822-1823), militia general (1835-1838); *Biographical Directory*, http://bioguide.congress.gov/scripts/biodisplay.pl?index=H000533.

[31] Dr. John McLemore, later Major in the Florida militia; Sprague, 150-153; Mahon, 101.

[32] Richard K. Call, West Florida militia general (1823), Governor of Florida Territory (1835-1840, 1841-1844); *Biographical Directory*, http://bioguide.congress.gov/scripts/biodisplay.pl?index=C000050.

[33] Col. Richard C. Parish, FL Vols., supported regular troops at Battle of Withlacoochee (December 31, 1835); *A&NC* 5 (December 32, 1837), 387; Woodburne Potter, *The War im Florida*, Enhanced Edition (Dade City, FL: Seminole Wars Foundation, Inc., 2013), 101, 111-112.

[34] Lt. Col. William J. Mills, FL militia, supported regular troops at Battle of Withlacoochee (December 31, 1835); Sprague, 92; *A&NC* 5 (December 21, 1837), 387; Potter, 115.

[35] Col. Leigh Read, FL militia officer, later Major and Brig. Gen.; Sprague, 136, 150-154, Mahon, 153, 272-273; Potter, 101.

[36] The ruins of some of these plantations can be visited. The Seminole Wars Heritage Trail Guide is available free of charge from the Florida Department

316

of Historical Resources at
dos.myflorida.com/historical/preservation/heritage_trails/seminole-wars-heritage-trail/.

[37] Refers to King Phillip, father of Coacoochee (Wildcat) and one of the major Seminole leaders.

[38] Spring Garden Plantation is located within the De Leon Springs State Park, 601 Ponce De Leon Blvd., De Leon Springs, FL. Machinery and stonework from the water-powered sugar mill is on display near a beautiful spring. https://www.floridastateparks.org/parks-and-trails/de-leon-springs-state-park.

[39] The Bulow Plantation Ruins Historic State Park is three miles west of Flagler Beach on CR 2001, south of SR100, and contains the ruins of an antebellum plantation and its sugar mill, built of coquina sedimentary rock, made up of crushed shells. It was the largest plantation in East Florida. It was developed beginning in 1821 by Major Charles Wilhelm Bulow, who acquired 4,675 acres on a tidal creek (later Bulow Creek). At Christmas 1831 into January 1832, Bulow's son hosted the artist and naturalist John James Audubon, who explored the area in his continuing study of American birds. The plantation was destroyed in the Seminole War of 1836.

The property and ruins were acquired by the State of Florida in 1945 and dedicated as a State Historic Park in 1957. It was added to the National Register of Historic Places on 29 September 1970. By Brian M. Powell, CC BY-SA 3.0, https://commons.wikimedia.org/w/index.php?curid=8207951.

[40] Maj. Benjamin A. Putnam, lawyer and St. Augustine resident, commanding officer of the FL volunteer St. Augustine Guards; Sprague, 216; Mahon, 112, 137.

[41] Capt. George Woodbine of the Royal Marines; Heidler and Heidler, 38.

[42] William Bartram (1739-1823) was America's first native born naturalist, artist, and botanist and first author in the modern genre of writers who portrayed nature through scientific examination as well as personal understanding. The son of noted botanist, John Bartram, William, from his mid teens, was noted for the quality of his botanic and ornithological drawings. His role in the maintenance of his father's botanic garden sparked William's interest in the scientific field, adding many rare species to it. In 1773, William embarked upon a four-year journey through the eight southern colonies ranging from the foothills of the Appalachian Mountains, to the Carolinas, Florida and Mississippi. *The Travels of William Bartram* is an account of this journey that combines the natural sciences, travel and philosophy in a literature style that is not just solely scientific. The book entails the many native flora and fauna he discovered, encounters with the intrepid Seminoles Indians, battles with aggressive alligators, and observations on God's device for Nature.

[43] Dr.William H. Simmons's *Notices of East Florida* was published more than a decade before hostilities began. It was recommended reading to those who needed to traverse the terrain.

[44] Maj. Francis Langhorne Dade, 3 Lt. 12 Inf. (March 1813); 2 Lt. (Jan. 1814); transferred to 4th Inf. (May 1815); 1 Lt. (Sept. 1816); Capt. (Feb. 1818); bvt. Maj. (Feb. 1828) for 10 years faithful service in one grade; killed by Seminole Indians on the march to Fort King, December 28, 1835; Heitman, 350.

[45] Maj. Francis Smith Belton, commanding officer at Fort Brooke, Maj. Adj. Inspector General (1820-1821) after being reinstated, Capt. 2nd Arty. (1821), Maj. 1st Arty. (July 1838) and 4th Arty. (Sept. 1838), Lt. Col, 3rd Arty. (1845), bvt. Col. (1847) for gallantry in battles of Contreras and Churubusco, Mexico, Col., 4th Arty. (1857); Mahon, 101; Heitman, 209.

[45] Brig. Gen. Joseph M. Hernandez, Florida Territorial Delegate to U. S. Congress (1822-1823), militia general (1835-1838); *Biographical Directory*, http://bioguide.congress.gov/scripts/biodisplay.pl?index=H000533.

[46] Capt. Upton Sinclair Fraser, 3rd Arty. (1828), killed at Dade's Battle December 28, 1835; Heitman, 434; Frank Laumer, *Dade's Last Command* (Gainesville: University Press of Florida, 1995), 39-40.

[47] Capt. George Washington Gardiner, graduated MA (1814), bvt. Capt., 2nd Arty. (1828), Capt. (1832), killed at Dade's Battle December 28, 1835; Heitman, 445; Cullum, 111; Laumer, 108.

[48] Lt. Robert Rich Mudge, graduated Military Academy (1833), 2nd Lt., 3rd Arty. (1835), killed at Dade's Battle December 28, 1835; Heitman, 734; Cullum 546-547; Laumer, 142-144.

[49] Lt. John Low Keais, graduated Military Academy (1835) and promoted bvt. 2nd Lt., 3rd Arty. (July 1835), killed at Dade's Battle December 28, 1835; Heitman, 586; Cullum, 594-595.

[50] Lt. Richard Henderson, graduated Military Academy (1835), promoted bvt. 2nd Lt., 2nd Arty. (July 1835), killed at Dade's Battle December 28, 1835; Heitman, 522; Cullum, 594.

[51] Lt. William Elon Basinger, graduated Military Academy (1830), promoted bvt. 2nd Lt., 2nd Arty. and 2nd Lt., 2nd Arty. (1830), killed at Dade's Battle December 28, 1835; Heitman, 197; Cullum, 448; Laumer, 42-44.

[52] Dr. John Slade Gatlin, Asst. Surgeon (1834), killed at Dade's Battle December 28, 1835; Heitman, 450.

[53] Maj. John Mountfort, 2nd Arty., bvt. Capt. (1814) for gallantry in attack on Plattsburg, NY, bvt. Maj. (1829) for faithful service in one grade; Heitman, 733.

[54] Many of the facts stated in Smith's account are inaccurate. For a detailed account of the Dade Battle see *Dade's Last Command* by Frank Laumer, (University Press of Florida, 1995).

[55] News reports contemporaneous with the Dade Massacre spoke of the horrific fate of the men who died there, thus creating a sense of national outrage among the American people. The region that included the site would only be sparsely populated for more than sixty years, at which time political leaders began to bring public attention back to the significance of the battle that most agreed marked the beginning of the Second Seminole War.

Through the determined efforts of a number of state and federal lawmakers, most notably State Legislator and later County Judge J.C.B. Koonce, in 1921 the State of Florida purchased the Dade tract as only the second parcel of land to be set aside as a state preserve. Funding for development came from government and especially private sources, and the story of what happened there in 1835 was once again made to be a part of the public knowledge. As of this writing, an annual reenactment of Dade's Battle has been conducted forty times, with a cumulative number of visitors and participants exceeding 100,000 persons. And although drawing fewer observers, a solemn wreath ceremony on the conflict's actual anniversary date each year is perhaps the most moving gesture of remembrance of that melancholy time of so long ago.

[56] Maj. Alexander C. W. Fanning, graduated Military Academy (1812), bvt. Maj. (1814) for gallantry in defense of Ft. Erie, bvt. Lt. Col. (1824) for ten years faithful service in one grade, Maj., 4th Arty. (1832), bvt. Col. for gallantry at Withlacoochee (1835), Lt. Col, 4th Arty. (1838); Heitman, 412-413; Cullum, 107-109.

[57] Maj. John S. Lytle, paymaster (1834), acting aide-de-camp to Gen. Clinch; Sprague, 92; Heitman, 651.

[58] Capt. William Montrose Graham, graduated Military Academy (1817), Capt., 4th Inf. (1832), commanding officer at Fort King, bvt. Maj. for gallantry at

Withlacoochee (1835), Maj., 2nd Inf. (1847), Lt. Col., 11th Inf. (1847), killed in
Battle of Molino del Rey, Mexico; Mahon, 87, Heitman, 468, Cullum, 157.
[59] Lt. Campbell Graham, graduated Military Academy (1822), promoted bvt.
2nd Lt. and 2nd Lt., 3rd Arty. (1822), bvt. Capt. for gallantry at Withlacoochee
(1835), bvt. Capt. Asst. Topo. Eng. (1837), Capt. Topo. Eng. (1838), Maj.
(1857); Heitman, 467, Cullum, 281-282.
[60] Lt. Thomas P. Ridgely (Ridgely), 2nd Lt., 2nd Arty. (1835), 1st Lt. (1836), Capt.
(1846); Sprague, 92; Heitman, 830.
[61] Cooley Massacre Memorial Monument located at Colee Hammock Park,
1500 Brickell Drive, Ft. Lauderdale. William Cooley Marker, where he moved
after loosing his family, is located at Tour Boat Landing on W. Fishbowl Drive
behind Ellie Schiller Homosassa Wildlife State Park, 4150 S. Suncoast Boule-
vard, Homosassa. Florida Seminiole Wars Heritage Trail Guide, 34, 42.

William Cooley was one of the first American settlers, and a regional leader, in what is now known as Broward County in the state of Florida. His family
was killed by Seminoles in 1836, during the Second Seminole War. The attack,
known as the "New River Massacre", caused immediate abandonment of the
area by whites. Cooley was born in Maryland, but little else is known about his
life prior to 1813, when he arrived in East Florida, a province of Spanish Florida, as part of a military expedition. He established himself as a farmer in the
northern part of the province before moving south, where he traded with local
Indians and continued to farm. During the period in which the region was
transferred from Spanish to U.S. governance, he sided with natives in a land
dispute against a merchant who had received a large grant from the King of
Spain and was evicting the Indians from their lands. Unhappy with the actions
of the Spanish, he moved to the New River area in 1826 to get as far possible
from the Spanish influence.

In New River, Cooley sustained himself as a as salvager and farmer, culti-
vating and milling arrowroot. His fortune and influence grew: he became the
first lawman and judge in the settlement, besides being a land appraiser. Local
Indians held him responsible for what they saw as a misjudgment involving the
murder of one of their chiefs, and attacked the settlement in revenge on January 4, 1836. Cooley survived the attack and lived for a further twenty-seven
years. He held administrative positions in Dade County, moved to Tampa in
1837, and had a short stint working for the U.S. Army as a guide and courier.
He moved to the Homosassa River area in 1840, where he became the first
postmaster and was a Hernando County candidate for the Florida House of
Representatives. Returning to Tampa in 1847, he was one of the first city
councilors, serving three terms before he died in 1863.
[62] Brig. Gen. Abraham (Abram) Eustis, bvt. Brig. Gen. (June 1834) and Col.,
1st Arty. (Nov. 1834), acting Florida commanding officer, commanded left
wing during Maj. Gen. Scott's campaign; Sprague, 106, 125-126; Heitman, 408.

[63] Captain Giles Porter, graduated Military Academy (1814), 2 Lt. Corps Arty. (1818), transferred to 1st Arty (1821), 1st Lt. (1823), bvt. Capt. (1833) for 10 years faithful service in one grade, Maj. 4th Arty. (1847); Heitman, 799.

[64] Lt. Col. William Gates, graduated Military Academy (1806), Maj., 2nd Arty. (1836), Lt. Col., 3rd Arty. (1836), Col., 3rd Arty. (1845), bvt. Brig. Gen. (1865) for long and faithful service in the Army; Heitman, 449; Cullum, 67-68.

[65] Maj. Gen. Winfield Scott, Lt. Col. 2nd Arty. (1812); Col. (1813); Col. Adj. Gen. (1813); Brig. Gen. (1814); bvt. Maj. Gen. (1814) for distinguished service in the successive conflicts of Chippewa and Niagara and for uniform gallantry and good conduct as an officer in army; Maj. Gen. (1841); Lt. Gen. (1847) for eminent service in war with Mexico; commander in chief of the army (July 5, 1841 to Nov. 1, 1861); Heitman, 870.

[66] John Henry Eaton, Secretary of War (1829-1831) and Governor of Florida Territory (1834-1836); *Biographical Directory*, http://bioguide.congress.gov/scripts/biodisplay.pl?index=E000024.

[67] Col. R. H. Goodwyn, commanded regiment of mounted SC Vols. in left wing during Maj. Gen. Scott's campaign; Potter, 167; Mahon, 156.

[68] Col. Persifor Frazer Smith, LA Vols. (1836), Brig. Gen. LA Vols. (1846), Col. mounted rifles (1846), bvt. Brig. Gen. for gallantry during conflicts at Monterey, Mexico and Battles of Contreras and Churubusco, Mexico; Brig. Gen. (1856); Heitman, 902.

[69] Naval Surgeon Dr. Frederick Leitner, killed by Seminole Indians at Powell's Battle, January 15, 1838; *A&NC*, 6 (February 22, 1838), 125; Mahon, 232.

[70] Governor of South Carolina George McDuffie. Later a US Senator.

[71] Col. William Lindsay, War of 1812 veteran, Col., 2nd Arty. (1832); Heitman, 634.

[72] *Mens consciarecti:* a mind aware of its own rectitude. The phrase comes verbatim from Virgil's Aeneid. (1604)

[73] Hamburgh Volunteers from South Carolina under command of Capt. S. W. Cunningham; Potter, 126.

[74] French adjective meaning, "correct in behavior or etiquette. Literal translation "as is necessary."

[75] Moultrie Creek runs west from the Matanzas River [now a part of the Intracoastal Waterway] approximately five miles south of St. Augustine. It was called Woodcutters Creek until James Grant, the first British Governor of Florida, granted 500 acres of land to John Moultrie in 1770. John Moultrie called his property Bella Vista and the point where the creek meets the river is still a beautiful view. John Moultrie built a lovely house and had hundreds of acres planted, but was only able to enjoy his plantation for a short period for in 1783 Florida again returned to Spanish control. He moved his family to Britain, abandoning the property, which was later destroyed by Indians. http://moultriecreek.us/journal/bella-vista/.

[76]*Fruges consumere nati*: "Born to consume the produce of the soil," disgrace every department in the Christian Church. They cannot teach because they will not learn. 2 Timothy 2:5. And if a man also strive for masteries, yet is he not crowned, except he strive lawfully.

[77]Common Box Turtle. Original Name: *Testudo carolina* (Linnaeus), 1758. Nomenclatural History: Davis & Rice (1883). List of Batrachia and Reptilia of Illinois. Bulletin of the Chicago Academy of Sciences. vol. 1, no. 3) used the junior synonym Testudo clausa Gmelin, 1789.

[78] Battle of Dunn Lawton (Dunlawton, Anderson's Plantation). For more information see John and Mary Lou Missall, *The Seminole Struggle: A History of America's Longest Indian War*, (Palm Beach, FL: Pineapple Press, 2020), 137.

[79] McRae Plantation. http://ormondhistory.org/the-dummett-plantation-the-mcrae-plantation-and-the-addison-blockhouse/.

[80] In 1825, brothers Kenneth and Duncan McRae purchased about one-fourth of the former Addison Plantation owned by Thomas Dummett. In 1832, they built a plantation and steam-powered sugar mill using the Addison house and outbuildings already on the property. They grew and processed sugar at the site from 1832 to 1836, when the Second Seminole War suddenly ended their visions of profit. After four successful years of sugar production the winter of 1835 brought a severe freeze, and with the Seminoles approaching, the family fled. In early 1836, the plantation was burned; in late February 1836, the Carolina Regiment of Volunteers fortified the detached kitchen for use as a defensive bulwark. A cannon named after a fallen comrade, "McDuffie," was placed on the roof of the former kitchen, which we now know as the Addison Blockhouse. The main house and other buildings were destroyed, although the slave quarters were left undisturbed, as was the custom of the Seminoles. Troops assembled near the Blockhouse, but the Seminoles often ambushed those who ventured out. Three were killed and more wounded. The men received orders to abandon the camp and move west. So on March 15, 1836, most of the volunteers of Camp McRae left on a three-day march to the fort at Volusia on the east side of the St. Johns River. They left many of their wounded behind in a nearby wooden stockade with volunteers to care for them, where they were rescued later. After this, the plantation was abandoned. McRae Plantation ruins and the Addison Blockhouses are located in the wilderness about a mile west of Ormond Lakes, which is off U.S. 1 north of Ormond Beach.

[81] Latin for of "its own kind," and used to describe a form of legal protection that exists outside typical legal protections -- that is, something that is ... https://www.merriam-webster.com/dictionary/sui%20generis.

[82]The Romans had a saying, "Punica fides" (the reliability of a Carthaginian) which for them represented the highest degree of treachery: The word of a Carthaginian (like Hannibal) was not to be trusted, nor could a Carthaginian be

relied on to maintain his political relationships.
http://www.csun.edu/~hcfll004/fides.html.

Index

www.ingramcontent.com/pod-product-compliance
Lightning Source LLC
Chambersburg PA
CBHW031233090426
42742CB00007B/178